1595

Coming Out in College

Critical Studies in Education and Culture Series

Between Capitalism and Democracy: Educational Policy
and the Crisis of the Welfare State
Svi Shapiro

Critical Psychology and Pedagogy: Interpretation
of the Personal World
Edmund Sullivan

Pedagogy and the Struggle for Voice: Issues of Language,
Power, and Schooling for Puerto Ricans
Catherine E. Walsh

Learning Work: A Critical Pedagogy of Work Education
Roger I. Simon, Don Dippo, and Arleen Schenke

Cultural Pedagogy: Art/Education/Politics
David Trend

Raising Curtains on Education:
Drama as a Site for Critical Pedagogy
Clar Doyle

Toward a Critical Politics of Teacher Thinking:
Mapping the Postmodern
Joe L. Kincheloe

Building Communities of Difference:
Higher Education in the Twenty-First Century
William G. Tierney

The Problem of Freedom in Postmodern Education
Tomasz Szkudlarek

Education Still under Siege: Second Edition
Stanley Aronowitz and Henry A. Giroux

Media Education and the (Re)Production of Culture
David Sholle and Stan Denski

Critical Pedagogy: An Introduction
Barry Kanpol

Coming Out in College

The Struggle for a Queer Identity

Robert A. Rhoads

Critical Studies in Education and Culture Series
Edited by Henry A. Giroux and Paulo Freire

BERGIN & GARVEY
Westport, Connecticut • London

Library of Congress Cataloging-in-Publication Data

Rhoads, Robert A.
    Coming out in college : the struggle for a queer identity / Robert
A. Rhoads.
        p. cm. — (Critical studies in education and culture series,
ISSN 1064–8615)
    Includes bibliographical references and index.
    ISBN 0–89789–378–6 (alk. paper).—ISBN 0–89789–421–9 (pbk.)
    1. Gays—United States—Identity. 2. Gay college students—United
States. 3. Coming out (Sexual orientation)—United States.
I. Title. II. Series.
HQ76.3.U5R48 1994
378.1′98′08664—dc20   94–16454

British Library Cataloguing in Publication Data is available.

Library of Congress Catalog Card Number: 94–16454
ISBN: 0–89789–378–6
    0–89789–421–9 (pbk.)
ISSN: 1064–8615

First published in 1994

Bergin & Garvey, 88 Post Road West, Westport, CT 06881
An imprint of Greenwood Publishing Group, Inc.

Printed in the United States of America

∞™

The paper used in this book complies with the
Permanent Paper Standard issued by the National
Information Standards Organization (Z39.48–1984).

10 9 8 7 6 5 4 3 2 1

To my family for their ongoing love and support. And to Bill Tierney for his help and friendship.

With thanks to Estela Bensimon, Phil Fuentes, Andrew Gitlin, Christine Jawork, Michael LeFlam, Yoshi Takei, Lee Upcraft, and Craig Waldo for their feedback on various drafts of this book.

Contents

Series Foreword

Within the last decade, the debate over the meaning and purpose of education has occupied the center of political and social life in the United States. Dominated largely by an aggressive and ongoing attempt by various sectors of the Right, including "fundamentalists," nationalists, and political conservatives, the debate over educational policy has been organized around a set of values and practices that take as their paradigmatic model the laws and ideology of the market place and the imperatives of a newly emerging cultural traditionalism. In the first instance, schooling is being redefined through a corporate ideology that stresses the primacy of choice over community, competition over cooperation, and excellence over equity. At stake here is the imperative to organize public schooling around the related practices of competition, reprivatization, standardization, and individualism.

In the second instance, the New Right has waged a cultural war against schools as part of a wider attempt to contest the emergence of new public cultures and social movements that have begun to demand that schools take seriously the imperatives of living in a multiracial and multicultural democracy. The contours of this cultural offensive are evident in the call by the Right for standardized testing, the rejection of multiculturalism, and the development of curricula around what is euphemistically called a "common culture." In this perspective, the notion of a common culture serves as a referent to denounce any attempt by subordinate groups to challenge the narrow ideological and political parameters by which such a culture both defines and expresses itself. It is not too surprising that the theoretical and political distance between defining schools around a common culture and denouncing cultural difference as the enemy of democratic life is relatively short indeed.

This debate is important not simply because it makes visible the role that schools play as sites of political and cultural contestation, but because it is within this debate that the notion of the United States as an open and democratic society is being questioned and redefined. Moreover, this debate provides a challenge to progressive educators both in and outside of the United States to address a number of conditions central to a postmodern world. First, public schools cannot be seen as either objective or neutral. As institutions actively involved in constructing political subjects and presupposing a vision of the future, they must be dealt with in terms that are simultaneously historical, critical, and transformative. Second, the relationship between knowledge and power in schools places undue emphasis on disciplinary structures and on individual achievement as the primary unit of value. Critical educators need a language that emphasizes how social identities are constructed within unequal relations of power in the schools and how schooling can be organized through interdisciplinary approaches to learning and cultural differences that address the dialectical and multifaceted experiences of everyday life. Third, the existing cultural transformation of American society into a multiracial and multicultural society structured in multiple relations of domination demands that we address how schools can become sites for cultural democracy rather than channeling colonies reproducing new forms of nativism and racism. Finally, critical educators need a language that takes seriously the relationship between democracy and the establishment of those teaching and learning conditions that enable forms of self- and social determination in students and teachers. This not only suggests new forms of self-definition for human agency, it also points to redistributing power within the school and between the school and the larger society.

Critical Studies in Education and Culture is intended as both a critique and a positive response to these concerns and the debates from which they emerge. Each volume is intended to address the meaning of schooling as a form of cultural politics, and cultural work as a pedagogical practice that serves to deepen and extend the possibilities of democratic public life. Broadly conceived, some central considerations present themselves as defining concerns of the Series. Within the last decade, a number of new theoretical discourses and vocabularies have emerged that challenge the narrow disciplinary boundaries and theoretical parameters that construct the traditional relationship among knowledge, power, and schooling. The emerging discourses of feminism, post-colonialism, literary studies, cultural studies, and post-modernism have broadened our understanding of how schools work as sites of containment and possibility. No longer content to view schools as objective institutions engaged in the transmission of an unproblematic cultural heritage, the new discourses illuminate how schools function as cultural sites actively engaged in the production of not only knowledge but social identities. *Critical Studies in Education and Culture* will attempt to encourage this type of analysis by emphasizing how schools might be addressed as border institutions or sites of crossing actively involved in exploring, reworking, and translating the ways in which culture is produced, negotiated, and rewritten.

Emphasizing the centrality of politics, culture, and power, *Critical Studies in Education and Culture* will deal with pedagogical issues that contribute in novel ways to our understanding of how critical knowledge, democratic values, and social practices can provide a basis for teachers, students, and other cultural workers to redefine their role as engaged and public intellectuals.

As part of a broader attempt to rewrite and refigure the relationship between education and culture, *Critical Studies in Education and Culture* is interested in work that is interdisciplinary, critical, and addresses the emergent discourses on gender, race, sexual orientation, class, ethnicity, and technology. In this respect, the Series is dedicated to opening up new discursive and public spaces for critical interventions into schools and other pedagogical sites. To accomplish this, each volume will attempt to rethink the relationship between language and experience, pedagogy and human agency, and ethics and social responsibility as part of a larger project for engaging and deepening the prospects of democratic schooling in a multiracial and multicultural society. Concerns central to this Series include addressing the political economy and deconstruction of visual, aural, and printed texts, issues of difference and multiculturalism, relationships between language and power, pedagogy as a form of cultural politics, and historical memory and the construction of identity and subjectivity.

Critical Studies in Education and Culture is dedicated to publishing studies that move beyond the boundaries of traditional and existing critical discourses. It is concerned with making public schooling a central expression of demo-cratic culture. In doing so it emphasizes works that combine cultural politics, pedagogical criticism, and social analyses with self-reflective tactics that challenge and transform those configurations of power that characterize the existing system of education and other public cultures.

--Henry A. Giroux

Key Characters

Jerry Sandaval--senior who identifies as gay/queer but occasionally has attractions for women

Tom Beal--closeted first-year student who identifies as a homosexual, fears coming out because of the "traditional values" of his family

Branden Conners--gay sophomore, closeted in his hometown but out at school, from a conservative area near Clement University

Shane McGuire--bisexual junior, closeted in the beginning of the academic year 1992-1993, later steps forward to assume a leadership role in a gay student organization

Roman Washburn--gay African American junior, "pulled out" of the closet by a friend

Karsch Palmer--gay/queer senior, came out his first year in college, out to his mother but not to his father

Roger Desko--serious-minded senior, identifies as gay/queer, a military brat, came out his first year in college

Tito Ortez--Puerto Rican senior who identifies as bisexual/queer, came out his sophomore year

Ben Curry--gay/queer graduate student, came out his first year in college to his roommate who also was gay

Andrew Lempke--gay/queer senior, came out his first year in college, sees everything about being gay as political

Deandre Witter--unidentified senior who acknowledges having mostly same-sex attractions, out to only a few friends

Coming Out in College

I

CONSTRUCTING CULTURAL BORDERS

The gay community is essentially a sense of connection and identity with other people who you have something in common with--a similar sexual orientation.

--Roger Desko, 25-year-old senior

Cultural borders serve to divide people; they separate "us" from "them" (Anzaldua, 1987). Yet, at the same time, borders enable people to connect, to identify with others in a similar position. For Roger Desko, who identifies the gay community as his family of choice, the sense of connection he has with other lesbian, gay, and bisexual people shapes much of his college life. In what follows, I explore the borders of sexual orientation and what these borders mean to students such as Roger as they struggle to develop a sense of identity.

1

The Struggle for Identity

Gay men and lesbians are orphans and our community is a collection of orphans. . . . We are like strangers who have been dropped on an island together.

--Brian McNaught, *On Being Gay*

A fog-like drizzle steadily fell upon a crowd of pink and lavender. The temperature was in the low 40s, but a cold north wind made the October day seem almost wintry. It was certainly no day to be standing outside for any length of time. Despite the cold and dampness, some thirty or so students had gathered on the steps of the auditorium on the campus of Clement University[1] for a local celebration of National Coming Out Day. Another 200 students stood on the adjacent sidewalk; they were there to offer support or to venture out of their closets in their own way. Shane, a handsome junior who majors in engineering, commented after the rally: "It was so exciting just to be in the crowd. The whole rally was very emotional, even just standing there watching." On this chilly day in 1992, Shane was content to be a silent voice, listening and offering support to others as they talked about what it was like to be queer and proud.

The term "queer" is an identifier adopted by a majority of the gay students who will be heard throughout this work. For these students, identifying as queer connotes a sense of pride and openness about one's same-sex desires as well as a degree of hostility toward heterosexism. Among other characteristics, being queer involves a certain attitude about one's sexual identity. This attitude was expressed by Shane some nine months after participating in National Coming Out Day: "Sometimes I feel like being very out and telling people who have a problem with it to piss off!" As another student explained, "To be queer is to be open about your sexual orientation. It means not being ashamed in any way." These students offer one interpretation of what it means to be queer. Other students argue that "to be queer means to be political" (in the sense of engaging in gay/queer politics). Still others use "queer" rather loosely as a unifying term for all lesbian, gay, and bisexual people regardless of whether those individuals identify as queer or not. Queer is a contentious term within the gay community. Gay authors such as Frank Browning (1993) discuss queer in terms of power and projecting that power in public settings. "Mall actions" are examples of Browning's conception of what it means to be queer:

> Gay men and lesbians, usually in a three-to-one male-to-female ratio, mount "queer visibility" expeditions, walking hand in hand into stores, shopping a lot, buying a little, and engaging in exaggerated mimicry of the straights who surround them. Occasionally, there is a kiss-in. The look is punk, drag, leather, bleached hair, dyed hair, earrings, ear cuffs, nipple rings, nose pins, scarves, streamers, and balloons. It's demonstration as picnic, picnic as political action. (p. 33)

For Browning, queer involves a degree of "rage" toward heterosexism and is often expressed in organized political activities. Alexander Doty (1993) offers a different conception of queerness when he writes that his notion of queer "does not limit queer expression to a certain political agenda. Any 'queerer than thou' attitude, based on politics, style, sexual behavior, or any other quality, can only make queerness become something other than an open and flexible space" (p. xv). For Doty, queerness "is a quality related to any expression that can be marked as contra-, non-, or anti-straight" (p. xv). One of the points of this text is to highlight how various students think about queerness and how their construction of a queer identity might differ from others within the gay community.

Although Shane was content to take a first step and simply be seen at a pride rally, other students at Clement University were there to be heard. These lesbian, gay, and bisexual students would be silent no longer.

> Hi. I'm Toni. I'm one of the co-directors for the department of Womyn's Concerns. I've come out to speak because lots of us are here and some of us are queer. Not to mention the fact that I've fucking had it up to here. There are people who feel justified in teaching and preaching the suppression of love. There is a lot of shit that goes on in our world, therefore we need all the love we can get. So, how do they justify it all? By calling this love bad love, sinful love, the wrong kind of love. To them I say that's a fucking oxymoron. There's no such thing as bad love. I speak for all of us, and I mean all of us everywhere, when I say that love feels good. As for those who say that queer love isn't love at all, you simply have no idea how very wrong you are. But no matter what anybody else says or thinks or does, I, as a bisexual/sensual womyn with a "y," reserve the right to love and to receive love on my terms. And so help me goddess above and below, no one will ever take that from me!

Next, a gay student took his turn at the podium. He told a story of having been beaten up over the summer by a couple of students and showed the subsequent scar left on his forehead. His attackers did not appreciate his flamboyant mannerisms. "I'm a queen and I'm not ashamed. I wear this scar as a badge of freedom--freedom that no one will ever take away from me." Another student stepped through the makeshift door frame erected at the top of the steps. The door frame symbolized the passage from "the closet" to a public identity--from a state of hiding to a state of openness about one's same-sex attractions. "I came out to my dad so he would stop asking me about girlfriends. I came out because I'm a gay man. I don't want anyone to accept me--I want them to respect me for who I am." Then Andrew, a tall senior and one of the leaders of the campus queer movement, spoke next:

> When I was little I was attracted to boys, not to girls. I lived with this feeling for years, without anyone knowing, without knowing what to do about it. It wasn't until I came to Clement that I realized it was possible to live happily as a gay man. Lesbian, gay, and bisexual people have two choices: come out or stay in your closet and continue hating yourself. Coming out is better than hating yourself. . . . Coming out is more than saying the word. It's about celebrating yourself. I'll never forget the time some fraternity guys beat me up while their gay brothers stood and watched. They chose to remain closeted. Coming out is about standing next to your real brothers.

One by one lesbian, gay, and bisexual students climbed the steps of the auditorium. Steps that must have seemed like years to them. They were all there for the same purpose: they came to publicly announce their sexual identity.

From time to time I heard background noise from across the sidewalk and lawn separating the auditorium from the campus's main classroom building. The classroom building had been the hub of student activity at Clement University for years, mostly because of its central location. This was the site where the "Clement Preacher" regularly proclaimed his conservative Christian views in an attempt to convert students. Although the Clement Preacher was often criticized by other Christians, even by some campus fundamentalists who saw his methods as more alienating than "discipling," he nonetheless seemed to galvanize conservative opposition to gay rights. While some 200 students stood around the steps of the auditorium in support of the lesbian, gay, and bisexual students, a similar-sized crowd formed around the Clement Preacher.

The crowd at the classroom building was boisterous, and I struggled to maintain my focus on the steps of the auditorium. No sooner had I regained my concentration than another round of uproarious laughter arose from the Clement Preacher's crowd. He was on a roll: "So a guy puts his penis in another guy's butt" was all I could make out; the laughter from his surrounding audience was too loud. And now people around me were laughing; something humorous had occurred on the steps of the auditorium. Then the Preacher had his crowd going again. Their laughter was louder than before. Back and forth the two crowds competed.

"What does the Bible say about homosexuals? The Bible says that it is unsightly in the eyes of God. That it is offensive to God. That it is abominable in the eyes of God," yelled the Clement Preacher. He turned and pointed toward the steps of the auditorium: "They would have you believe that it is ok. That Christian morality is archaic. That it doesn't apply to us today. But God's word is eternal. The same yesterday, today, and tomorrow."

His words struck a chord in my own mind. Two or three years earlier, I held similar views about homosexuality. I had tossed around the very issue he was now raising. Eventually, I came to the same horizon that Toni challenged others to reach: when it comes to the love of other people, there is no such thing as bad love. In the end, my belief in Christ's teachings about justice and love brought me to support gay rights; and later, student narratives about abuse and discrimination brought me to join the struggle myself.

"I kind of hope I get through this without crying," continued one student. "I think there is going to be a lot of finger pointing and I hope no one takes this personally. But I have some things that need to be said." The student paused as if to catch his breath and prepare himself for what was no doubt to be an emotional outpouring. Several seconds passed . . . they seemed like leg irons.

> This goes out to the queer community. To those who don't know where they are.
> I am sick and tired of being good enough to suck your dick but not good enough
> to know your name. I am sick and tired of being good enough to be your friend
> at a nightclub on a Sunday evening but not good enough to be your friend
> anywhere else. I am sick and tired of being beat up and abused while you stand
> by and do nothing. I am sick and tired of those who are politically out but who
> forget where they came from not so long ago. I am sick and tired of being good
> enough for you to talk to but not good enough to be a guest in your home. And
> most of all, I am sick and tired of being sick and tired.

This book is about the experiences students at Clement University face in their personal struggle to come to terms with same-sex attraction and their communal struggle to change both the culture of the institution and, in turn, the general culture of American society. The remaining sections of this chapter provide a context for this work and highlight the theory and methodology employed in the study.

THE STRUGGLE FOR A PUBLIC SPACE

The voices presented thus far were all heard on National Coming Out Day on the campus of Clement University, a university with over 30,000 students. National Coming Out Day at Clement symbolizes the larger societal struggle faced by lesbian, gay, and bisexual people as they strive to create a public space in which they can be visible and live without fear and discrimination. Their space is a source of identity situated within a culture that seeks to keep them hidden. Like Clement students, lesbian, gay, and bisexual students across the country are struggling to claim their own place on campus and in public life (Dale & Soler, 1993; D'Emilio 1992). Some have already spoken out, others do so now, more will follow. "We're here, we're queer, get used to it" is the Queer Nation slogan that fits many of these most visible and politically active students.

The students at Clement University highlight campus oppression faced by lesbian, gay, and bisexual college students. The fact that oppressive campus environments exist is well documented (D'Augelli, 1989a, 1989c; Herek, 1986, 1993; La Salle & Rhoads, 1992; Low, 1988; Nelson & Baker, 1990; Nieberding, 1989; Shepard, 1990; Tierney et al., 1992). Although we know that many campus environments are hostile for lesbian, gay, and bisexual students, we know very little about the ways in which these students actually endure, and in some instances challenge, campus climates.[2] To highlight this point, I call upon the results of a literature review from 1970 to 1993. Out of more than 200 pieces of research reviewed, 77 percent focus on heterosexual attitudes toward gay students whereas only 23 percent actually discuss their experiences in academe. Of the latter group, only 21 pieces of research offer any substantial insight into the problems faced by lesbian, gay, and bisexual college students. I discuss this literature in chapter 2 as a way to consider sexual identity issues.

The first step in the development of a lesbian, gay, or bisexual identity is "coming out." Coming out is the process of openly acknowledging one's same-sex attractions. It is a process that all individuals who identify with same-sex attractions must confront. For individuals who think of themselves as queer, coming out represents an initial step in becoming engaged in the politics of sexual identity.

The political and cultural goal of queer students at Clement University is to create a public sphere free of heterosexism and homophobia. Heterosexism is "the belief that everyone is, or should be, heterosexual," notes Richard Friend (1993, p. 211). He goes on to add:

> Based on the assumption of universal heterosexuality . . . a systematic set of institutional and cultural arrangements exist that reward and privilege people for being or appearing to be heterosexual, and establish potential punishments or lack of privilege for being or appearing to be homosexual. Heterosexism is prejudice against homosexuality which is maintained by a pervasive set of societal institutions that sanction and promote this ideology. (p. 211)

Similarly, Audre Lorde (1985) describes heterosexism as "a belief in the inherent superiority of one pattern of loving over all others and thereby the right to dominance" (p. 3). The dominance of heterosexist ideology and culture leads to homophobia.

Lorde describes homophobia as "a terror surrounding feelings of love for members of the same sex and thereby a hatred of those feelings in others" (pp. 3-4). Likewise for Friend, homophobia is seen as "the fear and hatred of homosexuality in one's self and in others" (p. 211). Whereas heterosexism relates more to a set of ideologies pervasive throughout a culture, homophobia is the acting out of heterosexist beliefs and attitudes. The coming out process and the more general process of establishing a public persona are crucial to the political and cultural struggle to eliminate heterosexism and homophobia. As one student noted, "I think it is really important to become highly visible once you come out. You need to work hard at changing people's views."

For some students, being political means identifying as queer. A student voice is helpful here: "Queer to me is different than gay. Not just because it includes lesbians and gays, but it's more of an attitude. There is a political aspect of being queer. You have to be political to be queer, but you don't have to be political to be gay." Another added: "For me queer means any gay, lesbian, or bisexual person who is out. If they're not out, then they are not queer. It has a political connotation."

There is another meaning of the term "queer" beyond the political. To some, queer is a unifying term that describes all lesbian, gay, and bisexual people. Although not every gay person would use the term, nonetheless it is used frequently by queer-identified people to name all lesbians, gay men, and bisexuals. In part, this is because the term is easier to use than the expression "lesbian, gay, and bisexual people." But even in this unifying sense, there is a political overtone to the term "queer." For queer students, use of the term as unifier is a statement of sisterhood and brotherhood. The term represents a call to all closeted and non-political members of the lesbian, gay, and bisexual community to unite. Throughout this work as well as in other writings (Browning, 1993; Doty, 1993; Signorile, 1993), it may be difficult to determine what sense of the term is implied. The problem is that the term itself is caught in the midst of a cultural struggle related to how lesbian, gay, and bisexual people are represented. This makes clarity difficult at times, but usually the context provides clues as to which meaning is intended.

A central theme of this book is "coming out"--the process of proclaiming one's queer identity (queer in a unifying sense). Although for some individuals the term "queer" is understood as a negative expression used to oppress lesbian, gay, and bisexual people, much in the same light that "nigger" might be used to insult black people, I purposefully select this term. Many people with same-sex attractions identify as queer in an effort to dismantle and then reconstruct their own meaning of a lesbian, gay, or bisexual identity. They have turned a weapon of their adversaries--queer used as a negative term--into a cultural tool to battle the politics of silencing. The reclamation of the term "queer" is akin to Evelyn Brooks Higginbotham's (1992) discussion of how black people have traditionally conceptualized the term "race": "Black people endeavored . . . to dismantle and deconstruct the dominant society's deployment of race. Racial meanings were never internalized by blacks and whites in an identical way" (pp. 266-267). In making this argument, Higginbotham builds upon the work of Mikhail Bakhtin

(1981):

> The word in language is half someone else's. It becomes "one's own" only when the speaker populates it with his own intention, his own accent, when he appropriates the word, adapting it to his own semantic and expressive intention. Prior to this moment of appropriation, the word does not exist in a neutral and impersonal language (it is not, after all, out of a dictionary that the speaker gets his words!), but rather it exists in other people's mouths, in other people's contexts, serving other people's intentions: it is from there that one must take the word, and make it one's own. . . . Language is not a neutral medium that passes freely and easily into the private property of the speaker's intentions; it is populated--overpopulated--with the intentions of others. Expropriating it, forcing it to submit to one's own intentions and accents, is a difficult and complicated process. (pp. 293-294)

Higginbotham concludes: "Blacks took 'race' and empowered its language with their own meaning and intent" (p. 267). In a similar sense, lesbian, gay, and bisexual students at Clement University are involved in a cultural battle to expropriate the term "queer." They desire to give it their own meaning, one that has a positive denotative and connotative value--a term to be celebrated. The following comment from a student at Clement sheds light on this notion:

> The other day I told my roommate about the queer dance we planned. I asked him if he wanted to go. I told him there would be a lot of straight supporters there. But he laughed when I used the word queer to refer to myself and other gays. Then I explained to him its different meaning and why some of us call ourselves queer and that we refuse to let others use this word against us. "Yes, I'm queer and I'm proud of it." It's that kind of thing.

Language changes with social and cultural contexts. The same can be said of the language of identity. "Cultural identity. . . is a matter of 'becoming' as well as 'being.' It belongs to the future as much as to the past" (Hall, 1990, p. 225). At one time, few people used the term "black" to identify people of African descent. The same is true of "African American." Still today, many blacks do not identify themselves as African American. The term "queer" may be examined in this same light. Although queer may be used to describe all people who identify as lesbian, gay, or bisexual, many do not adopt this term as a personal identifier. The same might be said of the term "gay," which once (and still does for many) included any person identifying with same-sex attractions but, recently, has come to refer mainly to men with almost entirely same-sex attractions. Many bisexual men and women, as well as lesbians, reject the term "gay" as a self-identifier. Gay as a unifying term for lesbians, gay men, and bisexuals may be on its way to the scrap heap of words. Twenty years from now, queer may be assigned to that same heap.

I highlight the term "queer" in this text for two reasons: first, because of its political and cultural potential to change how lesbian, gay, and bisexual people are represented; and second, because most of the students involved in this project use the term.

The conceptions that students at Clement have about what it means to be queer are probably different from those in other parts of the country. Shane's discussion of queer as an attitude of *wanting* to tell someone off for making heterosexist remarks may differ from a queer student in New York City who may be totally belligerent in addressing heterosexism. Then again, there may be other queer students at Clement who in certain settings might "read" someone for making heterosexist remarks in conversation.

Language is circumscribed by individual and collective identity. Students at Clement not only are engaged in a struggle for individual identity but are also in the process of creating a sense of community. For many of these students, the group struggle revolves around what it means to be queer. That great variance exists from one individual (or one locale) to the next in terms of what it means to be queer is hardly surprising. For example, students living in a relatively non-violent rural area (such as where Clement University is located) may have a different conception of queerness than students in a large urban area beset with violence. The notion of a queer identity at Clement University (as well as elsewhere) is in its infancy, and as such, differences are to be expected. The point is that words and meanings are never static and always contestable.

The expropriation of the term "queer" calls attention to the general theoretical framework undergirding this study: critical postmodernism. Critical postmodernists recognize the significant role that language and culture play in shaping individual and group identities. As Michel Foucault (1970) notes, "The fundamental codes of culture--those governing its language, its schemas of perception, its exchanges, its techniques, its values, the hierarchy of its practices--establish for every man, from the very first, the empirical orders with which he will be dealing and within which he will be at home" (p. xx). One such fundamental code is heterosexuality.

The norm of heterosexuality is a cultural code that has been passed from one generation to the next through social institutions such as education. In general, this view is discussed as social reproduction theory (Giroux, 1983b). Social reproduction theory relates to how dominant cultural patterns are continually reconstituted in subsequent generations. Schooling has been one of the principal foci of reproduction theorists. From critical studies of schooling, researchers have uncovered student resistance--attitudes and behaviors students exhibit that resist the norms and values conveyed in schools. Resistance is a response to cultural forces that attempt to reproduce and, in effect, silence those alienated by the values and norms being taught. Resistance may be envisioned as a form of cultural work on the part of a marginalized group. By cultural work, I refer to the process of utilizing political and educational means to modify cultural codes and patterns. In chapter 2, I argue that the actions of queer students at Clement move beyond traditional notions of resistance and in fact are more oppositional in nature. As we shall see, this has significant implications for how we conceptualize queer students as a cultural enclave.

With the preceding discussion in mind, the intent of this work is to highlight the experiences of queer students at Clement as they struggle to gain a private and public voice. The private voice relates to the initial aspects of the coming-out process. A public voice pertains more to becoming politically active and struggling for gay rights in general. Five questions direct this project:

1. What does it mean to "come out" and what changes do students go through as a result of this process?
2. What does it mean to adopt a queer persona?
3. What role does the queer subculture play in the coming-out process and in the larger process of identity development?
4. How can a critical postmodern perspective help us to understand identity issues related to gay and bisexual students?
5. What can be done to improve campus environments for lesbian, gay, and bisexual students?

BORDER CROSSING

This work is based on an ethnographic study of gay and bisexual male students enrolled at Clement University. By students, I refer to individuals enrolled full- or part-time in either undergraduate or graduate courses.

Although the study includes some observations of lesbian and bisexual women, for the most part the focus is on gay and bisexual men. I have not included women in this study because ethnographic research is demanding work that requires crossing cultural borders that are typically foreign to the investigator. Developing a sense of trust among groups of gay and bisexual college students was difficult enough without adding problems compounded by gender differences. This is not to say that I do not deal with gender. As I elaborate in later chapters, issues of sexual orientation and gender are highly interactive and, therefore, difficult to separate.

Another cultural border not addressed in this work, at least not to any significant degree, is that of race. This was not by choice but by necessity. In nearly two years of participant observation within the lesbian, gay, and bisexual community at Clement University, I met eight male students of color who identified as queer, gay, or bisexual. This is in large part due to the fact that Clement University has a disproportionately small minority student population (only 9 percent are minorities). Of these eight students, seven agreed to participate in formal-structured interviews, hardly enough to draw significant conclusions about the unique experiences of gay or bisexual students of color. Nevertheless, I include comments from the seven men in the hope that they generate further inquiry into the dual oppressions of race and sexual orientation.

The preceding two paragraphs highlight a significant issue about lesbian, gay, and bisexual people: Does a singular gay community exist? One could argue that there are multiple communities: lesbians make up a community, as do bisexual women; gay men compose another community, as do bisexual men. Additionally, some might even point out that within these four distinct communities are further subdivisions based on race, age, or even the degree to which one is out. Perhaps the politically active queer students, who form the focus of this study, could be seen as composing their own community. Although the argument against a singular community can be made, I argue that there is a sense of solidarity among these diverse groups. In essence, the gay community is a community of difference. As I discuss in chapter 8, I believe there is a common bond that unites all lesbian, gay, and bisexual people--a sense of solidarity that derives from their marginalized status. As one student poignantly noted, "You know what makes the gay community? You and me against the whole world. The only way we can keep from being pushed into the corner or back into our closets--our cages--is to unite, to stand together. We have to stand together or be crushed. It's that simple."

CULTURE/ORGANIZATIONAL CULTURE

Lesbian, gay, and bisexual students at Clement University go to classes, attend parties, socialize, sleep in residence halls or off-campus apartments, and participate in sporting and cultural events. They do not exist in a vacuum; they are actively engaged in the everyday social life of the university. What students experience at Clement is a socialization process during which they establish, experiment with, and reestablish a sense of identity. By identity, I refer to *the sense of self that emerges from the interaction between the individual and social experience* (Mead, 1934).

Culture serves as a guiding framework for socialization. By culture, I adopt an interpretive perspective wherein culture is shaped by, and in turn shapes, social interaction (Smircich, 1983). This is the classic notion of culture put forth by Clifford Geertz, who theorized that "man is an animal suspended in webs of significance he himself has spun" (1973, p. 5). In this light, "culture is both the medium and the outcome of discourses" (McLaren, 1991, p. 237). Moreover, culture is not merely a meta-phenomenon that exists at the societal level and nowhere else; indeed, all social organizations exhibit unique cultures. As Burton Clark (1970, 1972) and William Tierney (1988) delineate in their work, colleges and universities as organizations also have distinctive cultural characteristics typically thought of as organizational culture. For students at Clement University, the organizational culture shapes their experiences and, in general, their socialization.

To understand the socialization of lesbian, gay, and bisexual students at Clement University, it is helpful to contextualize the organizational culture. All organizations exist within specific societies that place an indelible mark upon those organizations. Therefore, before examining the culture of Clement University, I explore aspects of American society that relate to lesbian, gay, and bisexual people. Additionally, Clement University represents an institution of higher learning and shares common traits with other colleges and universities. I also discuss research on campus environments that pertains to lesbian, gay, and bisexual students. I organize my discussion from the larger reference point--the culture of U.S. society--to smaller reference points-- campus cultures, and then the culture of Clement University.

The Culture of U.S. Society

One way of contextualizing the culture of a society is to examine some of the key social and political issues--the points of contention. In American society, for example, Oregon barely voted down Ballot Measure 9, which "equate[d] homosexuality with sadism, masochism, and pedophilia" (Woestendiek, 1992, p. A1). While Oregon nearly passed Measure 9, conservatives in Colorado succeeded in passing their own measure (Amendment 2) which made it illegal to pass legislation protecting lesbian, gay, and bisexual people from discrimination and also voided existing protective legislation. The backlash from the passage of Amendment 2 resulted in a Colorado boycott where gay-supportive individuals, businesses, and associations excluded Colorado as a site of vacation and business plans.

On a national level, concern over the military ban on lesbian, gay, and bisexual people resulted in President Clinton passing a "don't ask, don't tell, don't pursue" policy. This policy has received mixed reviews. Some see it as a step in the right direction, but others define the policy as a major victory for conservatives who seek to deny openly gay people the opportunity to serve in the military. Even though the new policy took effect on October 1, 1993, gay activists and the American Civil Liberties Union plan to challenge the policy on two counts. First, lawyers are prepared to argue that the policy restricts the speech of lesbian, gay, and bisexual people in the military (they would not be able to talk about their sexual orientation), thereby violating First Amendment rights. Second, lawyers contend that the new policy violates the Fifth Amendment, which prohibits the federal government from denying "equal protection under the law." However, based on previous federal and Supreme Court decisions (which have essentially argued that soldiers do not have the same constitutional rights as citizens), gay activists are approaching this round in the courts with guarded optimism (Labaton, 1993).

Homophobia and heterosexism are revealed not only through national issues such as military service or legislation but also through acts of violence and intimidation. Gregory Herek (1989) points out that lesbians and gay men are prime targets of hate crimes. Of 2,074 individuals surveyed by the National Gay and Lesbian Task Force, nearly all respondents had at one time or another been harassed, threatened, or attacked. A Minneapolis study revealed that out of 289 lesbians and gay men who responded to a questionnaire, 72 percent had experienced verbal harassment because of their sexual orientation. In a Philadelphia study, 73 percent of the gay men and 42 percent of the lesbians had experienced criminal violence at some point in their lives as a result of their sexual orientation. Furthermore, high rates of verbal abuse were also reported in the Philadelphia study: 92 percent for gay men and 81 percent for lesbians. Herek also provides the following contextual data. In Bucks County, Pennsylvania, a gay man was found with multiple stab wounds and his throat slit. In Portland, Maine, three women were assaulted after being verbally abused with anti-lesbian epithets. One of the women suffered a fractured jaw, several broken teeth, and bruised ribs. In Boston, a gay man was attacked by three men after leaving a bar. The three assailants raped him with bottles, lighted matches, and other implements while stating repeatedly, "This is what faggots deserve." In Stockton, California, a gay minister was found dead in his car with his skull crushed and his throat slit. In Greensboro, North Carolina, a cross was burned outside the home of a gay man who hosted a group working on an AIDS project.

What can we conclude about the culture of American society in relation to lesbian, gay, and bisexual people? First, we live in a society where daily harassment and violence occurs against lesbian, gay, and bisexual people. Second, despite evidence of abuse, legislative efforts to protect the basic rights of gay people are often met with resistance, as the cases of Colorado and Oregon demonstrate. Third, we live in a country where lesbians, gay men, and bisexuals who profess patriotism to their country and a willingness to take up arms and die if necessary cannot do so if they are open about their sexual identity--at least not during peacetime (Shilts, 1993).

Campus Cultures/Climates

One might expect that our college and university communities as "ivory towers" of intellect would be bastions of equality where persecution of individuals based on sexual orientation is nonexistent. Such is not the case. Research demonstrates that homophobia and heterosexism are rampant on American campuses.

> Despite the changes in the last two decades, gay people are still swimming in a largely oppressive sea. Most campuses do not have gay student groups. Most gay faculty members and administrators have not come out. Even on campuses that have proven responsive to gay and lesbian concerns, progress has often come through the work of a mere handful of individuals who have chosen to be visible. . . . There are still many campuses in the United States where no lesbian or gay man feels safe enough to come out. From a gay vantage point, something is still wrong in the academy. (D'Emilio, 1990, p. 17)

Although John D'Emilio points out the general problem of hostile campus environments, a number of specific campus assessments provide more concrete evidence. Arthur Reynolds (1989) reports that gay men rate the climate at the University of Virginia lower than do straight men in regard to emotional support. Jane Low (1988) notes that students at the University of California at Davis rate campus intolerance of homosexuality as more serious than racial intolerance. Several universities report investigations of campus climates wherein lesbian, gay, and bisexual students are significantly more likely to face harassment and discrimination than heterosexual students (Cavin, 1987; Herek, 1986; Nelson & Baker, 1990; Nieberding, 1989). In separate studies conducted at Pennsylvania State University, Anthony D'Augelli (1988, 1989c) discusses high rates of victimization among lesbian and gay students, faculty, and staff, with three-fourths reporting that they had been verbally harassed and one-fourth reporting that they had been threatened with physical violence.

The Culture of Clement University

Clement University is a large research university situated in the eastern portion of the United States. Recently, Clement adopted a sexual orientation clause as part of the university's official statement of non-discrimination. The clause was passed after much hard work and lobbying on the part of students, faculty, and staff. The adoption of the clause situates Clement University among a handful of other major universities such as the University of Illinois, Rutgers University, and the University of Massachusetts that have enacted similar policies (Nelson & Baker, 1990). In fact, only about 10 percent of all postsecondary institutions have enacted protective clauses for gay people (NGLTF, 1992).

Students at Clement University have become increasingly involved in the campus political arena; this is seen in the growth and prominence of LGBSA (Lesbian, Gay, and Bisexual Student Alliance), the Graduate Student Coalition (GSC), and ALLIES (a group of straight and unidentified students formed to battle homophobia). A changing political climate at Clement is also evident in the creation of a campus committee concerned with homophobia and heterosexism. These groups established a formidable alliance at about the same time a new president began his tenure at Clement. Concurrent developments such as these make for a dynamic state of affairs at Clement University.

The climate for gay students at Clement is somewhat of a paradox: to the casual observer, Clement University might be seen as a university actively dealing with gay issues. Yet serious problems still exist. Despite the adoption of the sexual orientation clause and the emergence of LGBSA as a prominent student group, a strong conservative aura permeates the culture of the university. This may, in part, be due to its geographic location--situated in the middle of a conservative rural area. Many students who attend Clement come from the surrounding area and reflect the conservative values of the region. One student noted: "Part of the problem is that Clement has a high percentage of students with rural backgrounds. It's hard to get around that, and the rural nature tends to promote conservatism." To provide evidence of the conservative nature of Clement's culture, I call upon the results of a campus survey conducted in 1991. The study was designed to evaluate the climate for lesbian, gay, and bisexual students. The study revealed high degrees of homophobia among the student body. For instance, 68 percent of heterosexuals indicated they would feel uncomfortable if they found out that their roommate was lesbian, gay, or bisexual. Additionally, 65 percent indicated that lesbian, gay, or bisexual students should remain "closeted." Alarmingly, 54 percent of the students believed gay students would be harassed if they were open about their sexual orientation. About 46 percent of heterosexual students said they would tell a derogatory joke about gay students.

Among the lesbian, gay, and bisexual students surveyed, the following results were noted. Approximately 67 percent believe they will be harassed on campus because of their sexual orientation. Eighty-seven percent agreed that a lesbian, gay, or bisexual student should remain closeted to avoid harassment. Fear of being labeled as a gay was also noted: 33 percent reported that they stay away from areas of campus where gay students hang out, and another 29 percent reported fear of being seen socializing with other lesbian, gay, or bisexual students.

Written comments obtained from the campus survey also indicated a high degree of intolerance. These comments were in reference to an open-ended question asking the respondent to comment on issues related to sexual orientation at Clement. Fifty-two percent of the written comments were oppositional or hostile in nature. The following are typical of the attitudes expressed by the hostile and oppositional comments:

• "Gay, lesbian, and bisexual lifestyles are immoral and should not be accepted as an ok lifestyle. I don't want my children to grow up thinking because everyone's doing it, it is all right. The Bible calls it sin!"
• "Homosexuals should not force their beliefs onto me and should stop trying to justify their insane actions."
• "I feel too many resources are being devoted to minority groups. If you can't fit in, get the hell out!"
• "I'm fed up with kow-towing to sexual perverts! It's enough to have to coexist with people who are tearing down the traditional family structure. Don't cram them down my throat. If we extend special privileges to them, why not do the same for child molesters, etc.? They're perverts too!"
• "It is obvious that homosexuals are genetically inferior to heterosexuals, and therefore should be eliminated, before they contaminate the rest of the 'straight' world. If I were in a position of power I would implement a program to eliminate homosexuals to make the world a better place to live."

The last comment brings to mind one of the darker chapters in recent history of campus life at Clement University: in 1989 a student sent a campus computer message offering a rationale for "killing homosexuals." Not long after this incident, a coach at Clement told a national newspaper that homosexual students would not be permitted on the team.

Additional evidence of the conservative nature of Clement is the Christian fundamentalist assault on lesbian, gay, and bisexual students and the support given by a member of the board of trustees to a right-wing student newspaper. I discuss the fundamentalist assault first.

In the fall of 1991 one of the campus fundamentalist ministers challenged any homosexual student, faculty, or staff member to a discussion of the Biblical interpretation of homosexuality as sin. A similar challenge was put forth recently by a Hidden Falls minister (Hidden Falls is the community within which Clement University is situated) who proposed an open debate entitled "Is sodomy a civil rights issue?" The pejorative language used to frame the debate highlights how sexual orientation issues and issues of sexual identity in general are frequently reduced by conservatives to the sexual act. Lost in such argumentation is the fact that issues of attraction and identification--whether physical, emotional, spiritual, or intellectual--are complex, multifaceted matters and deserve deeper analyses than simply equating them with the sexual acts that might occur between two men or two women.

Although the case of the Hidden Falls minister did not occur on campus, I mention this incident because of the interconnectedness of Clement University and Hidden Falls. Clement University is roughly the same size as Hidden Falls, and each is defined in part by the other. Whether this is the result of their similar size or a host of other factors (such as the prevalence of university staff who live in and identify with Hidden Falls), it is difficult to separate the identity of Clement University from the surrounding community and its cultural morass.

During the course of the 1992-1993 academic year, a highly contested issue in Hidden Falls was the addition of a sexual orientation amendment to the town's fair housing ordinance. This issue was often the focus of the official Clement University student newspaper. The sexual orientation amendment was also a source of great division within the religious community of Hidden Falls, where conservative clergy came out against the clause and moderate to liberal clergy supported the clause. After much clamor and repeated delays, the amendment was adopted.

Another significant example of the generally conservative climate of Clement is a newly formed student newspaper, which gets much of its support from a member of the board of trustees. This paper, known as *The Student Voice*, has sided against multicultural education, affirmative action, women's studies, gay rights, feminism, and virtually every other form of cultural and social change related to diversity. The paper reflects an editorial stance similar to the *Dartmouth Review* and other conservative student publications that have emerged over the last ten to fifteen years (Smith, 1993). The following are excerpts from two articles that appeared in *The Student Voice*:

I just can't see how people who are concerned about the ozone layer, rain forests, and other aspects of nature are not worried about the preservation of the human race. Homosexuality isn't natural and it shouldn't be treated as such. . . . Maybe instead of trying to gain sympathy and acceptance from a population which thinks homosexuality is wrong, homosexuals should seek help to fit in with society, instead of trying to change it for themselves. Homosexuality should be treated as a problem which impedes one socially, and we [should] give help and counsel to gay people to [achieve] a better and healthier life-style.

AIDS is a terrible disease and those who obtain it innocently should be greatly pitied, but those who get it through their behavior deserve no pity whatsoever. Those who engage in homosexuality, fornication or intravenous drug use are taking a calculated risk. Every time they engage in their behavior they are gambling that they will not contract the HIV virus. As in any gamble, they will win or lose. If they win, they're lucky; if they lose, they're dead. Either way it was a risk they chose to take. If they choose to gamble with their life, they deserve no pity if they lose. In my opinion, those who contract AIDS through risky and sinful behavior are fools. They deserve no sympathy other than that which we commonly reserve for those who have a want of intelligence.

Few people at Clement University openly question the right of students to express such opinions. The issue here is not freedom of speech but the message that a campus community sends to gay students when this kind of discourse is supported by a high-ranking official of the university. Would such an assault be permitted were this any group other than gay students?

The preceding pages not only highlight the oppressive aspects of the culture of Clement University but also allude to some advances for lesbian, gay, and bisexual students and staff. Again, the culture of Clement University is somewhat of a paradox: although there is a conservative aura underlying the university, queer students and staff have pushed issues of homophobia and heterosexism to the forefront in an effort to achieve fair treatment. In some areas they have had great success, with perhaps the best example being the adoption of the sexual orientation clause. In a very real sense, sexual orientation has been invented as a topic for discussion. Queer students and staff have forced gay rights into the discourse of the university. In the past, incidents of homophobia and heterosexism likely would have gone undiscussed at official university settings. However, they certainly might have been discussed by lesbian, gay, and bisexual students and staff, but most likely behind closed doors. Because sexual orientation and related issues are at the forefront of much of the discourse at Clement, it makes an ideal site for this study.

Within the overall cultural setting of Clement University, queer students struggle to create their own discourse and ultimately claim their own space. As D'Augelli (1989b) points out, "Control of the right to speak--the privilege of beginning discourse, shaping it, and setting its limits--is a critical tool in the production of knowledge and truth, and, therefore, power" (p. 126). The lesbian, gay, and bisexual student organization at Clement leads the way in this cultural and political struggle to gain voice.

THE LESBIAN, GAY, AND BISEXUAL STUDENT ALLIANCE (LGBSA)

LGBSA has two co-directors, one male and one female student, who take turns leading meetings. Meetings are held on Monday nights at the student cultural center in a room about the size of a small classroom, with chairs lining the perimeter. Typically the meetings begin with an icebreaker, in which students get a chance to introduce themselves to the group. On one occasion students were asked to describe the most unusual job they ever held. A gay student who once worked as a phone-sex operator got the biggest applause. On another occasion students had to select a flavor they would be if they were ice cream: "latex" got the most laughs. Although sexual innuendos are commonplace, the tone of the meetings is nonetheless serious and there is frequent disagreement. Perhaps the most heated debate during the 1992-1993 academic year related to whether LGBSA would endorse candidates for student government president and vice president. After almost two hours of hearing candidates and debating qualifications, the group finally agreed, by a slim margin, on whom to endorse.

Despite its tendency to get bogged down in various controversies, LGBSA has played a significant role in pushing for campus change. For example, the organization was instrumental in getting a sexual orientation clause added to the campus non-discrimination policy and has been on the forefront of practically every discussion or decision related to gay issues.

LGBSA was founded in 1985 as LGSA, the Lesbian and Gay Student Alliance. LGSA added bisexuals to its charter in 1991 and thus became LGBSA, the current organization. LGSA followed in the footsteps of HOCU--Homophiles of Clement University. HOCU was founded in 1971 and met a great deal of resistance from the university administration. In fact, Clement lawyers investigated the chartering of HOCU in an attempt to prevent its right to occupy campus space. Eventually the university revoked HOCU's charter, which led members of the organization to file a federal suit arguing that their constitutional rights under the First and Fourteenth amendments had been violated. Nearly two years later the case was settled out of court and HOCU had reestablished itself as a legitimate student organization.

More than twenty years have passed since the initial confrontation between the University administration and the first gay student organization. Today, LGBSA forms the heart of the queer student movement at Clement. Because of LGBSA's role in the political arena, and because LGBSA members were the most accessible research participants, many of the observations and much of the discussion contained in this work pertain to these students. Students who are less out, or even closeted, are difficult to meet; and to convince them to participate in an interview is not easy. I did, however, convince several students and they are included in the sample. In this regard, the data and discussion that follow are not based on a representative sample of gay and bisexual male students at Clement. In sampling gay college men, no one really knows what a representative sample would or should look like, because we can only guess how many students are closeted. Because of the difficulty in reaching closeted students, involving students who are out and politically active is the best available avenue.

WHAT FOLLOWS

In the next chapter, "Critical Postmodernism," I highlight the theoretical underpinnings of this study. The focus is on the synthesis of critical theory and postmodern social theory. I examine how critical perspectives have been utilized in education. Additionally, I discuss issues related to culture and subculture and how queer students as a social collectivity might be conceptualized from a subcultural perspective. Finally, I explore literature related to lesbian, gay, and bisexual students.

In chapter 3, "The Study," I explore the methodological aspects of the project. I discuss key epistemological questions related to critical postmodernism and its compatibility with critical ethnography. Additionally, I delineate the basic elements of ethnographic research and relate them to this project.

In chapter 4, "The Closet and a Negative Existence," I explore what Eve Kosofsky Sedgwick describes as the "epistemology of the closet." I rely upon student narratives to provide concrete evidence of the heterosexism and homophobia inherent in the cultures of Clement University and American society. Also highlighted is what I describe as "negative existence" in which life is defined not by possibility but, instead, is rooted in inhibition, denial, and negativity. The work of Foucault and his notion of "the power of the norm" provides theoretical support.

Chapter 5, "Coming Out in College," reveals the experiences of gay and bisexual men as they struggle to claim a sense of identity. For most of the students in the study, coming out is experienced as a rebirth. Throughout this chapter we hear stories of transformation as gay students enter a new realm of public recognition and visibility. As one student noted, "Coming out was like the whole world was taken off my shoulders, and every time I come out to someone else my burden becomes even lighter." Theoretically, this chapter relates to the politics of gaining voice discussed in the work of Henry Giroux, Tierney, and feminist scholars such as Lorde and bell hooks.

Chapter 6, "Cultural Workers and the Politics of Silencing," details the political and cultural struggles queer students face in battling heterosexism and homophobia. I interweave theoretical discussions of silencing tactics exhibited by the promotion of dominant cultural beliefs, mores, and norms with incidents of harassment and discrimination experienced by gay and bisexual men. For many members of the gay community, coming out to oneself and then to others is only an initial step in a larger, equally important process--the development of a group identity. Once out, some gay and bisexual students begin the process of becoming politically active and identifying as queer. These students may be thought of as cultural workers who seek to empower both those who are closeted and those who exist in the gay social sphere. The work of Foucault and Giroux frames the theoretical discussions in this chapter.

In chapter 7, "Culture/Subculture," I examine queer students at Clement as a subculture. More specifically, I argue that because of their oppositional stance to heterosexuality, queer students are best conceptualized as a contraculture. Even though queer students exhibit common social patterns, which warrants their treatment as a contraculture, they also reveal a great deal of diversity. With this in mind, I highlight various issues that continually challenge the queer contraculture as a basis for group identity. Finally, just as culture serves as a general framework for identity, I maintain that the queer contraculture serves as a source of identity for lesbian, gay, and bisexual students at Clement University.

In chapter 8, "Identity and Socialization," I examine the constructivist/ essentialist debate over sexual orientation and move toward a synthesis of these divergent perspectives. I discuss a notion of a gay identity that includes elements of both constructivist and essentialist views. Whereas traditional ethnic groups are socialized as youth, through primary socialization, lesbian, gay, and bisexual people are predominantly socialized later in life, through secondary socialization. At Clement University, the queer contra-culture serves as the principal source of socialization to gay ethnicity. The work of Steven Epstein helps to frame this chapter.

With regard to achieving educational and social change, Dolores Grayson (1987) maintains, "Simply understanding what it is like to be gay or lesbian is not the answer" (p. 137). With these words in mind, I conclude with chapter 9, "Toward Communities of Difference," by focusing on praxis. I highlight the participation of Clement University students in the March on Washington and focus on their efforts to change the culture of American society and the university. I delineate various problems uncovered by this project and offer solutions based on student suggestions and my own interpretations. I summarize the main points of the study and return to the idea of communities of difference.

Finally, throughout the text I discuss my role in this project. Situating oneself within the text falls within a critical postmodern view of the role of author/researcher, who is seen as an intimate part of the research process. For critical postmodernists, the separation of the researched from the researcher is rooted in a Cartesian dualism that enforces binary oppositions, which, in the end, create a false sense of objectivity and neutrality. By highlighting my own engagement with research participants, I hope to avoid the dichotomization of the researcher and the researched. Thus, throughout the text I offer personal insights that focus primarily upon the following questions: What does it mean to undertake research of gay and bisexual students? How has my own sense of identity been reframed? In essence, I place myself as a subject of my own study.

NOTES

1. All personal nouns, such as Clement University, are pseudonyms. This includes those names used for students involved in this project. However, I note that many of the students wanted me to use their real names in order to express openness and pride about their sexual identities.

2. Throughout this text I use the terms "climate" and "environment" interchangeably and think of them as indicators of the larger concept of campus culture.

2

Critical Postmodernism

> Oppositional paradigms provide new languages through which it becomes possible to deconstruct and challenge dominant relations of power and knowledge legitimated in traditional forms of discourse.
> --Henry Giroux, *Border Crossings*

Gay students at Clement University have forged a group identity that has enabled them to enter their agenda into the political terrain of the University. Without a sense of communal struggle, this would not have been possible. The most politically involved lesbian, gay, and bisexual students recognize the importance of a group identity and have rallied around the expropriation of the term "queer" as a means to forge that identity. In redefining what it means to be queer, these students have contributed to a new representation of a gay identity.

Of the forty students involved in this study, twenty-seven (68 percent) use the term "queer" either as a personal identifier or in reference to the larger lesbian, gay, and bisexual community. All leadership positions in LGBSA are filled by queer students. Roger and Tito are two leaders of the queer student movement at Clement. Tito, a senior, became actively involved in LGBSA and gay politics soon after coming out: "Once I came out to myself I became a lot more political. I have always been very vocal about gay and lesbian rights and about the fact that sexuality is more gray than we want to accept. When I came out what became different is that I took the label queer and before I didn't." For Tito, queer students are those lesbian, gay, and bisexual students who are "political and proud."

Roger, a junior, believes that "heterosexual culture is very set on making gay and lesbian people invisible, whether they use physical violence or institutionalized violence. Coming out is a way of battling back." Roger talked about the community aspect of a queer identity: "It is essentially a sense of connection and identity with other people whom you have something in common with--a similar sexual orientation." In this light, community is defined by one's sexual orientation and the acceptance of that orientation by the group members. This is unique to lesbian, gay, and bisexual people in that few heterosexuals identify as their community of choice "the straight community." In fact, by most definitions of community, no such social collectivity exists.

Although Roger is proud of the queer community, at the same time he is often disappointed by it: "The times when people won't stand up for what is right and fight courageously for fundamental rights all people should have. Like walking down the street holding hands with your lover without facing harassment." Roger believes that if more people would come out and become politically active, "things would be better for all of us."

In the narratives of Tito and Roger, one gains a sense of the two different meanings of the term "queer." Tito uses the term in reference to only those lesbian, gay, or bisexual students who are "political and proud," whereas Roger uses queer as a blanket term for the entire community of lesbian, gay, and bisexual students. Throughout my interactions with Roger and Tito, both used queer in these two different manners. Queer, thus, has both a political and a unifying sense. Without a unifying quality, a call for a group identity, the politics of sexual identity is reduced to individual struggle. The hope of students like Tito and Roger is not so much that other students adopt the term "queer" as a self-identifier but that, instead, queer students work for the day when all lesbian, gay, and bisexual people will be out and proud about their sexual identity. Queer students see visibility as a necessity if they are to achieve social and economic justice. The importance of visibility is highlighted by Lauren Berlant and Elizabeth Freeman (1993) in their analyses of Queer Nationality: "Visibility is critical if a safe public existence is to be forged for American gays" (p. 201).

The manner in which Roger and Tito employ the term brings to mind a previous era when African Americans employed the phrase "Black Power." Berlant and Freeman (1993) note a similar parallel in discussing the Black Panthers and the queer version--the Pink Panthers:

> The Panthers, a foot patrol that straddles the "safe spaces" . . . and the "unsafe spaces" of public life in America, not only defend other queer bodies but aim to be a continual reminder of them. Dressed in black T-shirts with pink triangles enclosing a black paw print, they move unarmed in groups, linked by walkie-talkies and whistles. In choosing a uniform that explicitly marks them as targets, as successors of the Black Power movement, and as seriocomic detectives, the Panthers bring together the . . . embodied threat implicit in individual queers crossing their subcultural boundaries, and the absurdity that founds this condition of sexual violence. (p. 206)

As with so many identity terms used by racial or ethnic groups, such as the way Black Power once was used by some African Americans, the concept of queer is contested terrain. On the one hand we hear nearly all student leaders at Clement calling themselves queer, and we hear other students who are in various stages of coming out explicitly rejecting the idea of being called queer. For the latter group of students, their attitude toward sexual orientation is something that ranges from a private matter that ought not be discussed to a liberal notion that gay people are quintessentially similar to everyone else.

The concept of queer rejects the notion that everyone is alike. The idea is confrontational and accentuates difference. Ultimately, one of the central tensions in discussions about sexual identity revolves around the notion of difference. Are people who have same-sex attractions similar to heterosexuals? How do similarity and difference get played out?

I use the term "queer," then, in two manners. Whenever one of the central characters speaks of himself as queer, I echo his definition. I also use it in a broader sense to force us to consider throughout the text one of its central dilemmas: How might we define sexual orientation in the late twentieth century, and in doing so, how does it aid our understanding of identity?

Central to understanding the struggles of Tito and Roger, as well as other lesbian, gay, and bisexual students at Clement, are the concepts of language, culture, and power. Language serves as the medium through which power gets enacted, while at the same time language achieves relevancy through the enactment of power. Power circumscribes social interactions, which are all shaped by the confines of culture. In turn, social interactions serve to reshape culture. In this light, language, culture, and power form a never-ending web of complex meaning.

Critical postmodernists concern themselves with how language, culture, and power interact to shape social experience. The focus is on human agency--the process of engaging in emancipatory struggle. Queer students at Clement are engaged in such a struggle.

Critical postmodernism is the synthesis of two theoretical traditions: critical theory and postmodern social theory (Tierney & Rhoads, 1993). Postmodernists describe an advanced society that has moved beyond modernism, whereas critical theorists typically focus on an advanced stage of capitalism. In either case, both describe the confining nature of culture and the degree to which human agency might play a role in reconstituting culture and identity.

Postmodernism has its roots in French intellectualism, in which the work of Jean Baudrillard, Jacques Derrida, Michel Foucault, and Jean-Francois Lyotard stand out (Agger, 1991; Benhabib, 1986; Kellner, 1988, 1990). Critical theory largely derives from the Frankfurt School in Germany, where Herbert Marcuse, Max Horkheimer, Theodore Adorno, and Jurgen Habermas advanced a Marxist view of culture and society (Agger, 1991; Benhabib, 1986;

Geuss, 1981; Jay, 1973; Kellner, 1989).

In what follows, I explore the basic tenets of critical postmodernism and relate them to the social context faced by lesbian, gay, and bisexual students at Clement University. I also call upon feminist theorists, such as bell hooks and Patti Lather, who have made significant contributions to our understanding of language, culture, and power. Based upon an extensive review of literature on critical and postmodern social theory (Tierney & Rhoads, 1993), I organize the discussion around the following themes: the critique of positivism, culture and identity, power/knowledge, marginalization and empowerment, and the union of theory and practice. I synthesize the discussion by highlighting queer students at Clement University as a student subculture engaged in opposition. In doing so, I highlight previous research on lesbian, gay, and bisexual college students.

THE CRITIQUE OF POSITIVISM

Foucault (1978) argues that prior to the early 1800s a homosexual identity did not exist. David Greenberg (1988) and John Boswell (1980) point to different time periods in which homosexual identities might have emerged. In any case, even though homosexual acts are likely to have existed previously, at various points in history the emergence of categories of people labeled as "homosexuals" took root. From an early Judeo-Christian perspective, homosexual acts were deviant, along with other acts such as adultery, fornication, and sodomy, but there was no social category known as homosexuals.

With the advance of positivism, homosexuals became labeled by the medical and psychiatric professions as a deviant subpopulation. Positivism is the generalized scientific process whereby complex phenomena are reduced to the observable, and then operationalized in order to be measured. Scientific objectivity and rationality are fundamental to positivistic science. In this light, positivism goes hand in hand with instrumentalism--the use of rationally calculated means toward achieving precisely defined ends. Fay (1987) discusses positivism as the "representation of natural phenomena in quantitative terms [and] the use of experimental procedures to test hypotheses" (p. 87). He relates positivism (modern science) to instrumentalism:

> Instrumental action . . . advocates a particular conception of explanation, namely, one that is non-teleogical, causal, and nomological. This is pertinent because explanations cast in this form are precisely the sort suitable for effective instrumental action by providing a firm foundation for an agent's expectations as to the behavior of objects. That is, knowing the natural causes and effects of various events, agents will have a basis on which they can successfully intervene

in the flow of events to bring about efficiently the results they desire. (p. 87)

Once categorized as a deviant subpopulation, early social science practitioners sought to identify, explain, and then "cure" homosexuals. They followed what seemed like a fairly rational path. However, an essential ideological question was left unasked: Who decides what is normal?

Although positivism has produced many scientific advances in the natural and physical sciences, critical postmodernists argue that such a view is incompatible with both the complexities of and the desire to improve social life. Along this line, Habermas (1973) argues that positivism has become so prevalent that any other form of critical investigation is seen as irrational or even worse--as dogmatic. "Any theory that relates to praxis in any way other than by strengthening and perfecting the possibilities for purposive-rational action must now appear dogmatic" (p. 264). The non-teleological nature of positivism renders certain questions, such as those related to justice and equality, moot. As Stanley Aronowitz points out in the introduction to Max Horkheimer's (1972) book, "Positivist thought, by accepting the role of science as the careful recording of the facts and limiting its generalizations to the unity of apparent reality, leaves the question of historical development aside and becomes instrumental to the prevailing system of power" (p. xiii). For critical postmodernists, positivism contributes to the marginalization of lesbian, gay, and bisexual people because fundamental ideological questions have been left out of the equation.

Positivism perpetuates a view of homosexuals as fundamentally different from heterosexuals. Such an essentialist position runs counter to more recent postmodern interpretations of sexual orientation as socially constructed. In chapter eight, I argue that both the traditional positivist view (essentialism) and the more recent postmodern perspective (social constructivism) are inadequate in explaining the diversity of gay identities.

The intent of critical postmodern researchers and theorists is to consider how theories shape the ways in which we think about, and then define, society and individuals. Central to understanding this process are the concepts of culture and identity.

CULTURE AND IDENTITY

Foucault (1980) argues that culture is more than a mere byproduct of social life. Culture shapes social life. Discourse plays an essential role in understanding the shaping power of culture. Foucault "deals with discourse's role in producing a 'Kafkaesque' system which constrains and frames human potentialities. He analyzes knowledge and truth as bases for the institutionalization of mechanisms of control, and as resources for excluding deviants and framing the context and terrain of social life" (Lamont & Wuthnow, 1990, p. 296).

Normalization lies at the heart of Foucault's views on culture. One significant way that normalization is accomplished is through the "importance of the action of the norm" (Foucault, 1978, p. 144). The norm becomes the prescribed code that societal members must follow. Cast in this light, all organizations have similar qualities in that they constrain individual action: "prisons resemble factories, schools, barracks, hospitals, which all resemble prisons" (Foucault, 1979, p. 228).

Modern societies have become sites of social imprisonment in which the observance of norms governs daily life. Prior to modernization, violators of the social order faced physical punishment such as public torture. With modernization came population growth and urban expansion. These changes dramatically altered the very nature of social life. Physical punishment was largely replaced by a system of constraints and privations in which surveillance moved from the "state" to the responsibility of "faithful" citizens. "From being an art of unbearable sensations punishment has become an economy of suspended rights" (Foucault, 1979, p. 11). Social control is achieved by inducing in citizens a state of conscious and permanent awareness of expectations and social repercussions. This is the power of normalization that Foucault highlights.

Heterosexuality is one source of identity that has become normalized through social surveillance and vigilance. In turn, an economy of rights and privileges revolves around compliance with heterosexuality. Those who comply benefit. Those who do not face social scrutiny and suspended rights.

Gay students at Clement University have experienced this economy of suspended rights firsthand. Roger dreams of someday being able to walk down the street and hold hands with his lover, a privilege most heterosexuals take for granted. Likewise, Tito hopes someday to go to parties and nightclubs with a best friend who out of fear remains closeted. Shane longs for the day when he will not have to screen everything he says. And Andrew envisions a world in which being gay does not have to be the exhausting political statement that it is now for him.

The irony, of course, is that the dream of these students who want to accentuate their difference by using terms such as "queer," and, as we shall see, a host of other confrontational tactics is in part a dream to be respected and accepted for who they are. In a way, these students are revolutionaries who want to overthrow the social order, yet, at the same time, be of that order --as defined in their own manner. This touch of irony raises a key concern of the text: How do we decenter norms and at the same time maintain viable communities? Indeed, in a postmodern world, how do we define community?

In framing heterosexuality as the norm, culture acts as a source of identity, distributing power in the form of status to some and marginalizing others. In conferring the label of deviance upon homosexual behavior, the normalizing society has created a social identity through which people who exhibit same-sex attractions are categorized and scrutinized as abnormal, sick, or perverse. By the same token, the emergence of "homosexual" as a distinct category of people has made it possible for lesbians, gay men, and bisexual people to organize around a common identity. Without a sense of a group identity, there cannot be a unified effort to legitimize homosexual identities. Steven Epstein (1987) notes: "How do you protest a socially imposed categorization, except by organizing around the category?" He goes on to add: "Just as blacks cannot fight the arbitrariness of racial classification without organizing as blacks, so gays could not advocate the overthrow of the sexual order without making their gayness the very basis of their claims" (p. 19).

The overthrow of the sexual order is the goal of students like Roger, Tito, Andrew, and Shane. Their strategy is fairly simple: take control of the language and discourse associated with sexual identity. In essence, their struggle is over self-representation and the power to name.

POWER/KNOWLEDGE

Few theorists have done more to unravel the complexity and interrelatedness of power and knowledge than Foucault, who maintains that power must be understood beyond its ability to limit or constrain. It must also be seen as a shaper of knowledge:

> Power would be a fragile thing if its only function were to repress, if it worked only through the mode of censorship, exclusion, blockage and repression, in the manner of the great Superego, exercising itself only in a negative way. If, on the contrary, power is strong this is because, as we are beginning to realize, it produces effects at the level of desire--and also at the level of knowledge. Far from preventing knowledge, power produces it. (1980, p. 59)

Foucault, and critical postmodernists in general, argue that all knowledge is particular; there are no grand narratives that convey universal truth.

The focus of the critical postmodern critique of knowledge is science and empiricism. As Lyotard (1984) makes clear, science exists within its own truth claims and therefore cannot be challenged outside of those claims. Likewise, Peter McLaren (1991) posits that "empiricism seeks vainly to transcend the political, ideological, and economic conditions that render the world into cultural and social formations" (p. 37).

For critical postmodernists, there is only narrative--localized claims to understanding based on subjectivity and personal experience. Lyotard (1984) elaborates:

> Truisms are fallacious. In the first place, scientific knowledge does not represent
> the totality of knowledge; it has always existed in addition to, and in competition
> and conflict with, another kind of knowledge, which I will call narrative in the
> interests of simplicity. I do not mean to say narrative knowledge can prevail over
> science, but its model is related to ideas of internal equilibrium and conviviality
> next to which contemporary scientific knowledge cuts a poor figure, especially
> if it is to undergo an exteriorization with respect to the "knower" and an
> alienation from its user even greater than has previously been the case. (p. 7)

Lyotard's work is helpful in that he poses the following question: "Who
decides the conditions of truth?" (p. 29). In dealing with questions related to
sexual orientation, critical postmodernists ask: Who decides which sexual
identities are normal or abnormal, acceptable or perverse, healthy or sick? The
answer lies in who possesses the power to define; in this light, critical
postmodernists uncover knowledge by locating power itself.

In terms of Clement University, heterosexuality has been inscribed as the
norm and lesbian, gay, and bisexual people have had little or no voice in the
matter. Queer students at Clement have participated, along with staff, in
raising sexual orientation as an issue, thus challenging the normalcy claims of
heterosexuality. Power defines knowledge. And "sexuality is never simply a
set of acts unconnected to questions of power" (Goldberg, 1993, p. 7). In
raising fundamental questions about same-sex attraction, queer students have
staked their claim to power and to the discourse of sexual orientation.

The manner in which queer students have challenged the traditional views
of sexual orientation at Clement University underscores the relational quality
of a critical postmodern view of power. Power is inherent in all social
relations; all groups and individuals have at their disposal some degree of
power. Nicholas Burbules (1986), in building upon the work of Foucault,
elaborates two key points of a relational conception of power. First, he argues
that power is neither chosen nor avoided by social actors; power is the
necessary byproduct of circumstances that bring people into social interaction.
Second, he argues that within all power relations a tension exists between
compliance and resistance. Although one agent in a social relation may be
successful in prescribing to another, a certain degree of autonomy is lost by the
advantaged agent in trying to "preserve" the relation. Also, the advantaged
agent is in many ways dependent upon the compliance of the disadvantaged
and must grant a degree of resistance to the disadvantaged agent. The idea
that the advantaged must depend on the involvement of the disadvantaged is
important in understanding social reproduction and resistance theory, which I
discuss later in this chapter.

Power is revealed by the dominance certain ideologies have over others, evident in the way advantaged groups shape the lives of disadvantaged groups. Often, one group's power over another is exercised not so much in an organized strategy but is more subtly evident in the way various aspects of their culture--their narrative knowledge, their discourse, so to speak--become legitimated by institutional mechanisms. Jeffrey Weeks (1988) points out that the prevailing discourse of sexuality "tells us what sex is, what it ought to be, and what it could be" (p. 208). An illustration at Clement University is the way in which instructors frequently offer heterosexual couples as examples in class, as if same-sex couples were nonexistent. One student noted:

> I get tired of all the heterosexist assumptions teachers and students make. They're always asking questions like "what do you look for in the opposite sex?" They didn't ask me those questions, thank God. I mean my sexual orientation is not something I want to bring up in class. It gets on my nerves. When they say things like that I go, "Well, I don't go out with women." It just seems that if they had more knowledge of queer lives, more sensitivity, I wouldn't have to even worry about it. A lot of the examples in classes are always, you know, "Janet and Dave or Bob and Carol." And when you get married . . . blah, blah, blah.

The comments from this student provide an example of the frustrations gay students often face in classes, the result of their lives being excluded from the academic experience.

Gay students at Clement exist within a culture in which their narrative knowledge and experiences have been rejected as irrelevant. Power has been exercised to define heterosexuality as the norm and homosexuality as deviant. Kenneth Gergen (1991) describes the postmodern condition as "marked by a plurality of voices vying for the right to reality--to be accepted as legitimate expressions of the true and the good" (p. 7). Queer students at Clement are engaged in a struggle to have same-sex attractions accepted as "legitimate expressions of the true and the good." Once again, the irony of their struggle is apparent. By accentuating their *difference* as queers, they seek *acceptance* within the culture of both the university and American society.

MARGINALIZATION AND EMPOWERMENT

Critical postmodernists concern themselves with issues of marginalization and empowerment. The endeavor is to help individuals and groups understand how society and psyche have structured people's lives in such a way that they might organize around self-determination. Only through such an awareness is social and psychological emancipation possible.

Douglas Kellner (1989) points out in his discussion of society and psyche that ideology plays a significant role in human oppression. Sexism, for instance, has been at the root of much of the feminist critique of women's oppression, and heterosexism at the root of oppression of lesbian, gay, and bisexual people. Whereas some social theorists and practitioners focus on specific ideologies, others note the interwoven nature of all oppression. Hooks (1984) elaborates:

> Individuals who fight for the eradication of sexism without supporting struggles to end racism or classism undermine their own efforts. Individuals who fight for the eradication of racism or classism while supporting sexist oppression are helping to maintain the cultural basis of all forms of group oppression. While they may initiate successful reforms, their efforts will not lead to revolutionary change. Their ambivalent relationship to oppression in general is a contradiction that must be resolved or they will daily undermine their own work. (p. 39)

I cite hooks for two reasons: first, she highlights some of the overlapping assumptions critical postmodernists and feminists share; and second, she sheds light on the major project of critical postmodernism--to confront oppression by uncovering cultural and ideological constraints that, in turn, assist groups in the process of self-determination. Hooks maintains that people can become accomplices in their own oppression. As we shall see, students such as Roger and Tito believe that their friends who remain closeted or who only participate in the social life of the gay community contribute to their own and others' oppression.

THE UNION OF THEORY AND PRACTICE

Critical postmodernism is grounded in the Marxian imperative: "To comprehend the world in order to change it" (Marcuse, 1972, p. 216). Critical postmodernists seek to bridge the chasm between research and action, a gap that they argue has been promoted by traditional positivist research. Habermas (1973) claims that the dominance of positivism has buried practical questions related to social action and emancipation. Positivism, he argues, inevitably leads to practical questions that only concern themselves with technical issues. Habermas elaborates on the basic problem of positivism: "No attempt at all is made to attain a rational consensus on the part of citizens concerning the practical control of their destiny. Its place is taken by the attempt to attain technical control over history by perfecting the administration of society" (p. 255). Instead of asking what the social consequences are of a process and who is marginalized by it, an emancipatory question, positivism has led many social scientists instead to ask how a process can be made more efficient, a technical question.

The goal for critical postmodernists is to reestablish the relationship between research and praxis by invoking our reflective nature. Richard Bernstein (1976) is helpful in his discussion of critical theorists:

> Critical theorists see the distinction between theory and action which is accepted by advocates of traditional theory, as itself an ideological reflection of a society in which "theory" only serves to foster the status quo. By way of contrast, critical theory seeks genuine unity of theory and praxis where the theoretical understanding of the contradictions inherent in existing society, when appropriated by those who are exploited, becomes constitutive of their very activity to transform society. (p. 182)

Critical theorists see theory itself as a form of social transformation. They do not reject empiricism but argue that empirical reality is grounded in one's theoretical positioning.

As Lather (1986b) notes, "Rather than the illusory 'value-free' knowledge of the positivists, praxis-oriented inquirers seek emancipatory knowledge" (p. 259). The challenge for this study is to utilize theory in a way that enlightens our understanding of oppression and contributes to human agency. How can a researcher/theorist make sense of the complex lives of gay students at Clement University in a way that aids in self-organization and empowerment? This is the task that lies ahead.

SYNTHESIS: QUEER STUDENTS AS A CULTURAL ENCLAVE

One of the first researchers to explore the cultural aspects of student life was Howard Becker (1963), who defined student culture as "a set of understandings shared by students and a set of actions congruent with those understandings" (p. 12). Queer students at Clement University share certain understandings about sexual identity and marginality. For example, they have "shared" understandings of "the closet" and what it means to "come out." As a cultural enclave situated within the larger cultural setting of Clement University, queer students may be conceptualized as a student subculture. Although the preceding conclusion seems self-evident, a review of previous research on student culture and subculture raises some doubts.

Numerous researchers have explored college students from a cultural/subcultural perspective (Horowitz, 1987; Kuh, 1990; Moffatt, 1989). This type of research was especially popular in the 1960s and early 1970s (Becker, 1963, 1972; Bushnell, 1962; Clark & Trow, 1966; Leemon, 1972; Wallace, 1966).

Recent research on student subcultures has tended to adopt a more critical focus than early studies, which were largely descriptive. Present-day research often examines how student groups and subcultures offer resistance to the schooling process. Discussions of resistance are found in a range of theories described as social reproduction theory (Giroux, 1983a, 1983b). Theories of social reproduction examine educational institutions as sites where dominant cultural patterns get reconstituted through the schooling process.

The interests of society's dominant cultural groups are served by schools through "prescriptions" provided to students. Paulo Freire (1970) notes: "Every prescription represents the imposition of one man's choice upon another, transforming the consciousness of the man prescribed to into one that conforms with the prescriber's consciousness" (p. 31). The influence of prescriptions can be seen in similar fashion to Foucault's notion of the "action of the norm." Although certain prescriptions and norms are promoted in schools, compliance is not altogether guaranteed. The lack of compliance on the part of students has led to a reformulation of reproduction theory in which the analyses of student resistance is central. Resistance relates to student behaviors and attitudes that are reactions to the oppressive structures within the school. In terms of resistance research and theorizing, the work's of Giroux (1981, 1983a, 1983b, 1986) and McLaren (1986, 1989) stand out.

Resistance is evidenced in a variety of ways but frequently results in students forming their own subculture. A number of researchers have documented resistance within K-12 settings (Eckert, 1989; Fine, 1986; Friend, 1993; MacLeod, 1987; McLaren, 1986; McRobbie, 1978; Ogbu, 1988; Willis, 1977). Consistent throughout much of this research is the notion that student subculture contributes to social reproduction. In other words, the subculture enacted by marginalized students frequently serves to continue their own exploitation.

The role that subcultures play in contributing to the marginalization of students also has been observed in postsecondary settings. For instance, Dorothy Holland and Margaret Eisenhart (1990) highlight the effects that college socialization--especially a peer culture related to dating--has on lowering the aspirations of college women. Others have observed similar phenomena among varying collegiate social groups (Rhoads, 1991, 1992; Sanday, 1990; Tierney, 1992; Weis, 1985).

Subcultures inherently run counter to some degree to the dominant culture of the organization or society. Research on student subcultures has demonstrated how students adopt norms, values, and beliefs that tend to resist the prescriptions of the educational setting. However, in the case of queer students at Clement University, these students move beyond resistance and, in fact, oppose the dominant norms of sexuality. The concept of subculture falls short here in that it fails to distinguish the degree of opposition to the dominant culture. The dilemma is that a more precise concept similar to that of subculture, but different from it, is needed.

J. Milton Yinger (1960) makes a distinction between subculture and "contraculture." He criticizes the careless use of the subculture concept and suggests a more precise delineation:

> To sharpen our analysis, I suggest the use of the term contraculture wherever the normative system of a group contains, as a primary element, a theme of conflict with the values of the total society, where personality variables are directly involved in the development and maintenance of the group's values, and wherever its norms can be understood only by reference to the relationship of the group to a surrounding dominant culture. (p. 629)

Yinger's work highlights the fact that queer students at Clement University are best conceptualized as a contraculture and not as a subculture. Their stance toward heterosexuality and heterosexual culture is more than resistance; it is oppositional in nature.

In highlighting queer students as a contraculture, I offer the following definition: *a social collectivity engaged in on-going interaction in which shared understandings are evidenced, some of which define the collectivity in opposition to the dominant culture.* Shared understandings may be thought of as similar values, beliefs, and attitudes. This definition derives from Yinger's insights as well as other interpretivists' work on culture and subculture (Becker, 1963, 1972; Smircich, 1983).

Elane Nuehring, Sara Beck Fein, and Mary Tyler (1989) examined the informal structure of lesbian and gay communities in terms of Yinger's (1960) concept of contraculture. "As a basic element, the gay collectivity manifests a system of sexual preference based on norms that conflict with the values of the broader society. Its existence cannot be understood except in relation to the conflict with the dominant culture" (Nuehring et al., 1989, p. 69). They also note that an important function of the lesbian and gay contraculture is that it generates and validates a positive self-image as well as serving as a source of identification.

As Nuehring, Fein, and Tyler point out, the contraculture in effect is defined by its opposition to mainstream culture. Queer students then face a complex postmodern dilemma: their struggle to decenter the norms of heterosexuality poses a risk to their own sense of oppositional identity. In seeking respect, acceptance, and equal rights, they face the possibility of losing the sense of "queerness" by which they define themselves. Yet, in allowing heterosexism to endure, they face prejudice and discrimination.

In their struggle to change the culture of Clement University, queer students have helped to get a sexual orientation clause added to the university's non-discrimination policy. On the surface, passage of the clause seems to be a step toward denorming heterosexuality. But on a deeper level, little has changed. Lesbian, gay, and bisexual students still face harassment and discrimination, and their experiences are still largely excluded from the classroom.

By their increased visibility and inclusion on various campus committees (the campus committee for equity is one example), queer students have opportunities to shape the discourse of the university and thereby challenge the norms of heterosexuality.   However, as a result of their participation in university governance and decision making they face the possibility of being co-opted by a system they seek to alter dramatically. In seeking to subvert the norm, the norm subverts them.

The question queer students must confront is: How to achieve the same rights and privileges afforded heterosexuals, and retain a sense of queer identity, thereby avoiding assimilation?   The question hinges upon how communities are conceptualized, an issue some critical postmodernists discuss in terms of "communities of difference" (Tierney, 1993b).   For critical postmodernists, dialogue about difference can serve as a connective fabric among diverse peoples. In this light, difference is not something to be erased but is instead something that can bring people together. I return to this issue later in the text.

In defining queer students at Clement University as a contraculture, I argue that "out" and politically involved lesbian, gay, and bisexual students share a common experience that is in opposition to the mainstream culture of the institution. Such a definition fits a significant number of students at Clement University, who frequently describe themselves as "family." However, not every lesbian, gay, or bisexual student shares this experience. In chapter 7 I highlight the diversity of the gay student community and how issues such as race and bisexuality impact the solidarity of the queer contraculture.

Some students select the queer contraculture as their family of choice, but others look elsewhere for social involvement, support, and validation. For example, Tom is a first-year student who prefers socializing in Random House, a group of gay and bisexual men who meet biweekly at an anonymous site. Students such as Tom, those not actively involved in gay politics, frequently come under criticism from queer students. "Outness"--the degree of being out and politically active--is another issue that serves to divide the lesbian, gay, and bisexual community.

Defined as a contraculture, queer students at Clement constitute a highly amorphous social collectivity whose membership is unclear to nearly everyone. Nonetheless, one requirement is fairly obvious: membership requires identification with same-sex attraction. As a unique cultural group comprised of lesbian, gay, and bisexual college students, what does previous literature tell us about these students?

Literature on Lesbian, Gay, and Bisexual Students

As I noted in chapter 1, an extensive review of the literature related to lesbian, gay, and bisexual college students for the period 1970 to 1993 turned up over 200 articles and books. The majority of these studies relate to issues of campus climate, homophobia, and attitudes toward gay people. Even though these studies may be helpful in understanding the nature of campus environments with which gay students must contend, they shed little light on their everyday experiences of coping with such environments. In essence, the lives of lesbian, gay, and bisexual students are rendered invisible. In what follows I discuss only those studies that identify some of the unique qualities and experiences of gay students. I divide this research into two categories: (1) developmental issues, and (2) general characteristics.

Developmental Issues. A number of researchers have examined developmental issues faced by lesbian and gay students with a variety of stage theories proposed (Cass, 1979; Finnegan & McNally, 1987; Marso, 1991; Miranda & Storms, 1989). Consistent throughout this body of research is the notion that self-labeling as a lesbian or gay student and self-disclosure of sexual orientation are related to the development of a positive lesbian or gay identity.

Ann Fleck Henderson (1984) argues that developmental issues are different for lesbian and gay students. For women, sexual orientation is generally established later than for men and is seen as less psychologically and interpersonally threatening. D'Augelli (1991a) describes a study of identity dilemmas faced by gay men in college, reporting that students' first disclosure to another person and their coming out typically occur in college. He also reveals that students' most significant fears relate to telling family members of their sexual orientation and that mothers tend to be more supportive than fathers.

Jane Banzhaf (1990) examines gay white males who attended college during the 1960s, 1970s, and the 1980s, focusing on their selection of role models. Of significance, she concludes that subjects from the 1970s and the 1980s believe that they might have made different career choices had identifiable gay role models been more available. Bruce Etringer, Eric Hillerbrand, and Cheryl Hetherington (1990) also discuss career development concerns among lesbian and gay students, as well as heterosexual students, concluding that gay men show the highest level of career choice uncertainty and that lesbians demonstrate the lowest.

Characteristics. In examining dating relationship patterns, Rick Schwabish (1990) notes intimacy motivation to be more salient for gay men than for heterosexual men. In a study of perceptual differences in gender ideals, Dennis Hellwege, Katye Perry, and Judith Dobson (1988) report lesbians to be the most consistently androgynous and heterosexual men to express more traditional sex role standards, whereas heterosexual women and gay men fall between these two groups and, generally speaking, are more ambivalent about androgyny.

Loyd Wright and Sheila Fling (1983) reveal that lesbian and gay students report greater family stress than heterosexual students and that bisexual students tend to view themselves more negatively than heterosexual students. Joel Yager, Felice Kurtzman, John Landsverk, and Edward Wiesmeier (1988) highlight a higher prevalence of behaviors and attitudes related to eating disorders among gay students than heterosexual male students, although other studies examining self-concept and personality adjustment report no significant differences (Cullinan, 1973; Horstman, 1975).

A point that can be taken from the preceding literature is that gay men face developmental issues different from those faced by heterosexual men and women, and lesbians. An important aspect of identity development for lesbians and gay men revolves around the issue of openness: those students most open about their sexual orientation seem to be more comfortable with their sense of self. Another point is that although coming out may be beneficial in developmental ways, it often results in students becoming the targets of homophobia and harassment. Unfortunately, the literature tells us very little about bisexual men and women.

SUMMARY

Three points form the basis of my argument throughout this book. First, queer students constitute a contraculture in that they do not merely resist heterosexuality as the dominant norm; they reject it entirely. At the center of this oppositional stance is the notion of queer identity. Queer students seek to subvert the norms of heterosexuality while at the same time they run the risk of being subverted themselves by the norm: in their struggle to gain respect and equal treatment, they face possible assimilation. Critical postmodern notions of communities of difference shed light on this conceptual dilemma (Tierney, 1993). I return to this idea in chapters 7, 8, and 9.

Second, in adopting a queer persona, students highlight a belief that lesbian, gay, and bisexual people are inherently different from heterosexuals. At the same time, in their goal to gain respect and acceptance and their desire to decenter society's norms of sexuality, queer students oppose the socially imposed definition of the "homosexual" as deviant or abnormal. Their stance highlights the inadequacies of an either/or view of essentialist and social constructivist treatments of sexual identity. An alternative to the constructivist/essentialist dualism is the idea that sexual identity is "both inescapable and transformable" (Epstein, 1987, p. 34). The solution to this conceptual dilemma lies in the notion of gay ethnicity, which I discuss extensively in chapter 8.

Finally, few studies have been conducted on lesbian, gay, and bisexual students. The vast majority of the more than 200 works examined focus on campus environments and on students' attitudes toward gay students; few actually study the experiences of lesbian, gay, and bisexual students. Indeed, their experiences in academe remain largely a mystery. Therefore, throughout this work (especially in chapters 4, 5, and 6) I attempt to shed light on the experiences of gay students as they struggle to create their own place in academe.

3

The Study

A good interpretation of anything--a poem, a person, a history, ritual, an institution, a society--takes us into the heart of that of which it is the interpretation.

--Clifford Geertz, *The Interpretation of Cultures*

"Wow! What's going on here? I'm not different from anyone else. That's not right." These were Jerry's thoughts on a day back in eighth grade when his girlfriend broke up with him because students were saying he was gay. Jerry was confused. Their accusations made no sense to him. He played sports like other boys: "I played soccer in eighth grade. I couldn't see myself fitting the stereotypical gay." Being gay meant hanging out with girls and playing with dolls, the "sissy-boy" syndrome; Jerry was into sports, so how could other kids think he was gay?

Nearly ten years later, his junior high and early high school experiences began to make sense to him. "Looking back now, I was screaming gay. But you know, I just didn't see it at the time." Jerry became sexually involved with a male friend while in high school, but it was not until he developed strong emotional feelings for another friend that he first truly questioned his sexual identity: "It was during the end of eleventh grade that I had a very difficult period. I was falling for a really close friend of mine. That's when I first started thinking that I might be gay."

Jerry Sandaval is a senior who majors in English. His high-top red sneakers are his trademark, along with his red, wavy shoulder-length hair that he often wears in a pony-tail. Although Jerry is not sure what he will do when he graduates, he knows that eventually he wants to work in gay politics. Law school is a possibility. Jerry's career plans have been a disappointment to his father, a successful businessman who dreams of Jerry following in his footsteps. He feels he has let his father down twice: by his career choice and by coming out as a gay man.

Although Jerry identifies as gay, deep inside he feels he is really bisexual: "I realize that I'm capable of feelings for people of both genders. I just choose to be involved with men. I guess I have a lot of internalized biphobia. Bisexuality is even less understood than being gay." Jerry has plotted his attractions in his head, and every four months or so he meets a woman who intrigues him enough to consider dating. "Occasionally I go for it. But mostly I just try to ignore it."

Jerry came out two years ago and has become "fascinated" by the politics of sexual identity. "It's one thing to think about being gay and how that affects me, but I've become much more aware of the impact of anyone being gay in society, the politics of it all." As part of the politics of being gay, Jerry incorporates certain mannerisms into his behavior that he believes help to identify him as a gay man. For example, in conversation Jerry adopts some of the traditional stereotypes associated with gay men: his voice sometimes rises to a higher pitch when he speaks, and he often uses his hands in a limped-wrist fashion to make a point. Although Jerry believes it is necessary for lesbian, gay, and bisexual people to be highly visible, he also expressed some remorse about the political aspect of being queer: "It's almost a shame that it is so political and that people just can't be gay like if they were straight."

Why can't Jerry "just be gay"? What does it mean to be gay, or bisexual, or queer? What makes the experiences of lesbian, gay, and bisexual people so different? Or are they different? These questions relate to culture and identity and how people make sense of their lives. They are not the types of questions to be tested by the traditional tools of science. Answers to such questions require intense involvement in the lives of others. These are interpretive questions. In this chapter I lay out a strategy for pursuing such questions.

CRITICAL POSTMODERNISM AS A GUIDE TO METHOD

In the preceding chapter I described a theoretical framework built upon two related theories: critical theory and postmodern social theory. I now explore the research implications for conducting social analyses from a critical postmodern perspective. Critical postmodernism places certain obligations upon the researcher. Tierney and Rhoads (1993) delineate five specific premises upon which critical postmodern research is built:

1. Research is concerned with the structures in which the study exists;
2. Knowledge (and language for that matter) is not neutral but is contested and political;
3. Difference and conflict, rather than similarity and consensus, are used as

organizing concepts;
4. Research is praxis-oriented; and
5. All researchers/authors are intimately tied to their theoretical perspectives. We are all positioned subjects.

In the following paragraphs I relate each of these issues to the study at hand.

The first premise calls attention to *structures* in which a particular study resides. In the case of gay students at Clement University, what are the structures with which I must be concerned? What is the institutional culture of Clement University like? What is the nature of the larger societal culture that serves as a backdrop for the experiences of gay students at Clement? As I noted in chapter 1, both the wider societal culture and the more local institutional culture can be characterized as heterosexist and homophobic. The fact that gay students at Clement must contend with these two forms of oppression frames much of the discussion in chapters 4 through 9.

The second premise deals with the issue of *knowledge*. The question that must be asked in conducting critical postmodern research is this: Whose definition of knowledge is enacted, and whose is irrelevant? Another question relates to the types of knowledge that get enacted. In relation to this study, knowledge related to heterosexuality is elevated as superior to knowledge related to homosexuality. This is obvious in the literature related to lesbian, gay, and bisexual students, in which for the most part knowledge of these students is virtually nonexistent. In fact, until only recently, research related to gay people was categorized as studies of deviance (Tierney, 1993a). The elevation of heterosexuality over homosexuality also is evident in legislative issues in Colorado and Oregon as well as in communities such as Hidden Falls. No one suggests that heterosexual people should not be included in various laws and policies that protect personal rights. The fact is that heterosexuals are automatically included in any discussions of constitutional rights, whereas the rights of lesbian, gay, and bisexual people are always debated. The message is quite clear: heterosexuality has superior status to homosexuality.

A third premise of a critical postmodern perspective is that research must contend with *difference* and *conflict*. In the preceding paragraph, I pointed out how one form of knowledge is privileged over another. However, the privileged position of heterosexuality is not without its attacks. In this study I focus on the cultural contestation over the hierarchy of sexualities. Additionally, even as the gay community conducts its own battle with heterosexism and homophobia primarily outside its community, there is internal struggle as well. The internal struggle revolves around differences within a community that divide and re-create new and smaller cultural groups such as the queer contraculture. The issues associated with this third premise are discussed in chapters 7 and 8.

Critical postmodern research is *praxis-oriented*. Issues of praxis must be dealt with in order for this study truly to fall within the critical postmodern genre. My responsibility here is met in a variety of ways. First, much of this project focuses on the social agency of gay students at Clement University. Specifically, I focus on queer students who engage in political and pedagogical activities aimed at re-creating the culture of Clement and the larger societal culture. In and of itself, this is insufficient. A second point, however, relates to one of the goals of this project--to generate possibilities for future reorganization of college communities based on the ideas of students. I devote the concluding chapter to the overall issue of social agency and discuss problems and solutions based on input from gay and bisexual students. A third point relates to my own involvement in creating social change. As I discuss later in this chapter, I engage in a multitude of activities concerned with changing the oppressive conditions found at Clement University and throughout American.

Finally, the fifth premise relates to the explication of the *researcher/author* as a positioned subject. This entails informing the reader of the researcher's own stance and position in conducting a study. This relates not only to the theoretical perspective of the researcher (explained in chapter 2) but also to personal issues that the researcher as a positioned subject may bring to a study. For instance, how does the sexual orientation of the researcher/writer affect the research process and the overall findings? How does the author view sexuality and sexual orientation? If these questions could be answered simply, I would do so now. But they are complex questions that unfold with the text.

Research is about knowledge; and knowledge is contextual. There is no finality of knowledge or understanding of reality that a researcher must search out and reveal. Critical postmodernists argue that the world is composed of multiple narratives. The goal of critical postmodern researchers is to unravel local narratives told by diverse members of our society. In the case of this study, the goal is to make sense of the experiences of gay and bisexual students and provide a vehicle for sharing their narratives in a way that is enlightening and empowering for others. Such a task demands an intense and intimate understanding of those under study. I contend that such a goal requires the tools traditionally associated with ethnographic research. In this sense I follow in the footsteps of two classic works: William Foote Whyte's (1943) *Street Corner Society*, in which he utilizes ethnographic methods to explore the social structure of an Italian slum; and Howard Becker et al.'s (1961) *Boys in White*, in which the authors explore student culture in medical school.

Although ethnography provides the tools for uncovering complex social behavior, it falls short in its ability to link local behavior to the larger social structure. A solution lies in combining ethnographic methods with a critical lens such as critical postmodernism. In the following pages I discuss critical ethnography and highlight the methods used for this study.

CRITICAL ETHNOGRAPHY

Critical ethnography provides the opportunity to observe and record complex social behavior while incorporating a critical lens with which to decipher the complexities of culture. Gary Anderson (1989) talks about critical ethnography as follows:

> Critical ethnography . . . is the result of the following dialectic: On one hand, critical ethnography has grown out of dissatisfactions with social accounts of "structures" like class, patriarchy, and racism, in which real human actors never appear. On the other hand, it has grown out of dissatisfaction with cultural accounts of human actors in which broad structural constraints like class, patriarchy, and racism never appear. Critical theorists in education have tended to view ethnographers as too atheoretical and neutral in their approach to research. Ethnographers have tended to view critical theorists as too theory-driven and biased in their research. (p. 249)

Critical ethnography requires exploration of the structural constraints associated with class, patriarchy, racism, and *heterosexism*, in the case of this study. Such a demand frequently means that the researcher must be willing to confront difference. In fact, one of the goals of critical ethnography is to call attention to difference. This does not mean that the goal of the researcher is to divide communities by extricating differences within and between social groups; the concern is that difference is too often whitewashed over and never adequately addressed. This notion is rooted in postmodern notions of communities in which difference may be seen as unifying because of the dialogue it creates. In exploring postmodern notions of difference, Nicholas Burbules and Suzanne Rice (1991) note: "There is no reason to assume that dialogue across differences involves either eliminating those differences or imposing one group's view on others" (p. 402). They also contend that, "Dialogue that leads to understanding, cooperation, and accommodation can sustain differences within a broader compact of toleration and respect" (p. 402). Burbules and Rice go on to argue that what is needed is not an antimodern rejection of community but a postmodern notion of community rooted in more flexible and less homogeneous assumptions.

In addition to an emphasis upon difference, critical ethnographers recognize that they themselves are not removed from their settings but are participants within their own fieldwork. Traditional research tends to portray the researcher outside the production of knowledge, as one who merely goes about the gathering of facts. Critical ethnography, on the other hand, conceptualizes the researcher as intimately involved with research participants in the creation of knowledge. Andrew Gitlin (1990), in discussing what he terms "educative research" in schools, underscores this point: "Underlying most research methods is the assumption that knowledge is something that researchers extract from those studied; it is a one-way process that researchers use to put together a convincing story about the way things are or should be in school" (p. 447). Gitlin claims that what is lost in the traditional conception of research is the notion that knowledge also arises from dialogue between researchers and research participants.

To briefly summarize, critical ethnography links a specific method-- ethnography--to a general theoretical perspective--critical theory (in its broadest sense). I have discussed the "critical" aspect of critical ethnography. What is left is to elaborate the general techniques of ethnographic research and the specific methods employed in this study.

ETHNOGRAPHY

Ethnographic techniques have traditionally been the principal strategy for examining different cultures and complex social phenomena. James Spradley (1979) notes that ethnographic method yields "empirical data about the lives of people in specific situations. It allows us to see alternate realities and modify our culture-bound theories of human behavior" (p. 13). Henry Giroux (1983a) points out that because of the complexity of the relationships between students, schooling, and culture, ethnographic studies of schools have been the most illuminating.

Ethnographic research seeks as its goal what Clifford Geertz (1973) refers to as "thick description." One achieves thick description through extensive and intensive involvement in the culture of a group under study. There are several tools available to ethnographic researchers as well as some key issues with which they must deal. In the following pages I combine discussions of methods and issues in order to help the reader understand the process I employed.

Getting In

To conduct this research, I spent nearly two years studying the lives of gay students at Clement University (the academic years 1991-1993). The first year of the study was spent primarily reading literature on or about lesbian, gay, and bisexual students and following gay issues in the campus newspaper. I also made several initial contacts with lesbian, gay, and bisexual students. These contacts occurred through mutual acquaintances who were on staff at

Clement University. I attended two LGBSA meetings to get an idea of how the organization was run and to make myself visible. In a sense, the first year of this study was my own coming-out period.

Out of my initial contacts with members of the lesbian, gay, and bisexual community, a close friendship evolved with a queer student named Tito. Tito became one of my best friends and acted as a key informant for much of the early research. Tito first brought the term "queer" to my attention. He came over to my apartment for dinner, walked in the doorway, and proclaimed, "Rob, I'm not bisexual anymore. I'm queer." Tito took me to a number of social events during the first year of my study and served as interpreter on many occasions when conversations and jokes went over my head. He also noted homophobic behaviors I exhibited, such as the following incident recorded in my field notes:

> I was at The Odyssey, a downtown nightclub that hosts "alternative night" for lesbian, gay, and bisexual people on Sunday nights. But this was a Saturday and I was with some teammates from my summer softball team. We were drinking, hanging out, and checking out the scenery, when Tito and four or five other queer students came into the bar. The Odyssey is probably as big as a medium-size auditorium and it has a large dance floor in the center. You could plan to hook up with some friends there and never even bump into them. So I was pretty surprised when Tito and his friends showed up. I never expected to see queer students there on a Saturday. I walked over to say hello. I felt I had to or it would seem like I was homophobic. Well, as Tito of course pointed out later, I came across as "very homophobic." I must have looked over my shoulder at my softball buddies to see if they were watching me. Anyway, that's what Tito said. I can't remember feeling homophobic.

Along with Tito and his friend Stacy, I first attended Friendlies--the only gay bar in Hidden Falls. The three of us would go there on Sunday nights, around 1 a.m., after socializing and dancing at The Odyssey. Friendlies is a tiny place, about the size of two dorm rooms. The bar where drinks are served is on one side and a bench lines the other wall. Typically, there are four or five men seated on the bench. Not many women go to Friendlies. Some of the men are "not so subtle" in their "scoping": their heads often turn as they watch the butts of guys who walk past them. Many of the students I interviewed who were old enough to drink expressed a strong dislike for Friendlies. Some described the older men who hang out there as "trolls" and "closet cases." One student commented: "There are so many queer people there who are closeted and they feel they have to stay that way. People hit on me and they wouldn't even give me the time of day if I saw them on the street." Another added, "Friendlies is not the best place. There's too many trolls that hang out there. Trolls being fat, ugly, older men with beer bellies who think that you might actually want to have sex with them. 'Yeah, right!'"

When I walked into Friendlies for the first time, I was afraid that someone might see me enter "that gay bar." I was careful to make sure that no one was around who might have known me. The fear of entering was not nearly as bad as the panic that struck when I was about to leave. When people enter Friendlies they can look around and make sure no one sees them. But when they come out, they never know who might be standing outside the door or nearby. I remember the feeling I had every time I walked out of Friendlies: I was afraid to be seen by some of my straight friends. What would I say to them? I asked Tito about my fear and he said he felt the same way: "No matter how many people know that you are gay or bisexual, many more don't know and you never know when you might bump into one of the ones who don't know."

By the beginning of the second year, the fall of 1992, I was known by many students within the lesbian, gay, and bisexual community. At this point I began to participate actively in LGBSA meetings, eventually becoming a member of the organization. At the second meeting of the year, I explained my study and requested gay and bisexual men to participate in interviews. I also asked for volunteers to serve on an advisory panel that would assist me in various aspects of the project. When the meeting ended, Shane was one of the first students to approach me. This was about the same time of year as the National Coming Out Day rally discussed in chapter 1. Shane was in the initial stages of coming out and he was curious and suspicious about my project; he wanted more information. "What is it you hope to find?" he asked. I told him that I wanted to learn more about the struggles gay men face in developing a sense of identity. "So you're not out to try and figure out why we're fucked up?" I assured him that I was not. Shane agreed not only to participate in an interview but also to serve on the advisory panel. He is a central character in chapter 4.

Key Informants

Another aspect of the ethnographic process is developing relationships with informants. As Spradley (1979) points out, "Informants are a source of information; literally they become teachers" (p. 25). For the first year of my study, Tito served as my principal informant.

During the second year (Tito had graduated by now), members of the advisory panel acted in this capacity. I created the advisory panel primarily because of my lack of understanding of gay issues and culture. LGBSA meetings are very political. Some of the brightest and most politically astute students at Clement University participate in these meetings. Queer students can be demanding and intimidating at times, and my biggest fear was using the wrong word or phrasing something in the wrong way. The advisory panel provided me the opportunity to run ideas and questions by some of the more politically aware gay and bisexual students in a less demanding atmosphere. Typically we met at my apartment.

Participant Observation

Another important aspect of this study involves participant observation. To be immersed in a culture or subculture one must become a participant. "Participant observation combines participation in the lives of the people under study with the maintenance of a professional distance that allows adequate observation and recording of data," notes David Fetterman (1989, p. 45). Along with ethnographic interviews (to be discussed in the next section), participant observations provided much of the data for this project.

Participant observation affords the researcher an opportunity to corroborate data collected during structured interviews. People do not always behave the way they say they do. Participant observation can validate or take issue with interview data. This process of corroborating data is called triangulation, described by Norman Denzin (1989) as "the use of multiple methods" (p. 236). The typical instrument for participant observation is a notebook and pencil, or a good memory when discretion is warranted.

In this study, I participated in a number of activities. I attended nearly every LGBSA meeting during the academic year 1992-1993. I went to queer dances, parties, and movie nights. I hosted a pot-luck dinner and attended others. I went to The Odyssey on Sunday evenings and Friendlies too. I participated in local protests and days of celebration such as National Coming Out Day, where I stood on the steps of the school auditorium with other queer students and allies. And I rode on the bus with students and staff to join the lesbian, gay, and bisexual march on Washington, D.C.

Ethnographic Interviews

Another significant tool is the ethnographic interview. Spradley (1979) delineates three different types of questions that can be asked during interviews. Descriptive questions are used to obtain a sample of the native language and culture. Structural questions provide direction for understanding the basic units of an individual's cultural knowledge. And finally, contrast questions seek information related to the meanings of various words in the informant's language.

The following question is an example of a descriptive question. This question was designed to understand better the terminology used within the gay student community: *How do you identify in terms of sexual orientation?*

My initial expectation (before I became aware of the term "queer") was that the men I interviewed would describe themselves as gay or bisexual. However, I often got such responses as "gay/queer" or "gay socially but queer politically." This provided valuable information about language and terminology, which I used in subsequent interviews.

The next question is an example of a structural question: *What does coming out mean to you?* With this question not only was I trying to learn more about the personal feelings that coming out generates for different individuals, but I also wanted to learn if the process itself was conceptualized in different ways across individuals.

The following question is a contrast question. Here I wanted to learn more about the meaning of the terms "gay community" and "queer community": *What does the term "gay community" mean to you and how is it different from or similar to the term "queer community"?* This question helped me to understand the subtle differences between being gay and being queer. This last question emerged later in my research, after I began to understand the significance of a queer identity. It serves as an example of how qualitative research requires adjustments in interview questions.

As my understanding of the lesbian, gay, and bisexual community and language began to grow, it became apparent that many of my initial interview questions were poorly worded, imprecise, or unimportant. For instance, a question in my original protocol read: *Who else knows about your sexual orientation?* After learning more about the language used by gay students, I came to realize that this question was badly phrased. I changed this question to read: *Who else are you out to?* I altered the interview protocols several times as my understanding of gay identity and sexual orientation issues changed. Again, I emphasize the flexibility that ethnographers must employ in pursuing cultural understanding: to paraphrase Geertz, ethnographic research is not a scientific process (in a traditional sense of science) in search of some ultimate truth; rather, it is an adventure in search of meaning.

Other Forms of Data Collection

In addition to participant observation and ethnographic interviews, two other data collection techniques were utilized. A number of informal interviews were conducted throughout the two-year study. Informal interviews followed no set protocol and basically provided data about a range of issues. Informal interviews were helpful to get clarification about something I observed or reinterpreted in reading through interview transcripts. As an example, the term "read" as in "to read someone" was mentioned in a couple of interviews, but it was not until I had several informal discussions about the term that I began to fully comprehend its meaning. To "read" someone is to tell them off in an assertive and educational way. Typically, queer students do the "reading" while some heterosexist transgressor does all the listening.

Another form of data is the collection of documents that are examined as part of the data analysis process. Documents used in this study include newspaper articles on or related to gay issues, magazine articles, materials and handouts given out by LGBSA, and university materials related to lesbian, gay, and bisexual students and/or policies.

Validity and Reliability

In traditional research, issues of validity and reliability are central to evaluating the quality of a research project. Reliability typically is defined as the ability of another researcher using similar techniques to repeat a study, thus verifying the earlier researcher's findings. Validity refers more or less to the accuracy of the conceptual categories used to explain the phenomenon under study. As one might expect, these concepts take on different meanings when critical ethnography is employed. I first deal with validity.

Patti Lather (1986a, 1986b) argues that critical researchers ought to be concerned not with the traditional notion of validity but instead with face validity, catalytic validity, and construct validity. Face validity is simply a way of ensuring that the researcher's explanations and descriptions make sense to research participants. The assumption is that those under study have the right to interpret the explanations and findings of the researcher and then enter into dialogue with the researcher. This idea is similar to Yvonna Lincoln and Egon Guba's (1986) notion of member checks, which they describe as "the process of continuous, informal testing of information by soliciting reactions of respondents to the investigator's reconstruction of what he or she has been told" (1986, p. 77). Member checks are important in research where cultural borders are crossed, because the culture under study is typically foreign to the investigator. With regard to this study, the advisory panel served as a member check in that they reviewed written materials and as a group discussed interpretations. In several cases, alternate interpretations were offered that were then included in the written text.

The second issue relates to construct validity, which pertains to theory-construction. The idea is to demonstrate how one's original theoretical perspective has been altered by the data collected throughout the study. As Lather (1986b) notes, "Building emancipatory social theory requires a ceaseless confrontation with and respect for the experiences of people in their daily lives to guard against theoretical imposition" (p. 271). How has my understanding and interaction with gay and bisexual students changed some of my original assumptions? I had not anticipated the degree of conflict within the lesbian, gay, and bisexual student community at Clement. My assumption was that in light of social and institutional oppression, lesbian, gay, and bisexual students must obviously be a tightly knit group. This is not the case. Although certainly a bond of oppression exists within the many groups that constitute the gay community (which is itself a questionable social collectivity), lesbian, gay, and bisexual students are diverse groups of people. This has made me rethink the very notion of culture and subculture, community and difference, and related identity issues. These issues are paramount to chapters 7, 8, and 9.

Catalytic validity deals with whether the research is reality-altering and praxis-centered. Does the research contribute in some way to the social change? Tierney and Rhoads (1993) note: "Research is not undertaken simply to advance knowledge, as if knowledge were an abstract concept, but, rather, researchers engage in research to change the world, and most centrally, the worlds which the researchers inhabit" (p. 329). I already have devoted considerable attention to the praxis-oriented nature of this project in my discussion of how the basic assumptions of critical postmodernism relate to methodology.

Reliability relates to the consistency of a study. Will a repetition of the research procedure produce similar results? Critical ethnography seeks to affect the social setting one examines by engaging participants in dialogue. This makes traditional notions of reliability cloudy, because if successful, the critical ethnographer will have affected some aspect of the social setting and thus a future study structured in a similar manner may not--and, indeed, should not--produce the same findings or conclusions. Gitlin (1990) elaborates:

> Traditional notions of reliability are . . . altered when the central aim of the research process is to develop voice. Within traditional methods, reliability is understood in terms of the ability of independent researchers to come to the same conclusions when the same procedures are used. In contrast, when the aim is the development of voice, it is undesirable and not expected that independent researcher-subject teams would come to the same conclusions. (pp. 446-447)

Clearly, since critical ethnography seeks social change first and foremost, the issue of reliability must be interpreted in a different light. Traditional notions of reliability are replaced by basic judgments made by the reader in examining a study. Thus, the following questions serve to guide the analysis of this study (Tierney & Rhoads, 1993):

• Are the voices presented in the study believable?
• Is the situation plausible?
• Where does the author/researcher fit in the formation of the text and what other interpretations might be offered?
• Has the text enabled the reader to reflect on his or her own life and work?

These questions help to invoke a self-reflective quality in assessing the significance of a particular study. Ultimately, the test of reliability for critical ethnography in particular, and critical postmodern work in general, is whether the text relates to the life of the reader.

The Sample

The universe for this research project includes all gay and bisexual men enrolled at Clement University. However, locating gay and bisexual male students is difficult because many are closeted. Realistically, the universe from which to select a sample of interview participants is the total number of gay and bisexual men at Clement who are to some degree "out." The problem is in locating these students, as not all gay and bisexual men are open or political enough to participate in LGBSA meetings. I did, however, make extensive use of LGBSA because the organization was the most accessible way to meet gay and bisexual men. I interviewed nearly every gay and bisexual male member of LGBSA--which amounted to about thirty of my forty research participants. From this sample of students, I was able to obtain a great deal of information about the coming-out process in general and the process of becoming political in particular.

The rest of the interview participants were referred to me by members of the gay student community. Several of these students do not adopt the same degree of openness about their sexual orientation as do the students in LGBSA. One student who self-identified as a homosexual and rated himself a six on the Kinsey scale commented about his life: "I'm not out to many people. It's like living a double life. You have all these feelings that you really can't express. Sometimes it's very lonely, alienating. I sort of isolate myself so people don't get the wrong idea and figure out that I'm gay." Another student who self-identified as a "closeted bisexual man" had the following to say: "It's like I go to a pride rally and I see more people hanging around the Clement Preacher. Last semester I was hanging around a gay friend a lot and people threw eggs at my door. It makes you very apprehensive." This student majors in engineering and commented that he has never seen a pride pin in any of his classes. "The people in engineering are not the people I would want to come out to." The first student has yet to come to terms with many of his own negative feelings about same-sex attraction and sees the closet as a safer place to work through those feelings. The second student has in some ways moved beyond internalized homophobia (some students prefer the term "internalized heterosexism") but remains closeted largely because of his fear of harassment and discrimination.

In an ideal world, my sample would be representative of the various class years, including graduate students. However, research is a series of compromises; and sampling equally across class year was one goal I was forced to drop. Although students frequently come out in college, they are not necessarily out during their first or second year and they are not likely to be highly visible if they are out. This makes finding first- and second-year students difficult. Hence, my sample is largely skewed toward upper-class and graduate students: 8 graduate students, 17 seniors, 10 juniors, 2 sophomores, and 3 first-year students. Even though this sample certainly is not reflective of the overall gay and bisexual male student body, it may closely resemble the overall population of out male students at Clement University.

Another important sampling concern going into this study related to racial makeup. Only 9 percent of Clement University students are members of minority groups. My initial goal was to oversample students of color so that I could get some understanding of the different issues faced by these students. I achieved this goal in that I interviewed seven students of color (roughly 18 percent of my sample). However, interviewing seven students is certainly no grounds for drawing significant generalizations. Nonetheless, I include points these students offered about racial differences so that issues of dual oppression can be highlighted and investigated in the future.

Early in the study I thought I would only interview undergraduate students, but I decided to include graduate students in order to achieve a larger interview sample. However, the graduate students interviewed are similar in age to the rest of the sample: the average age of the 32 undergraduates is 22.2 years; the average age of the 8 graduate students is 23.6 years; and overall, 93 percent (37/40) of the cohort is within four years of the mean (22.5).

I also examined the sample by family income to get an idea of the relative SES (socio-economic status) of my research participants. As Table 3.1 reveals, the class standing was fairly high. Average family income was $64,600 with a range of $250,000 to $15,000. The sample average income is significantly

Table 3.1
Class Standing Breakdown

Social Class	Income	Frequency
upper class	($100,000 or more)	7
upper-middle class	($ 50,000 - $100,000)	18
lower-middle class	($ 30,000 - $ 50,000)	9
working class	($ 15,000 - $ 30,000)	6
lower class	($ 15,000 or less)	0

Note: Class estimates are based on Macionis, 1992.

higher than that of the Clement student body, which has an average family income of about $50,000. In terms of sexual orientation issues, research tends to support the view that homophobia is higher among working-class youth (Harry, 1986). One can only assume that identifying as lesbian, gay, or bisexual would be that much more difficult for students from lower-income families. Although significant conclusions should not be drawn here, the data lend support for such a view.

Although this study is based on interviews with forty students and observations that derive from hundreds of others, eleven students in particular are central characters throughout this work. Some of the key characters have already spoken. Andrew gave a coming-out speech on the steps of the school auditorium as part of National Coming Out Day. Shane was in the audience when Andrew spoke and later joined the advisory panel. Jerry, of the red hair and red shoes, was introduced in this chapter; he too became a member of the advisory panel. Roger is one of the leaders of the queer student movement at Clement; in chapter 2 he highlighted the inclusive sense of the term "queer." Tito served as a key informant during the first year of my study and became a close friend. I return to these students throughout the text and in turn introduce six additional characters. For now, I offer Table 3.2, which provides

Table 3.2
Summary of Key Characters

Pseudonym	Identifies As	Age	Major	Career Plans
Jerry Sandaval	gay/queer	21	English	Gay Politics
Tom Beal	homosexual	18	Biology	Medicine
Branden Conners	gay	21	Education	Teaching
Shane McGuire	bisexual	22	Engineering	Engineering
Roman Washburn	gay	23	Real Estate	Real Estate
Karsch Palmer	gay/queer	22	Environ.Sci.	Gay Politics
Roger Desko	gay/queer	25	Human Dev.	Counseling
Tito Ortez	bi/queer	22	Speech	Psychology
Ben Curry	gay/queer	22	Health Ed.	Counseling
Andrew Lempke	gay/queer	21	Psychology	Psychology
Deandre Witter	unidentified	22	Ed./French	Teaching

a summary sketch of these eleven men. I also note that they have granted me permission to discuss their lives in great detail and have approved of any descriptions or references that pertain to them.

Data Analysis

Geertz (1973) claims that cultural analysis "is guessing at meanings, assessing the guesses, and drawing explanatory conclusions from the better guesses, not discovering the Continent of Meaning and mapping out its bodiless landscape" (p. 20). He adds that cultural theory is not predictive, at least not in a strict sense. "The diagnostician doesn't predict measles; he decides that someone has them, or at the very most anticipates that someone is rather likely to get them" (p. 26). Clearly, in discussing coming to terms with culture, Geertz is not talking about the typical conception of science. Indeed, the methodology employed in my study is far removed from positivistic notions of predictability and control. The emphasis in the data analysis and in the project as a whole was to make sense of an unfamiliar (unfamiliar to me) aspect of student culture. This is and was an interpretive process that is never-ending. "Cultural analysis is intrinsically incomplete" (Geertz, 1973, p. 29).

In analyzing the data, I did not look for patterns that would assist me in developing predictions about the behavior of gay and bisexual students. I was in search of meaning. The theory and a priori assumptions a researcher adopts shape the way in which data are analyzed. Going into this study I had certain questions in mind: What does it mean to come out? Why do some students become politically involved? What role does the gay community play in terms of identity development? These questions are reflected in the interview protocols and form themes around which the data might be analyzed. I had certain questions in mind going into the study, but others surfaced later. The emergence of these questions and related categories falls in line with Michael Patton's (1980) idea that the grouping of data is an inductively derived process whereby salient patterns emerge from the data.

I began the analysis of data about a third of the way through the project. Ethnographers need to interpret and reinterpret as they conduct their cultural analyses (Rosaldo, 1989). The process is self-reflective. This means revising questions as well as theories. Thus, as I began to analyze the data I also revised and refined my theories. For example, I had a theoretical interest in the relationship between a student's gay or bisexual identity and the gay community. As my study progressed, and as I interpreted and reinterpreted data, issues related to identity and community became even more complex as the notion of a queer identity began to unfold. This resulted in the creation of new questions and new categories of data.

I did not create categories based on the statistical significance of certain key phrases or on their percentage of occurrence. Such a strategy is incompatible with critical ethnographic research. Instead, I relied on my own interpretation of statements framed by the context in which they were situated to draw conclusions about their significance. Although this may seem subjective, and it is, I stress the significant role the advisory panel played as a form of member check.

POSTMODERN NARRATIVE

Narrative is everywhere, as everywhere there exists a story. At the local nightclub, the residence hall, the classroom, or on the street corner, there is a story to be told. Postmodern narrative is more than merely a way of describing the world: it is a way of comprehending our social world. One goal of postmodern writers is to turn social settings into narrative events that assist others in understanding the complexities of social experience. Laurel Richardson (1990) is helpful:

> Narrative displays the goals and intentions of human actors; it makes individuals, cultures, societies, and historical epochs comprehensible as wholes; it humanizes time; and it allows us to contemplate the effects of our own actions, and to alter the direction of our own lives. Narrative is everywhere; it is present in myth, fable, short story, epic, history, tragedy, comedy, painting, dance, stained glass windows, cinema, social histories, fairy tales, novels, science schema, comic strips, conversation, and journal articles. (p. 117)

Critical postmodern narrative is concerned with events that relate to social conflict and difference. The goal is not to provide an idyllic portrait of human social life but to contribute to our understanding of human struggle and agency. In this light, postmodern narrative must be rich in detail in order to convey the social dramas that unfold. As Richardson also points out, narrative has transformative potential: "People make sense of their lives through the stories that are available to them and they attempt to fit their lives into the available stories" (p. 129). She goes on to add, "If available narrative is limiting, destructive, or at odds with the actual life, peoples' lives end up being limited and textually disenfranchised" (p. 129).

My goal, then, is to construct a narrative of gay and bisexual students that has meaning for people's lives (is it believable?); and at the same time, I must challenge those social contexts that form barriers to a more democratic and just society (is it praxis-oriented?).

SUMMARY: ORGANIZING ACROSS DIFFERENCES

In *I Am Your Sister*, the late poet Audre Lorde (1985) describes her anger over the disregard for difference:

> There was a poster in the '60s that was very popular: HE'S NOT BLACK, HE'S MY BROTHER! It used to infuriate me because it implied that the two were mutually exclusive--"he" couldn't be both brother and Black. Well, I do not want to be tolerated, nor misnamed. I want to be recognized. I am a Black Lesbian, and I am your sister. (p. 8)

Difference is something that attracts our focus; difference should not be concealed behind closet doors. In Tierney's (1993b) recent work he describes the need to create communities of difference--an apparent oxymoron until we see the possibility of dialogue as connective fabric. Tierney argues that in order to reconceptualize contemporary notions of community, we first have to let go of traditional modernist assumptions that undergird our understanding of communal life. We then can adopt a view of social life in which we "accept one another's differences and work from those differences to build solidarity" (p. 24). He elaborates on this perspective:

> It is curious, perhaps, that I am suggesting we build the idea of community around the concept of diversity, for communities generally suggest commonality. Such communities, however, have inevitably silenced those of us on the borders. Instead, we need to develop the notion of difference and engage in dialogues across border zones. (p. 25)

Indeed, what queer students at Clement University seek to accomplish involves crossing borders, entering into dialogue, and moving toward communities of difference.

II

INDIVIDUALS WITHIN THE BORDERS

It all started when I met the first openly gay people. I sort of made friends with these two guys who lived in my dorm who were gay. They showed me that it was something that could be acceptable, that being gay isn't something that is a bad thing. It helped me to start dealing with my feelings for a man on my hall whom I fell in love with.
                                                                                     --Karsch Palmer, 22-year-old senior

Like Karsch Palmer and so many other students across the country, college is a place and a time to establish and reestablish a sense of identity. For students who identify with same-sex attractions, college offers freedom from the constraints of high school and parental supervision. In the two chapters that follow, I focus upon individual students and their personal struggles with sexual identity issues.

4

The Closet and a Negative Existence

The closeted, as captives, suffer such profound psychological trauma that they develop a relationship to their closets similar to that of hostages to their captors: They defend them--lulled into a false sense of security and blind to the trauma they experience--and are threatened by those who are out.

--Michelangelo Signorile, Queer in America

The closet symbolizes the oppression of lesbian, gay, and bisexual people who have been forced to remain silent about their sexual identity. As Eve Kosofsky Sedgwick (1990) maintains, "The closet is the defining structure for gay oppression in this century" (p. 68). The normalization of sexuality has created and continues to reinforce the closet. Because heterosexuality is the norm, most people assume that everyone is straight. This makes leaving the closet an ongoing process, since one continually makes new acquaintances. Sedgwick is helpful once again:

> Even an out gay person deals daily with interlocutors about whom she doesn't know whether they know or not; it is equally difficult to guess for any given interlocutor whether, if they did know, the knowledge would seem very important. Nor--at the most basic level--is it unaccountable that someone who wanted a job, custody or visiting rights, insurance, protection from violence, from "therapy," from distorting stereotype, from insulting scrutiny, from simple insult, from forcible interpretation of their bodily product, could deliberately choose to remain in or to reenter the closet in some or all segments of their life. The gay closet is not a feature only of the lives of gay people. But for many gay people it is still the fundamental feature of social life; and there can be few gay people, however courageous and forthright by habit, however fortunate in the support of their immediate communities, in whose lives the closet is not still a shaping presence. (p. 68)

Heterosexuality in part has been normalized through discourse. Michel Foucault (1978) writes about how the discourse of the eighteenth century to the present has framed sexuality. He argues that the discourse that became prevalent was one of disparate sexual identities wherein heterosexuality--that which served the reproduction of society--was firmly implanted as the norm. Concurrently, homosexuality, which had previously existed merely as an act (often an aberrant act with severe social consequences), took on a whole new identity--a marginalized identity. As a result of normalization, homosexuality exists on the fringes of society or, worse yet, as an invisible, unmentionable aspect of society.

For the students involved in this study who recognized their same-sex attractions at an early age, this aspect of their identity had to remain for the most part invisible and unmentionable. One student reflected:

> I knew for quite a while, at four or five, that I was attracted to the same sex. I wanted to touch other boys, to kiss them, to hold them. It was pretty obvious to me that my attractions were for boys and not girls. My parents have always reacted to it with sort of disgust. At 11 or 12 they asked me if I was gay and before I could respond they said they would have to send me away so that I wouldn't influence my brother or sister. They were worried about me infecting them in some way. Well, after I heard "we'd have to send you away if you are," I knew that it was inappropriate to say yes.

A range of thoughts were expressed by students as they discussed their experiences of the closet. The following themes capture much of their discussions: thoughts of suicide, internalized homophobia, time in the closet, and sexual exploration from the closet. Before discussing these themes, I introduce three students from Clement University whose experiences in the closet serve to ground the remainder of this chapter. For these three men, being gay or bisexual was at first unmentionable. Their lives have been framed to a great extent by the closet.

TOM BEAL

Tom Beal is a first-year student who dreams of becoming a doctor. He is dark-skinned, stands about 5' 9", and weighs no more than 150 pounds. His black, straight hair dangles in front of his brown eyes like vertical blinds in a window. Whether intentional or not, keeping others from seeing what Tom is seeing or, more pointedly, what Tom is looking at is important; especially if what he is looking at is another guy.

Tom is reluctant to identify as a gay man: "I guess I would say I'm a homosexual but that word sort of freaks me out. I would say I'm gay but I'm still very uncomfortable with the whole idea. I'm just now beginning to come to terms with it." With both feet firmly planted in the closet, Tom is barely cognizant of what his life might be like as an out gay man. And although he fears coming out, he is miserable in the closet. What Tom despises is the constant deception: "I hate to have to play charades with my friends and lie to them. Like 'Hey Tom, do you have a girlfriend yet?' I just play along. I have to screen everything I say."

One of the reasons Tom has decided to remain closeted is fear of how his parents might react: "I think my mother would react very badly. She has very conservative values. My family is very traditional. I don't know how my dad would react. I don't want to find out either. I guess right now I'm just not ready for that." Tom also is not ready to be identified with any queer students who participate in LGBSA meetings. "I don't want to be associated with them at all. I don't want anyone to know I'm gay. It's kind of hard to explain. I want to be gay because I feel that's what I am, but I don't want anyone to know." I asked Tom about his fears: "I'm scared for my life. There are so many hateful people out there. Who knows what they might do?"

I met Tom for the first time at an LGBSA meeting in the fall of 1992. As it turned out, Tom lived across the street from me, so after the meeting we walked home together. The meeting had been Tom's first and he was soundly disappointed: "It was more political than I expected. I was looking more for a social-type thing. I didn't expect all the arguing, all the political stuff." He went on to explain that he is not out to many people and he only wants to become involved on a social level. This is why Tom never attended another LGBSA meeting and later became involved in Random House.

BRANDEN CONNERS

The walls surrounding the dance floor seemed to sway from side to side, the effect of a room full of students waving their arms back and forth over their heads to a Madonna tune. The volume was so loud that the speakers made a cracking sound from time to time, making it difficult to understand the words. The dance, the work of LGBSA and ALLIES, was planned for a Friday evening in December as an end-of-semester tension release as students prepared for finals. Most of the students who attended were lesbian, gay, bisexual, or straight supporters.

The dance floor was a mixture of amoebic-like groups: men dancing with other men, women with women, men and women together. Some students danced by themselves. They stuck out by the way they roamed the dance floor, starting out on one side and pirouetting to the other. Students danced in boots, black leather jackets, and vests. Others wore black T-shirts and baggy jeans riding low on their hips. Black Doc Martens were too numerous

to count. Nearly everyone in the converted gym of the student cultural center
was dancing except for a few men who stood in the darkness of the room's
perimeter. One of those men was Branden Conners. If Branden had things his
way, he would never be on the sidelines watching others dance.

Unlike Tom, who is afraid to be identified with other out gay or bisexual
men, Branden is actively involved in LGBSA. However, that is not to say
Branden's involvement has been wholly satisfying: "It's really been great to
come out and have the support of the gay community and LGBSA. But by the
same token, I feel like a lot of people don't really care if I'm here or not,
because I'm not attractive to them. They ignore me. They don't see that I'm
a person too." Branden is about 5'5" and is probably thirty pounds
overweight. Branden has little positive to say about his appearance, and his
feeling that he is unattractive is a heavy psychological burden: "I've been very
depressed and I'm trying to resolve my self-image and the way I'm treated by
LGBSA members. Gay men are more image conscious than straight women;
so if you're unattractive and you're gay then it's really hard."

Adding to the stress and anxiety in Branden's life is the fact that he leads
a double life: he is out at Clement but closeted at home. "Moving back and
forth between being out and being closeted is draining. Going home is like
going back in the closet all over again. It's like a little piece of me dies each
time I go home, but it's resuscitated when I come back to school." Back
home, Branden is out only to his mother. She took it hard at first but has
shown some progress. She even teased him once when he dressed in drag for
Halloween by remarking, "I know all transvestites aren't gay. I watch Oprah!"
His mother does not want him to come out to his father for fear Branden will
be shut off financially. She also does not want him to be involved in LGBSA:
"She was afraid that I was out on campus. She was afraid that I was involved
with 'that student group.' I lied to her and told her I wasn't."

SHANE MCGUIRE

Shane McGuire, first encountered at the rally highlighted in chapter 1, is a
junior who grew up in a major urban area along the East Coast. Since he
came out to himself, Shane's life has been a multitude of steps; and as we
shall see, like his reluctance on National Coming Out Day, he often fears
scaling those steps.

Shane identifies as a bisexual man and has been out of the closet for less
than a year. "I say I'm bisexual, but others in the gay community would be
upset. They expect everybody to define themselves as either straight or gay,
but things aren't so black and white." Shane is around 5'10", with long,
straight brown hair. Shane is a stark contrast to Branden in that Shane rarely
lacks attention from others in the gay community. Whereas Shane is slim with

the build of a swimmer, Branden is heavy and seen by other students as unattractive. Whereas Shane receives positive comments about his looks (mainly his dark eyes and soft brown hair) and is often asked to participate in various social activities, Branden is rarely mentioned and frequently excluded.

Shane majors in engineering but has recently begun to question his selection. "I wanted to be a civil engineer, but I have been having troubles. I seem to excel in liberal arts stuff. You know, the artsy-fartsy kind of stuff." Despite his ambivalence toward his major, Shane finds a certain degree of safety in engineering: "I think one of the reasons I'm in civil engineering is that it's safe. Maybe it's easier to look straight."

Whereas Tom is closeted to mostly everyone at Clement and Branden is out to nearly everyone he meets at school, Shane is out to some members of the Clement community (mostly members of LGBSA) but closeted to others. Being out to some and not out to others, all in the same locale, creates difficulties. Shane shared one of his more disturbing incidents. He was visiting with a friend from back home at the student center at Clement when two students from LGBSA walked by them. "They looked very gay and wore pink triangles on their T-shirts. They walked by us and said 'Hi Shane' and stopped to talk to me about signs up in the LGBSA office. I just kind of sat there wondering, 'What does my friend think?' I don't think I'm ready for that kind of scene yet."

In the fall of 1992, Shane felt members of LGBSA were pushing him faster than he wanted to go. He was just beginning to come out of the closet and the politics of being out were entirely new to him, yet some of the leaders of LGBSA had many expectations of him. Nonetheless, by the spring of 1993 Shane was an elected officer in LGBSA and actively involved in gay politics. He had moved so quickly that when he read the interview transcript a few months after the interview took place, he could not believe some of the things he had said. For instance, in April Shane added the following note to his interview transcript: "Now that I'm more out than in October, I find it very difficult to go back into the closet." Despite his changing view of the world, Shane's early comments provide insight into the nature of the closet. I return to some of his comments later in this chapter.

EXPERIENCES IN THE CLOSET

The experiences of Tom, Branden, and Shane are similar to those of other students I interviewed. Jerry, for example, remained closeted to his family while he came out to all his friends at Clement. Similarly, Andrew came out to his roommate during his first year but remained closeted to everyone else: "We were basically closeted to everyone but ourselves. For a while I was perfectly content to stay in our own little world." Eventually, Andrew met other gay men who, strangely enough to him, seemed happy. He began to realize that he could also find happiness as a gay man.

Gay and bisexual students who remain closeted must learn to live with a foot in two different worlds--a straight world and a gay world. As I noted in chapter 1, lesbian, gay, and bisexual people have good reasons for being closeted--especially as adolescents; our culture has created a climate of fear for youth with same-sex attractions and many remain closeted until their college years (D'Augelli, 1991a).

What does it mean to live in the closet and how did students in this study deal with their experience in the closet? One student noted that when he was in the sixth grade he first admitted to himself that he was gay: "I said to myself. 'Face it, you're a fag.' I was down on myself then. I thought it was something bad that I should keep hidden." Another student also knew since he was very young: "I had known for a long time that I was gay, but it wasn't until my sophomore year in college that I decided these feelings were not going away and that I could be happy as a gay man." This student lived for years believing that his ongoing depression was a normal part of life. A third student recalled admitting to himself in eighth grade that he had same-sex attractions. He made a conscious decision to remain in the closet until after high school: "I'm like ok this is what I am, deal with it. You know, get through high school, get out of here, and move on to better things." A fourth made a similar choice: "I was 13 or 14 when I finally admitted to myself that I was gay. I knew I was gay but no one else did."

Although many students who remain closeted during their high school and early college years have to deal with feelings of self-hatred projected from society, not all students fall prey to normalization. One student commented:

> By about 13 I pretty much knew that I was gay. I feel lucky because I never went through a period of self-hatred like so many other queer people do. I knew that eventually I would be able to deal with it, but now was not the time: living in the suburbs and all. I was pretty lonely and had only a few friends--no real close friends. I felt like I was the only one in my school who was gay.

Consistent throughout the preceding student narratives is the theme of forced denial. Other students offer similar evidence. During junior high school Andrew beat up a friend to squelch a rumor that he was gay. "As boys do, we fought and I beat the shit out of him and then I wasn't gay anymore. Obviously, right?" Another student endured years of his father's verbal abuse of "homosexuals," all the while knowing he was gay himself. The negative messages sent to lesbian, gay, and bisexual youth force them to deny their same-sex feelings. The byproduct of this continuous onslaught for many is low self-esteem, and some even contemplate escape from a life of pain and turmoil.

Thoughts of Suicide

The effects of being closeted are so devastating that suicide is a frequent thought. Paul Gibson (1989) points out that gay youth are two to three times more likely to attempt suicide than heterosexual youth. Several of the gay and bisexual men I interviewed considered suicide specifically because of their same-sex attractions and their related fear of not being accepted. One student discussed feelings of suicide he dealt with during the years preceding his coming out: "I was very suicidal before coming out. Between 12 and 23 I thought about killing myself so many times. It seemed easier than dealing with the whole thing." Another described how his general feelings of alienation led him to attempt suicide: "One day I just got fed up with everyone's bullshit and said I don't give a damn and I tried to commit suicide." He tried a drug overdose but woke up the next day. "I realized why I had tried to do it, and I have been a pretty pessimistic person ever since. This whole life has made me feel very old and distrustful."

These two students are not alone. Karsch, a well-groomed senior with a boyish smile, recalled his high school days: "I didn't socialize at all. I didn't have a really close group of friends. I went to my junior and senior proms with girls, but I never really dated. I had frequent thoughts of suicide. I even had a plan: I'd use pills to do it." One student sought help when he first began to realize he was gay: "It was a very difficult process. I had to wrestle with it for months. I saw a counselor in the counseling center, and I thought about killing myself all the time. I didn't really see any point in going through life as a gay man. I felt that suicide was basically my only option. Gay wasn't something that I wanted to be." Another reflected on his suicidal feelings: "When I was in ninth grade I was suicidal. I was like 'I can't believe I'm this way.' On and off through high school I was like that." For Roger, the realization that he was gay was just one more thing with which to deal: "In junior and senior high school I had suicidal thoughts all the time. When I started to sense that I might be gay that was just one more thing on top of everything."

Adolescence is a stressful period in life for anyone. It is a time when youth seek to clarify their own sense of who they are as a person. Erik Erikson (1968) maintains that adolescence is a period of intense personal turmoil: "Adolescence is not an affliction but a . . . normal phase of increased conflict . . . defined by a certain self-perpetuating propensity, by an increasing waste of defensive energy, and by a deepened psychosocial isolation" (p. 163). For gay and bisexual men, this period in life is even more traumatic because in addition to the typical stressors such as leaving home, dating, and thoughts of career, they also must come to terms with their same-sex attractions.

When youth with same-sex attractions internalize the hatred conveyed by society toward lesbian, gay, and bisexual people, it is hardly surprising that suicide is an option so many choose. But for those who survive, they still must come to terms with varying degrees of fear and resentment associated with their sexual orientation.

Internalized Homophobia

The preceding section calls attention to the idea that for many gay and bisexual students there are times when suicide seems easier than living in a culture that despises "homosexuals." Yet none of these men woke up one morning and decided to be gay or bisexual; for whatever reasons, they just were. And because of their sexual orientation they seemed destined to live a life of depression, with recurrent thoughts of suicide.

After years in the closet, several of the students in this study had built up such levels of self-hatred and guilt that stepping through "that fear," and literally out of their closets, seemed like a remote possibility. Branden discussed the closet as "all those walls that you build around yourself." For him, the walls represent all his feelings of denial, self-doubt, and self-hatred. Such feelings are described by some as internalized homophobia. Karsch described internalized homophobia as "all that shame that I had internalized. All the guilt I felt." Dealing with these negative feelings while in the closet is a difficult process, as the walls of fear and self-hatred only seem to reinforce the closet.

One student who is mostly closeted still seeks explanations for the "causes" of his "homosexuality": "I don't have particularly fond memories. My father is very distant. I've read that most gay men have distant relationships with their fathers. Growing up I was sort of afraid of him. I don't feel close to him at all. I think this lack of attachment contributes to my homosexuality." One can sense in this student's words the vestiges of being told for years that homosexuality is deviant and sick. As a result of internalized shame, he struggles with "why" his sexual orientation is what it is--a question most people who are heterosexual do not consider. A point this student fails to recognize is how his own feelings of same-sex attraction might have influenced his relationship and "closeness" with his father.

Shane's dark brown eyes took on a focused, almost trance-like quality as he spoke about the closet. His tone was one of half anger, half frustration: "Society tells gays they're sick. They are forced to remain hidden. Even the act has to remain confidential. It's like homosexuality does not exist." For Shane, being closeted is about "lying to yourself." The lying, the inability to admit the truth to oneself, is where much of the self-loathing comes from in Shane's thinking.

Jerry reflected on the closet in a similar manner to Shane when he talked about his experience in the closet as a period of "deceitfulness."   As a teenager, Jerry could not admit to himself that he was one of "them." Even after having a sexual relationship with two other boys, one of which was a significant "emotional involvement" for Jerry, he could barely face the idea that he was or might be gay. "It's weird, because I could see the sex as perfectly normal. It's just what happens. But that didn't make me gay?" Jerry's image of what it meant to be gay was so negative that he could not come to terms with his same-sex attractions until later in life, when he found himself falling emotionally for another guy.

Time in the Closet

Like Jerry, most of the gay and bisexual students involved in this project spent significant years struggling to understand their same-sex attractions, and then additional years passed before they shared those feelings with someone else. Of the forty gay and bisexual men in this study, twenty-four (60 percent) spent more than two years during which they were out to no one but themselves.

One way of looking at the temporal aspect of closetedness is to consider the time spent between identifying as gay to oneself (self-acknowledgment) and then revealing one's sexual identity to others (self-disclosure). Self-acknowledgment marks the beginning of the coming-out process, a process that is typically followed by a public phase in which feelings are shared with others. By this definition, self-acknowledgment does not mean the first recognition of feelings toward the same sex--something that typically occurs at a fairly young age. For instance, sixteen students indicated that they recognized feelings of attraction for the same sex at an age of less than 10 years old. Self-acknowledgment, as used here, refers to the distinct time or period during which the student finally proclaims to himself that he is gay or bisexual. A comment from a student highlights what is meant by self-acknowledgment as well as self-disclosure: "I put the name gay to myself when I was 13, but I came out to others when I was 16." For some, identifying a specific time is fairly easy. For others, there was no particular event that helped them finally to say, "Hey, I'm gay." These students had difficulty specifying precisely when they self-acknowledged, but nonetheless they were able to estimate an age. The average age at self-acknowledgment was 16.2 years.

An intentional sharing of personal information about one's sexual identity to one or more others is termed self-disclosure (Nelson-Jones & Strong, 1976). The average age of self-disclosure for the students in this study was 19.3 years. For some students, self-acknowledgment actually occurred through disclosure to someone else. This was the case for the student who made the following student: "Coming out to myself and coming out to someone else kind of happened at the same time. It was kind of like I had to come out to someone else in order to admit it to myself. Up until then, I was hesitant to say that I was gay even to myself. I figured I could change. I just had to find the right woman."

Leaving the closet is a lifelong process, but one can still get an idea of the extent of being completely closeted: the individual has acknowledged his sexual orientation to himself but to no one else. One could also include the years of self-denial as time in the closet, but that has not been done here. Of the forty participants in this study, the average number of years spent completely closeted was 3.1 years. Seven students came out to themselves by coming out to someone else and therefore spent no time fully closeted (as closeted is defined here). The greatest number of years spent completely closeted was reported by a student who self-acknowledged around the age of 13 but did not self-disclose until he was 26. Table 4.1 provides a percentage breakdown of time in the closet.

Table 4.1
Years between Self-Acknowledgment and Self-Disclosure

Years	Percentage of Students
0 to 1 year	37.5 %
2 to 3 years	22.5 %
4 to 5 years	20.0 %
6 or more years	20.0 %

At least seven of the students recognized, and in fact acted upon, attractions for the same sex at a much earlier age than their self-acknowledgment as a gay or bisexual male. Branden remembered as early as age six or seven getting sexually aroused when he watched actor Ron Ely in his role as Tarzan. Tom recalled his attraction to other boys when he went roller-skating as a child. Despite early hints of same-sex attraction, many students did not adopt a gay or bisexual identity largely because they did not know that such an identity existed or because they hoped or thought "these feelings" would go away. Another student's comments are helpful here: "Back in high school, maybe in ninth or tenth grade, I remember asking myself if I was gay or not. I remember saying to myself, 'I just like to sleep with guys, but I'm not gay.'" Similarly, Andrew described his attitude about various sexual experiences he had with other boys while in high school: "Well, I thought maybe if I do this it'll go away, or I thought I'd grow out of it. Basically that was the main thing. I thought it would go away." Andrew did not acknowledge his gay identity until his first year in college, although he had had several sexual experiences and recognized as a young boy that he had attractions for other boys. Andrew typifies several students who recognized their feelings and attractions for other boys at an early age but never thought of themselves as gay until later in life--after they realized their attractions were fairly permanent. The following student provides one more example: "I actually started to be conscious of my feelings toward guys in high school, probably my junior year." Despite this student's awareness of his feelings of attraction for the same sex, he did not come out to himself until four years later, and then only a month passed before he came out to one of his best friends--Jerry Sandaval.

Two points ought to be made here about the sample. First, the students involved in this project are probably atypical when compared to other similar-aged gay and bisexual men. They are college students who come primarily from middle-class families. And, as I noted in chapter 3, social class may have a significant influence on coming out and on one's attitudes toward lesbian, gay, and bisexual people. Second, many of the students in this study are the most "out" students at Clement and therefore may possess unique characteristics that set them apart (for instance, maybe they have more supportive family environments). With this in mind, the discussion here about "time in the closet" may not be representative. It is probably safe to say that other gay and bisexual men may self-acknowledge at a later age and spend a longer period between self-acknowledgment and self-disclosure.

Sexual Exploration from the Closet

When heterosexuals become more attuned to their sexuality, they often act on those feelings through sexual experimentation with themselves and others. The same is true of students with same-sex attractions. However, in a society that relegates gay and bisexual people to the closet, the possibility of developing meaningful relationships is next to impossible. There are, however, some options available; most of these alternatives are dangerous and involve casual sex. One student elaborated on one of those options--bookstore sex:

Before I came out I was a bookstore visitor. Socially, people are forced to go there. I used to go to this bookstore near my hometown to meet people. I feel very guilty about this. It's the same thing in one of the classroom buildings on campus. People are forced to do these disgusting things because they can't face who they are because society tells them they're sick. Yet their feelings are real. People are forced to remain hidden--even the act has to remain confidential. It's like homosexuality does not exist. I had no idea it was anything like that when

I first went to the bookstore. I went there to buy pornography. You know,
magazines or books. There are booths there where you can watch films and have
sex with other men. I met the first man I ever wanted to know there. That was
a big deal then. That was the first person I ever had a relationship with. I wish
I could have met someone in school because that would have been safer.

Another student, now in his early 20s, has engaged in restroom sex since
he was 14 years old. This student described restroom sex as sex with a
stranger whom one typically meets in a public restroom. He went on to note
that there are two places in his hometown where he has participated in this
kind of sex. He also commented on why some men's rooms have holes
between the toilet stalls. "The holes are not for putting your dick in them so
someone can suck it. They are more for looking out for other guys. Either
you're doing something and you don't want to get caught, or you use them to
look out for someone who might be interested."

This student engaged in restroom sex throughout his high school years
while denying that he was gay. "I was so afraid that I was gay, but it felt so
good to be with a man." This student brought up the fact that closeted men
frequent a building on campus late at night to have restroom sex, typically on
Friday and Saturday nights. This was confirmed by several other students who
were aware of the practice.

In efforts to keep pace with its expanding student body, Clement has
constructed newer classroom buildings on many of the grassy areas that once
decorated Clement's landscape. The result is a dense mixture of new and old
buildings spread about the university's main thoroughfare. Some of the
classroom buildings are popular sites for students who often "pull all-nighters"
in the solitude of a deserted classroom. One older building in particular is a
choice site. This building is also the favorite site of closeted gay and bisexual
men who participate in restroom sex.

Late one weekend night, a gay student in this study ventured to this
building for restroom sex. He met another student hanging out in one of the
stalls who also wanted to have casual sex. They decided to go somewhere
else, because too many people were outside the restroom in the hallway.
Neither could go back to his room because they were both closeted and had
roommates, so they went to another less-traveled building. "Most of the guys
that do the restroom scene are closeted. In fact some of them don't even
believe they are gay. It's just a sexual thing, they'll say." During a recent
semester the student ventured to this building on several occasions. His
rationale was simple: "I can't get any dates and yet I am a sexual person. I
don't really like having to resort to that kind of thing, but who really does?"

Another student who is politically active in gay issues at Clement
University found his participation in restroom sex to be somewhat of a
paradox. "Restroom sex is something I'm involved in. It's something I've

done a lot. I've gone cruising and have had anonymous sex. It's kind of amusing that I will be so politically involved yet at the same time engage in anonymous sex, since it basically encourages someone else to remain closeted."

Restroom sex is not the only vehicle for closeted gay and bisexual men to meet other men for relationships. Recently, at Clement University a new organization has sprung up known as Random House. Tom, whom we met earlier in this chapter, is a closeted first-year student who identifies as a homosexual. He described Random House as "a group of guys who are very closeted who meet at different places each week. It's a lot of guys who are uncomfortable with who they are." Tom went on to explain the dislike members of LGBSA have for Random House: "They consider it a meat market. But it's really not like that at all. It's just a place for guys who are not ready to come out." Tom found out about Random House through an ad in the student newspaper that informed interested students to call the lesbian and gay switchboard. The switchboard then provides a number for students to call. As Tom noted, "You call someone and meet with him and one other person and they check you out just to make sure you're ok."

Tom was only partially correct about LGBSA not liking Random House. Certainly, some of the most politically active students in LGBSA resented what Random House offered to students, but others saw a need in reaching men who--for whatever reason--did not want to leave their closets yet. The LGBSA members who were opposed resented the fact that men in Random House were able to enjoy their same-sex attractions while at the same time reaping the benefits of passing as straight. One student in LGBSA shared his feelings:

> Random House is a "boys' club." They were talking about establishing a group of very "straight" gay and bisexual men that could meet together and they basically said that it was not meant to be a meat market, but if people meet and hook up, so be it. "If it happens it happens" was kind of their attitude. When they started Random House they had good motives, but I think it has evolved into something different. It was intended to offer support for gay and bisexual men still in the closet but it has turned out to be more of a cover for those men who want to have sex with other men and then go back to their girlfriends and basically remain closeted.

On one occasion Andrew, a leader in LGBSA, hosted a queer party at his apartment. The advertisement for the party revealed some of the tension between Random House and members of LGBSA: "On Saturday, November 14. Party at Fiesta House. . . . There's nothing *random* [my emphasis] about it!"

Relationships are a challenge for students who are closeted, but some, nonetheless, found opportunities for exploration as adolescents. Jerry discussed how he "hooked up" several times in high school: "There was nothing emotional, though." Another student described an experience he had at a summer camp:

> I met this other boy and for four weeks we were just friends, but then just a couple of days before camp ended we got real involved sexually. We wrote every day for about a month or so, then I never heard from him again. I later found out that his parents read one of his letters, so they wouldn't let him stay in touch with me anymore.

Andrew slept with one of his best friends in junior high school. He found the experience to be eye-opening: "I thought 'oh wow, maybe this isn't so wrong.'" Andrew talked about how he learned all his life that having sex with a man was wrong, but his experience seemed to tell him something different: "I thought it seemed like he enjoyed it and I enjoyed it. So it was something we shouldn't do? I was like, 'Oh this is great. There's someone else that feels like I do.'" The next day Andrew's friend (the one with whom he had sex) spread it all over the school that Andrew had sexually assaulted him. "It was horrendous; I mean it was my first real encounter with homophobia."

The narratives throughout this chapter dramatize the debilitating effects of a culture and its related discourse that promote one form of loving over another. Despite these students' struggles to claim an identity rooted in their same-sex attractions, the past discourse has been so ingrained that it is difficult to escape its confining hold. The years spent hearing about the evils of homosexuality and homosexuals leave a tremendous impression upon young people. The discourse not only leads them to suffer years in the closet but also produces a sense of *negative existence*--in which life is defined more by what cannot be done than by what can be done; living is a matter of impossibilities rather than possibilities.

NEGATIVE EXISTENCE

Signorile compares the relationship between the closet and the closeted to "that of hostages to their captors" (1993, p. xviii). Being closeted provides a degree of safety from bigotry and prejudice. Based on the narratives heard throughout this chapter, however, the closet is not a place to develop a positive sense of identity. One student highlighted the negativity of the closet:

> Being closeted is totally negative. It provides no positive support or sense of self. People do it for protection. You're basically lying and being dishonest with people and with friends. Your initial justification is: "I don't know what

my friends will think." It's very unhealthy. It's just that you can't develop a real self-identity because you're too busy pretending to be something you're not. You are a totally different person depending on who you're around. All I remember is pain. It got more and more draining the longer I hid. It was kind of like acting, but the part gets tougher and tougher to play.

Another student provided insight into the closet by describing what is gained in leaving it behind: "Being able not to be afraid to tell people what my feelings are; not having to hide." As these comments indicate, living in the closet leads some students to think in terms of negatives: What can I *not* do?

The discourse of homosexuality weighs differently upon individuals: some internalize less of the negative than others. One student discussed how he "never really internalized the self-hatred that many queers do as a result of being told they are sick or abnormal. For me it felt perfectly normal. I never experienced the suicidal thoughts and depression like so many other gay people do." For whatever reason, at an early age some students are able to filter out what they are told about lesbian, gay, and bisexual people through their own lens of experience and feelings. For others, filtering out negative messages is more difficult. The power of discourse takes its toll. But even for the fortunate students who learn early on that what they are told may not be so, being gay or bisexual has its constraints.

One of the common experiences students noted about being closeted, or about interacting with people to whom they may not be out, is the fact that they have to "screen" what they say and do. Branden's life provides insight here: "I'm only out in Hidden Falls. I'm not out back home. I love being in Hidden Falls because I can be myself. I can say anything I want to, do anything I want. I can even watch guys walk by if I want." When Branden returns home, he goes back in the closet. "I hate being home. It's like having to live a constant lie--being afraid of what you might say or do."

Being afraid to say the wrong word or phrase that will give "the secret" away is a major concern when an individual is closeted. One student described how he felt he literally had to watch himself interact so that he did not give anything away. "You alter your behavior so that you don't appear gay. Like making glances toward women so that people think you're straight. Or making comments about them like 'what a body!' Also, I make sure not to look at guys when they walk by." The feelings described by this student portray a common dilemma for students who are out to some people but in the closet to others: they walk a fine line where they must constantly analyze their settings and filter what they say. Shane noted: "When you're gay and closeted you have to screen everything you say--everything. It's as if you have to listen to yourself say things before you say them."

SUMMARY

The closet symbolizes the effect of the normalization of other-sex relationships. The power of the norms associated with heterosexuality imprison those who feel differently, those who have attractions that do not fit the normalized version of how we are expected to be. For some, confinement is so severe that thoughts of suicide are prevalent. For others, fear of being found out leads them constantly to filter feelings and thoughts. These factors make it unlikely that one can establish deep relationships when a significant aspect of one's identity is kept secret. How well can our parents really know us when so much remains hidden? Likewise, how can our brothers, sisters, and our friends truly know who we are?

Being closeted is a socially derived form of imprisonment in which a significant aspect of one's identity remains hidden. Society serves as overseer of behavior, dealing out punishment to its violators. To resist society's norms is to face social retribution. To comply is to deny one's identity. Lesbian, gay, and bisexual people are faced with a choice: to come out, or not to come out. The majority of the students involved in this project have chosen to come out and face social scrutiny. Only through coming out can one begin to tear away the bars of the closet and move from a negative existence to a positive self-definition.

The closet is a byproduct of the politics of silencing. Coming out is one way of battling silencing tactics. Although it is reasonable to first discuss the politics of silencing, then the closet, and then coming out, I have switched the order in this text for a reason. Not all students who come out engage in cultural struggle to overturn the politics of silencing. Among Clement University's gay students, queer students are predominantly the ones engaged in cultural work. Their significant role in attempting to change the culture of Clement University warrants its own chapter. To ground students as cultural workers, it makes sense to discuss that work in light of the politics of silencing. Hence, although this chapter highlights students' experiences in the closet, and the next chapter coming out, chapter 6 deals with students and their cultural battle against the politics of silencing.

5

Coming Out in College

Coming out is not chiefly a means to happiness. It is a conscious giving up of power, a subjection to an increased prospect of discrimination, and an opening to a heightened awareness of the ways by which society despises gays--these are not the near occasions of happiness. Yet coming out--even in the face of social interdict--gives people a sense of self, a sense that for better or worse their lives are their own, that their lives have a ground.

--Richard Mohr, *Gay Ideas*

Coming out is the process of disclosing one's sexual orientation; it begins with self-acknowledgment and expands outward to others. Coming out marks the rite of passage to a lesbian, gay, or bisexual identity (Herdt, 1992). Because we live in a society in which nearly everyone assumes people to be heterosexual, coming out is a never-ending process; no matter how many people know about one's sexual orientation, there will be others to whom that individual will have to come out. For the out students involved in this project,[1] coming out was one of the most significant experiences in their lives.

On October 9, 1992, Andrew Lempke stood on the steps of the Clement University auditorium and proudly described coming out as an act of celebrating one's sexual identity. Only six days later, Andrew sat on my overstuffed living room sofa and reflected on another aspect of coming out: the fear of the unknown. For Andrew, the most frightening thought was telling his parents: "I think I stayed closeted because I knew I could never come out to them. I was like, 'There's no way.' That was just it for me, and I think it's a similar experience with a lot of people." Andrew related a story about a gay man he had just met who stayed married for seventeen years because of his parents. "He felt he could never come out to them." Andrew eventually came out to his parents, and his life has not been the same since. "Once my parents knew, life was a lot easier. From then on everything was easier."

Another student talked about how he knew even as a child that he was gay. But he was taught that being gay was wrong, so he tried to have a girlfriend. "I had one in junior high and in high school." Finally, this student gave up trying to be the person everyone else seemed to want him to be. "Within the last nine months or so I just said fuck it. People are going to like me or not. I started becoming more open about being gay." This student attended the coming-out rally on the steps of the school auditorium, where he was interviewed by a reporter. He used the interview as a way to come out to people with whom he worked.

For a second student, coming out is not about rallies and marches but is more a matter of being honest: it means answering questions about your sexual identity truthfully and openly. "I will not stand on the steps of the auditorium and scream out 'I'm gay.' I don't wear my heart on my sleeve. Coming out is achieving a state of honesty with my friends and people in general. It's not hiding anything. It's like achieving a new level of self-confidence." A third student described coming out as the "point of breaking":

> Coming out involves taking all the negative things that you've heard about yourself, heard about "those people," and just saying to yourself that none of it matters as much as you do. It means opening up the door and letting out all the internalized hatred, fear, self-doubt, and self-worthlessness. I think it's the point of breaking. You either come out or you sort of die.

One student's life changed dramatically at age 15 after he met another boy who was openly gay. He finally had someone with whom he could share his feelings. "It was kind of a relief. In a way I was coming out to myself through him." This student talked about never having the negative feelings that so many other lesbian, gay, and bisexual youth face. "I've never really felt guilty or suicidal, or abnormal. It was society's outlook on homosexuality, not mine. It was other people saying that, not me. I've always felt very positive about it. So coming out was basically a chance to share emotions with people in the same boat."

Anthony D'Augelli (1991a) maintains: "Although most lesbian and gay adults acknowledge their affectional orientation to themselves during adolescence, most have not come out by the time they enter a college or university" (p. 140). D'Augelli (1991b) points out that many, if not most, lesbian, gay, and bisexual people self-disclose by age 21. Gay college students will likely be at a point in their lives at which self-disclosure becomes an issue. College is a challenging time for students; for students who also have sexual identity issues to confront, the college experience may be even more difficult.

For college-aged adults, lesbian and gay sexual orientation issues are highly
psychologically salient, far overpowering in significance other psychosocial
issues at this time in their lives. The issues have been in their awareness for
longer periods than earlier cohorts. Denial becomes increasingly improbable, and
conflict intensifies. Emotional upset is normative for lesbian and gay college
students: whatever delicate balances had been forged in earlier years are easily
destabilized. These are their critical years, times of high risk. Greater societal
acceptance makes denial more difficult. (D'Augelli, 1991b, p. 3)

Coming out is an important step in ending self-denial and claiming a sense of
gay identity. For many it marks the beginning of the development of a
positive self-esteem.

For gay students as well as straight students, college life represents freedom
from parents and high school social networks. "The intense secrecies of high
school are dissipated as a result of diminished parental and peer monitoring,
as well as the possibility of the creation of new networks. The 'I'll wait until
college' syndrome is a powerful one" (D'Augelli, 1991b, p. 3). Seeing other
lesbian, gay, or bisexual students out and about on campus is added incentive
to self-disclose. Additionally, the parents of today's college students had
children after Stonewall and about the time that the American Psychiatric
Association deleted homosexuality as a form of mental illness from the
Diagnostic and Statistical Manual-II (DSM-II). These historical events have
left some middle-aged adults questioning prior definitions of sexuality,
possibly making the parents of today's college students more open to and
knowledgeable of people who identify with same-sex attraction.

From a critical postmodern perspective, coming out may be seen as
opposition to a normalizing society and culture that frames homosexuality as
deviant. Claiming one's lesbian, gay, or bisexual identity is a struggle against
the power of the norm. In coming out, gay students open themselves up to
social retribution. Their opposition may be seen not only as an attempt to
claim a sense of identity but also as an effort to reshape social norms.

We have heard about Shane's efforts to be out to some people and not to
others. We have listened to Branden talk about what it is like to be closeted
back home but out at school. And then there is Tom Beal, who is only out to
a few close friends at Clement. These three students stand in stark contrast to
Roger, Tito, Jerry, and Andrew, who are out to practically everyone who
knows them. In this chapter, I introduce two more Clement University
students who have come out to claim their gay identities: Roman Washburn
and Karsch Palmer. I share their stories and provide additional student
narratives related to three aspects of coming out that were stressed by students
throughout the two-year study: changes related to coming out, coming out as
process, and coming out to parents and family.

ROMAN WASHBURN

Roman Washburn is an African American student who was raised in an urban setting. Roman came to Clement University over five years ago but took a few years off from school while he lived and worked in Hidden Falls. He is about 6 feet tall with a medium build. Roman used to work at a clothing store and is always well-dressed and fashionable. At a party he co-hosted with another student from LGBSA, Roman wore a pair of black pleated pants with sharp creases aligned perfectly with the points of his black dress shoes. Over a light-colored, short-sleeve shirt with a button-down collar, he wore a black and silver finely striped vest along with a narrow black tie. As the finishing touch to his accessorized outfit, Roman added a shiny patent leather belt with a bright silver buckle. Everyone at the party commented about how good Roman looked. Whether it was his clothing, his looks, or some other unexplainable quality, Roman presented himself with self-confidence and control. But life was not always this way for Roman.

As a child Roman had problems. "I was a spaz. My parents separated when I was six and I lived with my mom. I got into a lot of trouble in school. I was in special education for three years. I was very hyper and had a lot of behavior problems. My mother sent me to live with my dad for a while. It wasn't that I couldn't do the work; I just didn't follow instructions." During high school, life began to change for Roman; most significantly, he began to do better academically. Today, Roman is an above-average student and hopes to work in corporate real estate.

Roman is very open about his identity as a gay man, although getting to this point has been a long struggle. "I remember one of my friends literally pulling me out of the closet. Finally I was happy. I could let myself be attracted to men. After all those years of denial." Although some things got better for Roman after coming out, everything was far from perfect. "What was bad was that I didn't talk to my father for three months. I knew he would be able to tell something was wrong, and I wasn't ready to let him know." Roman recalled the day that he finally called his dad:

Roman: Hi Dad. How are you doing?
Roman's Dad: Pretty good. How is school going?
Roman: Ok, but there's something I want to tell you. Are you sitting down?
Roman's Dad: Why?
Roman: I'm gay.
Roman's Dad: What does that mean?
Roman: Dad, it means I do guys.

His father went on to express a concern about whether Roman was practicing safe sex. Roman assured him that he was. "We talked about what it means to be gay, and he was pretty cool and supportive. It's funny, but now we talk all the time, probably a couple of times a week, which is way more than before. He teases me sometimes about being a wimp and telling him over the phone." Roman also talked with his father about the possibility of telling his mother, but they both agreed that it was better not to tell her. "She's a fundamentalist Christian. We're afraid that she'll quit her job and stay at home and pray all day for me."

KARSCH PALMER

Whereas Roman is out to his father but not to his mother, the opposite is true for Karsch Palmer: he came out to his mother during his first year in college. "My freshman year there were some clues that my mother picked up on. She met two of my friends whom I always talked about, and one of them is obviously gay. About a week later she asked me if I was gay, and I told her that I was." Karsch's mom did not take the news well. "She started crying and told me it was the worst thing she'd ever heard." Karsch never came out to his father--their relationship is cordial at best: "We don't really talk about feelings and important stuff, just work and the weather. It wasn't important for me to come out to him."

Karsch grew up in a rural area, where he spent most of his time helping his father with the family business. His neighborhood was small and he rarely socialized. As a child, Karsch did not fit in with the other children: "I couldn't interact with other kids. I hated being in social situations." Karsch's shyness continued into high school, where he never developed a close group of friends. He went to a few dances but was never comfortable. He said: "I didn't know when I was in high school that I was gay. I was not attracted to girls but neither was I attracted to boys. Looking back on my childhood, I think I tried to deny my feelings for boys and lead pretty much an asexual life."

With short, well-groomed hair and a boyish smile, Karsch looks like he could be a poster boy for Wheaties. Unless, of course, one looks more closely and notices his earring, his "Adam and Steve" T-shirt, or one of the many queer buttons on his backpack. Although Karsch made few friends in high school, his college experience has been quite different. He is well liked by other members of LGBSA (Karsch was included in most social activities in which I participated), and he has several friends with whom he frequently goes to The Odyssey.

Karsch's college friendships are a stark contrast to the loneliness and isolation he experienced throughout much of his childhood. He contributes much of the change in his life to coming out. "I feel more self-confident, more in touch with myself. I feel I have more genuine relationships. I'm not in a constant state of hiding now. I'm able to deal more honestly with people. I like myself for the first time in my life."

Karsch feels that coming out has made him more self-confident in social settings. As a result, he has the opportunity to make close friends for the first time in his life. But he also experiences disappointments. Karsch gets angry when people are not attuned to his sexual orientation: "I'm continually surprised at the people who don't know. It gets irritating sometimes because there are so many people who are clueless." Karsch has found that he has to come out time and time again. He imagined coming out as a one-time event: "After I came out, I was naive enough to believe that it was all over and that for some mystical reason everyone would all of a sudden know. No matter how many clues you give, they will miss most of them or ignore them because they don't want to believe it." For Karsch, "they" refers to a heterosexual world where most people, despite the efforts of queer students such as himself, continue to assume everyone is straight.

What can we learn from the sketches of Roman and Karsch?
One point relates to changes that occurred in their lives after coming out. Roman could finally admit openly that he liked men and was attracted to men. Karsch began to feel more confident about himself, socialized more, and for the first time made some close friends. Both also had serious challenges to face, such as deciding whether or not to come out to their parents or other people whom they met. Karsch, in particular, highlights a second point: the notion of coming out as a process. He noted his ongoing dissatisfaction with people who are "clueless" about his sexual orientation. Karsch is continually frustrated at having to come out; no matter how many people he tells, there are many more he meets who assume he is straight. The experiences of Karsch highlight coming out as an ongoing process.

Additionally, whereas Karsch is out to his mother and not his father, the opposite is true of Roman. Coming out to his father was a great relief for Roman, and it also brought them closer together. Roman and his father have decided that he should not come out to his mother. Karsch, on the other hand, sees no reason to come out to his father but has come out to his mother, who questioned him about his sexual orientation. His father has expressed little to no awareness or concern. The examples of Roman and Karsch raise numerous questions about coming out to one's parents as well as other family members. How important is it to come out to parents? Does the significance of coming out depend on the student's relationship with his parents? Do students come out to one parent but not the other? What about coming out to other family members? Issues such as these will be discussed further when I highlight student experiences of coming out to their parents and family.

CHANGES

Thirty-five of the forty gay and bisexual students involved in this project are out (keeping in mind that coming out is ongoing). Of these thirty-five "out" students, thirty (86 percent) described coming out as one of the most significant experiences in their lives. For these thirty students, coming out has been "a great relief" that has been "freeing," "empowering," "frightening," and "challenging." Even though none of the thirty-five students who are out suggested any regrets, six of these students (17 percent) did not find the process to be the overwhelmingly positive experience that the other students described. One student recalled the first time he came out to someone: "The first time was terrible. I came out to my best friend during a trip we were taking. We were talking about our lives, our fears, our wishes, and I ended up letting him know I was gay." His friend completely withdrew from him. They were supposed to rent a place together but their plans fell apart. "I found out later that he was in love with me. He just couldn't deal with it." Another student talked about experiencing periods of self-loathing after he came out. Eventually, however, those periods became less frequent. A third student highlighted the difficulties he faced: "It's kind of like I've got to make up for nineteen years of defining myself one way and now I have to redefine who I am. It's really frustrating."

We have already heard Andrew describe his coming out as a time of celebration (despite the fears he had of coming out to his family). Jerry became "a lot more political" after coming out, as did Tito and Roger. For the majority of interview participants, coming out has been a process that has brought about significant personal change. One student noted, "I became more confident, less afraid, more open, relieved. I'm about as happy now as I've ever been." Another described coming out as an "awakening." "It was a time when everything just hit me and made perfect sense. The whole self-realization was profound." A third student pointed out that both his self-worth and self-confidence increased. "I'm more interesting, more easygoing, more comfortable with who I am." A fourth mentioned that he was finally able to love the man he saw in the mirror every day. Coming out helped him to rid himself of internalized hatred and self-doubt that had developed over the years.

One student talked about coming out as "the greatest thing that ever happened to me. It's given me courage, strength, and a sense of identity to confront all kinds of things in my life." For another it was a little scary at first. He feared how his friends would react: "I'm always afraid of losing my friends. After they all found out, the reaction was overwhelmingly positive. It felt like a ton of weight being taken off my shoulders." Branden discussed his experience in similar terms: "Every person I've ever come out to has made me feel like a major weight has been taken off my shoulders each time I tell someone. The weight is really everyone's expectations of what I should be, a heterosexual.   But when I come out to them the weight or burden is removed."

Like Jerry, Tito, and Roger, other students described how they became more interested in politics, and especially gay rights. A student commented: "My politics have turned around 180 degrees. After I came out I went from being a staunch conservative to more radical politics. I moved from the right to the left almost overnight. I kind of 'crashed out' instead of coming out." The political aspects of coming out, alluded to by this student, are echoed by a graduate student:

> When I was an undergraduate, which was before I was out and proud and fighting for my rights, I might have gone to a gay pride rally but only to watch or offer support. But now, instead of merely supporting other advocates, I have become one myself. I have become more of a fighter for my own rights as opposed to a supporter of others fighting for my rights. I do that for myself and for the community. So that has changed.

Not all students "shift to the left" and take up gay politics. One student, who does not identify as queer, highlights some of the differences between queer students and their politics, and his more moderate stance: "Without queer pride we wouldn't have half the rights we have now. They make it easier for all of us. But it takes a lot of give and take, and I'm more of a give-and-take person. I don't mind compromising. That's hard for queers to accept." This student went on to point out that he is in a conservative field (sports administration) and if his sexual identity ever became an issue it could jeopardize his career. "I want to protect myself. It's really a shame that I have to make that decision. That's probably why I'm not queer, my business associations. I'm very conservative." This student sheds light on the political aspect of a queer identity, which I discuss in detail in the next chapter.

"I figured I could change. I just had to find the right woman," commented a gay undergraduate. This student tried to find the "right" woman, but his relationships with the other sex never worked out. He found himself feeling empty when he dated women, and his attractions for men remained strong. The example of this student highlights a common question some people tend to ask: Why don't or can't homosexuals change and become straight? The question hinges on the assumption that homosexuality is a preference and, thus, something that can be chosen or rejected.   But many students' experiences support a different perspective: that sexual identity is deeper than any conscious choice they make.   In fact, several students discussed their attempts to modify their sexual behavior in order to be straight.   One gay student, who dated girls in high school, described his experience trying to live as a heterosexual male. He took a date to the prom, a girl he had gone out with for a number of months. They got a hotel room after the prom and their plan was to spend the night together. The student came prepared with several condoms. There was one small problem, though: he was not able to get sexually aroused. Another student who dated girls in high school had a difficult time connecting emotionally with them. He had several sexual experiences that were "ok," but there was no emotional attachment--the kind of attachment he desired to have with other boys. A third student was physically attracted to some girls, but it was not the same kind of attraction he felt for boys, which included both physical and emotional qualities. A fourth student summarized a common response lesbian, gay, and bisexual students expressed toward questions about choice and changing one's sexual orientation: "Do heterosexuals wake up one day and decide to be attracted to the opposite sex?"

Many of the out students in this project went through intense periods of questioning in relation to their sexual identity; fourteen students, in particular, highlighted the beginning of the coming-out process as one such period. These students reflected on the confusion they felt when they first struggled to understand their same-sex attractions. Some asked questions like "Why me?": "For the longest time I couldn't even say the word 'gay.' I wished that I was not in this situation. I didn't want to have to explore this side of me. I wished I was straight and didn't have to explain this. 'Why me?' That was my attitude. 'I'm not like other gays.'"

For these fourteen students, the early realization that they were gay or bisexual brought about a period of reflection as they tried to make sense of their past. Roger noted: "It was funny because, when I look back, I remember always making friends with the best-looking guys so that I could hang around them. I don't recall being aware of this at the time." Roman reflected on his past:

> I never really sensed as a kid that anything was different about me, although one time when I was doing an educational program on queer issues something came to me. I remember there was a kid who lived down the street and I used to go to his house and we would play this game. One of us would walk by his bed and the other would jump on him and we would roll around on the bed together. We called it "mugger." I think that meant something, although at the time I didn't really pick up on it.

Whether the game mugger had significance beyond the conscious level is a point of confusion for Roman today. Although his mystery remains unsolved, what is important here is the reconstruction of the past that Roman and other gay and bisexual men go through as part of coming out. That people examine their pasts in light of the present--and vice versa--is a presumption that is probably no great leap of faith. For gay and bisexual students who come out, reflections on the past bring new insights. Like Roman, Karsch reexamined his childhood and adolescence after coming out. His shyness makes perfect sense to him now. Avoiding social contact was his way of not having to reveal a part of himself he feared: a part he could not explain--his same-sex attraction.

COMING OUT AS PROCESS

For Roman and Karsch, and for the other gay and bisexual men involved in this project, coming out is an ongoing process. Roger discussed coming out as something that has a beginning but never really ends. Jerry commented about the different levels of "outness" that people reach as time passes. A similar view was echoed by Shane, the engineering major, who described the number of people he is out to as expanding logarithmically with time. Gilbert Herdt (1992) recognizes the ongoing nature of coming out in discussing it as a rite of passage to a gay or lesbian identity: "Although the 'coming out' concept conveys a single event pinpointed in time and space, many writers today recognize a multiplicity of events stretching over years" (p. 30). A student voice is helpful here as well: "It's a continuous process that goes on every day. It's a process that never ends." Two others offer their support: "To me, coming out is a never-ending process. It's something that's easy to mark the beginning of but also something that never ends." "I really view it as a process. I don't think it's over. Every time I put myself in a new situation around new people, there's always the issue of when to come out to them."

Coming out is ongoing because of the pervasiveness of heterosexism. The following comments from a gay graduate student underscore this idea: "I participated in a seminar yesterday with faculty and staff. I think I came out to practically everyone there. I had to help them to understand what it means to be gay." Another student provided additional insights into the frustrations not only of coming out but also of being out: "Being out has created an awareness within me that everything I do is open to scrutiny by the rest of the world. I feel this incredible pressure at times, and sometimes I just want to blow people's minds by doing something very effeminate or campy [acting in an effeminate manner with an additional touch of flamboyancy]." This student went on to add: "I just get so tired of being questioned about why am I gay and what's it like."

The comments from this last student offer understanding of what life is like when one has to endure a culture that promotes one form of loving over another. The pervasive attitude that an other-sex relationship is the only legitimate expression of human attraction and affection is the essence of a heterosexist society. However, understanding the effects of heterosexism goes far beyond merely recognizing the attitudes people hold. Heterosexism infiltrates our organizations as well and becomes institutionalized in ways that deny lesbian, gay, and bisexual people the same basic rights that heterosexuals take for granted. At Clement University, for example, spousal benefits are geared toward heterosexual married couples. As Roger pointed out: "The heterosexual culture is very set on making gay and lesbian people invisible, whether they use physical violence or institutionalized violence. Coming out is a way of battling that."

In discussing coming out, students continually reinforced self-acknowledgment as the first step in the process. "Coming out to yourself is the first step, and then coming out to others follows," remarked Karsch. He later added: "There has to be a point at which you say to yourself 'I'm gay.'" Andrew noted that coming out basically means learning to love yourself first. Jerry maintained that coming out happens on a couple of different levels. "I guess coming out is just being aware of your sexual orientation, and I think first you have to admit it to yourself." Coming out, for Shane, first means recognizing your same-sex attractions: then, "You have to stop lying to yourself, stop fighting yourself, and slowly tell other people." Another student commented on the different layers to coming out, with the first layer involving self-admission: "Coming out involves accepting yourself, coming out to people in the gay community, coming out to people outside the community--like relatives, parents, and friends. You're coming out your entire life. It's a circle that keeps getting bigger and bigger."

Coming out as a process typically begins with self-acknowledgment, although sometimes another person may be involved in that self-admission, as was the case with Roman and another student involved in the project. This student shared his experience:

> It was last February that I really came out to myself and someone else kind of at the same time. I always kind of knew but I never really admitted it to myself. I met somebody in my biology class and I had a copy of *The Student Voice* [the conservative student newspaper recently started at Clement] and there was an article about how all the women in Womyn's Studies were lesbos and dykes. I said I was disappointed about the way they were portrayed, and he said he was in LGBSA. After class I kind of followed him and we talked about it. It was kind of like I had to come out to someone else in order to admit it to myself.

Although the vast majority of students in this project self-acknowledged before disclosing their sexual identity to another person, some, such as Roman, came out to themselves by admitting their sexual orientation to a friend. The coming-out process is a variable one. Some students come out to themselves and then wait years to tell someone else. Others are literally pulled out of their closets by a friend, as Roman was by Jerry. Some come out on the steps of the school auditorium, and others seek the solace of a one-to-one sharing. The variability that marks the coming-out process is also true of coming out to parents and family.

COMING OUT TO PARENTS AND FAMILY

Coming out to one's family has different meanings for students. Some see coming out to parents as crucial to a healthy view of oneself as a gay or bisexual man. For other students, particularly those who may not have close relationships with their parents, coming out does not seem so imperative. Karsch, for example, sees no reason to come out to his father. And for different reasons, Roman has chosen not to come out to his mother. In any case, coming out to family is a matter to which all students involved in this study have given serious thought. Table 5.1 provides a breakdown of how many students in the sample are out to both parents, only one parent, or neither parent.

Table 5.1
Out to Parents

Both	Mother Only	Father Only	Neither
17	7	2	14
42.5%	17.5%	5.0%	35.0%

Note: Two students have deceased fathers and one has no contact with his mother.

A gay student explained that he sees no reason to come out to his parents at this point in his life. "I have to set the time and make sure it's right. My mother will be disappointed. She's asked me about it in the past. My father would probably say, 'Oh well, it's a fact of life.'" This student made the following observation: "Mothers always know even though they may never admit it. They see you playing with other kids and they ask you about girls you might like. I tell her I'm just not outgoing enough to get dates. I'm not good-looking enough."

Besides this student, seven others noted the keen awareness of their mothers. One student came out to his mother, and her response was, "I already knew." "I guess because when I was little I liked to play with dolls and she probably noticed that I always looked at boys." Another student suspects his mother knows: "She came up to visit one weekend. We were at The Odyssey one evening [not on alternative night], and out of the blue she told me about her good friends who live above her who are gay."

Some students who came out to parents received a great deal of support and affirmation. Recall how Roman became closer to his father after coming out to him. They talk to one another on the phone on a regular basis now. Other students shared similar stories. One student went home for spring break with a spiked haircut and his dad teased him about looking like a "fag." "That really hurt my feelings. The next day I was pretty depressed and my mom asked me, 'What's going on? Are you gay?' I said no." About six months later he wrote his mother a letter and delivered it in person. "Basically I told her I was gay. I told my dad and brothers that same night and they pretty much accepted it. Three months later my mom was referring to me as 'my gay son.'" He recalled how his mother teased him while on vacation: "She said, 'Come on, my gay son.' That made me feel so good because she meant it in an affectionate way. I wouldn't be surprised if they started a PFLAG [Parents and Friends of Lesbians and Gays] chapter in my home town. They tell people off who are bad-mouthing gays or if anyone acts homophobic around them."

Another student talked about his experience in coming out to his parents and family. "My parents had no problems. They just wanted me to be careful. They were worried that other people would take their hatred of homosexuality out on me." He added that even his brothers and sisters were very accepting. "The thing about my house is if you're happy then they're happy." His family often asks him questions about whom he is dating. "They have really helped because I can talk about anything with them. I feel really lucky because I know a lot of guys don't have that kind of support."

Although many students received support from their parents and families, others were not so fortunate. For one student, coming out to his mother has been a mixed blessing. He described an argument he had with her about Madonna kissing a woman in a music video. They were in his mother's car on their way to a dentist's appointment.

> My mother was saying that such behavior had no place on television or in our society. We were yelling and screaming about the video and she got really mad and looked at me and said, "Are you gay?" Then she hit me with all these sexual questions about how I'm tearing my body apart. We sat in the dentist's office on opposite sides and she said we'd have to have a talk before I went back to school.

This student went on to explain that his mother was upset because his father was gay and now her son was too, "and she felt like it was destroying the family. Like I was destroying the family." For the longest time his mother would not speak to him: "A month and a half maybe. I was more suicidal during this period than I'd ever been." The tension eventually eased. "Eventually she talked to me. I remember I was talking to my sister on the phone and my mother got on and said, 'I'm washing my hair, baby, but just wanted to say hi.' My mother is a great person. I have a lot of respect for her." Another student discussed a similar reaction by his mother. They did not speak for about a week after he came out to her. "Finally, we had a heart-to-heart and she said that if she could pick things the way she wanted them to be she certainly wouldn't pick them this way, but if that's what I am then she could accept it. She was more open about the whole thing when she met my boyfriend. She liked him."

These last two students at first received a nonsupportive response from their mothers after coming out, but as time passed they became more affirming. Other students described a process that parents seem to have to go through in learning to accept their children's gay or bisexual identity. Jerry talked about how panic-stricken his mother was when he first came out to her and how she changed over the course of a year, slowly beginning to accept his gay identity. "She has come to accept it a little, but she will never bring it up. I think there's a process parents have to go through to accept their son or daughter as gay or lesbian." When Karsch first came out to his mother, she sent him religious tracts in an effort to convince him to change: "She's passed that now. She sends me stuff I can relate to--stuff that isn't trying to change me in some way. I bought her a book that she's reading now, *Beyond Acceptance*, published by PFLAG."

Another student came out to his parents when he was 22 years old. "It was interesting; it was a week of hysteria. Seven days of hysteria." This student discussed how his father "came around" eventually, but his mother did not. "My mother had a bad experience with her first husband. She was married once before she met my father. They were going to celebrate an anniversary by recommitting themselves when she found out that he was gay. It's left quite a scar for her." Today, his parents are divorced and his mother lives in Scotland. This student has not heard from his mother in years. However, he has a much closer relationship with his father. "My father had a seven-day nervous breakdown. He's become much more accepting though now. A parent's love should be unconditional, and his is kind of that way."

Students use different strategies in coming out to parents and family members. Kevin decided to come out to his family through the mail while he was still at school. He sent letters to all his family members on a Thursday, expecting that they would receive them on Friday or Saturday. His plan was to call them individually on Sunday evening, "give everyone a day or two for the dust to settle." Kevin called his father on Sunday evening and his father responded: "Tell me something I didn't already know." His father had long suspected that Kevin was gay and had asked him once when he was in high school. Kevin denied it then. What surprised him the most was his mother's reaction: "My mother was the most surprised. She didn't have a clue, which shocked me." He reflected on his conversation with his mom:

Kevin: Hi Mom. I guess by now you've got my letter?
Kevin's Mom: Yes. I'm shocked. I never even knew.
Kevin: But Mom, you should've had an idea. I never had a girlfriend or dated in high
  school. I never even talked about girls.
Kevin's Mom: I wish you had told me earlier, and then I could have gotten you some
  help.
Kevin: Gee thanks Mom. It's not a disease. It's the way I am. It's what I am.
Kevin's Mom: Does this mean you don't like women at all?
Kevin: Yes Mom! At least not sexually.

Kevin's brother and sister took the news much better: "They already had
a clue, so they weren't that surprised." His sister always answered the phone
when his friends called, so she had long suspected Kevin of being gay. His
brother walked in on him one time when he was sitting on the floor leaning
against the bed making out with a friend. They separated before his brother
saw them, but Kevin believes his brother knew what was going on.

Like Kevin, Branden also chose a letter as a way to come out to his mother.
While he was at school, he ripped a page out of his journal; "it was a page that
basically told the whole story." Branden attached a cover letter and sent it to
his mother. About a week after he mailed it, he got a call from her. "She was
crying and saying, 'It's just a phase. You'll meet the right woman. You still
could meet a girl you like. Have you done anything yet? How do you really
know? You're too young to know these things.'" Branden's whole semester
was ruined. He expended so much energy coming out that he did poorly in
school, getting a 1.2 grade point average. "I was emotionally drained but at
the same time relieved. My secret was finally out." Branden went on to note
that he and his mother both agreed not to tell his father for fear that his father
would "shut him off" and stop paying for his schooling.

Branden was by no means alone in getting a negative reaction from one or
both parents. Two other students discussed the reactions of their parents:

I thought my mother had already figured everything out so when I actually told
her I didn't expect much of a scene. Boy, was I wrong. She got very upset.
She was yelling and crying at the same time. She then told my father [his
parents were separated at this time]. He came and talked to me about it. He was
good about it all. My mother still gets a little upset, but she's beginning to make
a little progress, but only a little. Basically she has blocked it out and won't deal
with it. I brought some gay fiction books back home after working at Disney
World in Florida, and she found them and threw them away. I've thought about
getting her some literature but it would be a waste. She would just throw it
away.

I decided after I turned 21 I was going to tell my family. I knew I wouldn't
have to worry about financial support after that because I would be on my own
anyway. . . . I didn't want to have to lie about being gay, and I found myself

having to tell more and more lies. I found a reason to tell them--a friend of
mine was in town and I had to tell them that I wanted to see him. I just
eventually came out and said I was gay. Their reaction was about what I
expected, maybe a little worse. They're religious, so they brought up the Bible
and other things like the social inappropriateness of it all. They said, "How
could you choose this way of life?"

This last student went to therapy with his mother and father, and essentially
the psychiatrist's concern focused on how the family was going to deal with
the whole issue. "He didn't try to change me but instead it was a matter of
how can we, as a family, deal with it all."

For ten students in this study, coming out was initiated by their parents.
One student went away for a weekend (when he lived at home), and while he
was gone his parents went through his room. What they found shocked them:
love letters from other men, and gay magazines. "When my dad picked me
up at the airport he confronted me. 'Are you gay?'" All this young man
could think of was all those years of his father's verbal gay bashing, of
listening to his verbiage about "those fags," all the while never suspecting that
his own son was gay. "I thought about how much I hated this man and how
I could really hurt him by telling him, 'Yes, I'm gay.' I really surprised him
when I said yes. He didn't expect me to stand up to him and not be
intimidated."

Another student spent the summer of 1990 at home with his parents. Being
at home meant one thing in particular to this student: a return to the closet.
To help deal with his frustration and anguish, he kept a journal in which he
wrote about his experiences and feelings. That summer he spent a lot of time
with his gay friends. He was out late one night and his mother's curiosity got
the best of her: she rifled through his room and found his journal. She felt
compelled to read it. "That night when I came home my mom and father were
sitting on the front porch. When I got there they asked me to come inside
with them. We sat down at the kitchen table and she asked me if I was gay.
I said yeah. Just like that. Like it was no big deal."

Other students shared similar experiences. One student recalled how his
father found a paper he had written about his life as a gay man. He would
never forget his father's reaction: "'You're going to hell and your soul is lost.'
He wanted me to see a priest." Despite his concern, his father also expressed
support. "He said he would never turn his back on me. He still paid for all
my schooling." Another, an aspiring writer, had a manuscript returned from
a publishing company to his parent's home. Upon receiving the package, his
parents opened it and read the manuscript. "It was very autobiographical and
I was in New York at the time. At first they were quite shocked. They called
me up out of the blue and told me if I was still writing this kind of material
I wasn't to come home at all. They refused to speak to me for a couple of

months." This student eventually went home for summer break and the subject was never brought up. "They know now that I'm gay. They just don't want to face it."

A student who lives with his father and grandmother (his father and mother are divorced) discussed his experience and offered an explanation for why some students might be confronted by one or both of their parents:

> I consider my father and grandmother as parents. I didn't come out to them, but they know. They discovered this letter and some pictures in my room. The letter was from an ex-boyfriend. You can't keep hiding everything forever. That's probably why so many parents find out by finding something in your room. Their reaction was one of anger, bitterness, threats of being disowned, written out of my grandmother's will. My father was more bent on trying to get me back on track, straight again. To this day they still hold on to the belief that they can make me straight. "If you chose to live this lifestyle then we'll have to disown you from the family." That's what my grandmother said to me. It really hurt, her saying she would disown me, but what hurt even more was her saying that I chose this lifestyle--the notion that I have an option. They are still hoping, but the communications between us are becoming less and less.

Based on the narratives shared by these gay and bisexual men, coming out to one's parents is a challenging experience. In many cases, students are out to friends at school but not to their parents (fourteen students in this study are not out to their parents). This is the case for a student I interviewed who feels the time is not right to come out to his parents. "If I came out they would react pretty badly. My mom would turn right away to the Bible. After the initial shock, she would eventually inform the rest of the family and then tell the whole church and they would all start praying over me." This student also fears being kicked out of the house as well as being disowned by his family. He has questioned his father and mother from time to time, just to get a reaction. Unfortunately, the reactions have all been negative. "I mentioned Liberace to my dad one time to see how he would respond." His father's stance became crystal clear when he responded, "That fairy!" "Eventually I'll bring it up, but now is just not the right time. There are some things I have to work out still."

SUMMARY

What can we conclude from the voices heard throughout this chapter? First, coming out to parents and family is a difficult-to-predict process. Some loved ones react in a supportive, affirming manner, but others accept their son's gay or bisexual identity only with great reluctance. Still other parents deny their son's sexual identity and never bring it up again. In terms of coming out, D'Augelli (1991a) reports that fathers tend to be significantly more intolerant or rejecting than mothers.   Although my research is not designed to test such evidence, one senses in the stories told here that great variability exists in the way mothers and fathers react.   One also gets a sense from seven students that mothers may have a greater awareness of their son's sexual identity.   Nearly half the students in this study suggested that support from parents and family was important in helping them to deal with the social pressures of being gay or bisexual.

A second point about coming out relates to its processual nature.   Coming out is not a single, distinct event; coming out is ongoing.   It is a process that typically begins with self-acknowledgment of one's gay or bisexual identity and proceeds outward as one discloses that part of his identity to others. Coming out has both a personal (self-acknowledgment) and a public (self-disclosure) aspect.

Finally, coming out has produced significant changes in the students with whom I spoke.   Many reported feelings of tremendous relief--as if great burdens had been removed from their lives. Another significant change related to politics.   For most of the gay and bisexual students I interviewed (twenty-seven of the forty), coming out meant becoming political.   One student explained, "To be out is to be political and to let others, especially straight people, know that we exist." Roger, a serious-minded senior who is a major character in the next chapter, claimed: "Coming out is a way of breaking down a system that doesn't want you to exist. It's a way of changing what a society thinks of normalcy."   For the gay and bisexual men involved in this project, to be political is to be engaged in cultural struggle.

NOTE

1. Because coming out is an ongoing process, to say someone is either in the closet or out of the closet is problematic. But to provide insight into my sample, thirty-five students consider themselves to be out and five students think of themselves as closeted.   Even the closeted students, however, are out to a few individuals.

III

CULTURAL BORDERS AND THE GROUP

> It's one thing to think about being gay and how that affects me, but I think that I've become much more aware of the impact of anyone being gay. . . . There are politics behind being gay and I've become much more aware of it and the politics of being a member of any under-represented group.
>
> --Jerry Sandaval, 21-year-old senior

Jerry Sandaval calls our attention to the notion of group identity. For Jerry, coming out and identifying as a gay man was only an initial step toward his engagement in gay politics. Jerry highlights the sense of group commitment many of the students in this project emphasized. In the following two chapters I focus upon the group and how the borders of sexual identity shape group allegiance and struggle.

6

Cultural Workers and the Politics of Silencing

> I have come to believe over and over again that what is most important
> to me must be spoken, made verbal and shared, even at the risk of
> having it bruised or misunderstood.
>
> --Audre Lorde, *Sister Outsider*

ROGER DESKO

Roger is a 25-year-old junior who brings an air of seriousness to nearly every aspect of his life. Although he is shy in certain social settings, such as at The Odyssey on Sunday nights or at gay parties or dances, when placed in a different setting, like a meeting of LGBSA, he takes on an entirely different persona. His quiet self-confidence emerges as he often assumes the role of organizational leader. His insights and constructive criticism are highly regarded among other members of LGBSA. Roger explained his split social personality: "At meetings I have a good idea of what's going on and what is needed to be effective as a group. But in social settings there are just too many intangibles that I cannot control. That frightens me."

Roger grew up in a military family; his father is a lifetime officer in the Air Force. He has few fond memories of his childhood--at least from about the age of five to young adulthood. "I don't think I had a very good childhood. It isn't necessarily related to being gay either. I was abducted and sexually assaulted when I was five when we lived in Turkey." Roger spent much of his childhood trying to recapture that which was taken from him: "Before I was sexually assaulted, I remember being a pretty happy child. Then everything in my life changed. I no longer saw the world in the same way. It was as if I lost something incredibly important and I could never get it back. It was as if my childhood had been taken away from me."

As childhood gave way to adolescence, Roger faced another serious problem: he began to sense that he might be gay. "That was just one more thing on top of everything that had already happened to me. I thought of suicide a lot. I was very reclusive and nerdy. I never really fit in because I was so afraid of other people."

As time passed, Roger became more comfortable with his sexual orientation and came out at the beginning of his college career. "Coming out gave me a sense of self--a sense that I never felt before. Being gay finally was something that I knew for sure. It was a certainty in my life. It was a sense of identity, something I could grab hold of." Roger has emerged as one of the political leaders of the queer movement at Clement University. His identification as a gay man has influenced his vocational plans. A deep concern for the AIDS crisis along with his interest in human sexuality has led him to pursue a career in the helping professions, where he hopes to work as a counselor.

Presently, Roger has taken on the task of challenging the military's ban on lesbian, gay, and bisexual people. He helped to found a student organization committed to forcing the Clement University ROTC program off campus or into acceptance of gay students. "This issue is something that I felt I had to take on. It had to be addressed. I really feel that I am effective because of my family's background in the military. I feel that what I'm doing is the right thing." Roger and the organization he helped to found have created consternation among some administrators at Clement University. Some even agree with Roger's position but feel their hands are tied because ROTC ultimately falls under the jurisdiction of the federal government. Tension eased a little when Bill Clinton was elected, as many within the gay community anxiously anticipated what would happen next. However, when Clinton seemed to waver a bit on his commitment, Roger and other students increased their protests. One of Roger's ideas included a poster that read "Violate Clement University Policies" and listed several recommended violations: ride bikes on the sidewalks, keep library books, pay someone to take your exams, smoke in all your classes, drink a six-pack in front of Old Main, have sex on the golf course, plagiarize, and so on. The idea for the poster, of course, came from the fact that ROTC was in violation of university policy with regard to discrimination based on sexual orientation. Roger is determined to pursue this cause until change occurs or he graduates.

TITO ORTEZ

Tito was born in New York City and raised in Puerto Rico. His career goal is to get his Ph.D. in clinical psychology and return to Puerto Rico, where he wants to contribute to solving some of the social issues his people face. Before pursuing graduate school, however, Tito wants to work with disadvantaged people in New York City, maybe as an advocate. Tito and I became acquainted when we both volunteered for work camps coordinated by

United Campus Ministry at Clement University. Over the winter break of 1991 we went on a trip to Washington, D.C., to work with homeless citizens, and in the spring of 1992 we participated in a Habitat for Humanity trip to Maryland. Through these trips and subsequent social settings, Tito and I became best friends.

At the age of 20, Tito admitted to himself that he was bisexual. Not long after his self-admission, he identified for the first time as queer. Although he had always been vocal about gay and lesbian rights, for him, adopting "queer" as an identifier meant a higher degree of commitment to sexual orientation issues and to social justice issues in general.

Tito had little awareness of his own sexuality as a child and young adult. He believes his lack of awareness related to having been sexually abused as a child. From the age of 7 until around 11, Tito was sexually abused by three older men: an uncle in his 40s, a friend of the family who was in his 30s, and the friend's son, who was a teenager. "I remember them fondling me and my having to masturbate them. I think the son tried to penetrate me because I remember being hurt and his trying to pacify me. It's really hard to recall the details." Coming out was a great release for Tito and helped him to deal with years of sexual repression. "I started to be honest with myself and with others. Not only on issues of sexuality, but on a whole host of other things as well."

Many people who meet Tito find him intimidating. He is assertive, self-confident, direct. Some say Tito has an attitude. That is an understatement. "I have found within me an incredible strength. I do not do things to please others anymore. I do not need to. I have developed self-confidence and an attitude about being queer." Tito always says what's on his mind and he rarely holds back. Tito's directness was what I found so appealing about his personality and partially explains our close friendship. I always knew I could get the truth from him. One night prior to going out on the town the following conversation took place:

Rob: Tito, how do these clothes look? Does this shirt go with these pants?
Tito: Rob, you have jock written all over you. That belt cannot be worn with those shoes, and that shirt looks like something right out of *Saturday Night Fever*. Where did you get those clothes? Sears and Roebuck?
Rob: When did they come up with that one? The belt has to match the shoes?
Tito: Rob, where have you been for the past 30 years? In the closet along with your clothes?
Rob: I can't believe I'm asking a Puerto Rican princess for advice on clothing. What is wrong with me? Look at you. Those pants are three sizes too big.
Tito: At least no one can see every bulge in my body.
Rob: At least I have bulges.
Tito: That you do. One big one, I might add--sitting right on top of your shoulders.

The discussions between Tito and me followed one of two tenors: we either teased one another incessantly, with him almost always getting the best of me, or we talked about highly introspective and serious thoughts and feelings. Tito likes to analyze people and situations. As a result, he is keenly aware of other people's feelings, sometimes even their thoughts.

This chapter focuses on queer students at Clement who have forged a group alliance against the politics of silencing. Students such as Tito and Roger epitomize the attitude of these students, who have stepped out of their closets and engaged in the pursuit of political and cultural change. I have elected to introduce Tito and Roger in this chapter because both adopt a queer identity and both are committed to gay politics. They have been actively involved in the political setting at Clement University. Tito and Roger have one more thing in common: both are survivors of sexual abuse. This latter point created a dilemma for me. I feared that introducing them together might lead some readers to make connections between being gay and sexual abuse experienced as children. I discussed this matter with Tito.

Rob: I'm reluctant to introduce Roger and you in the same chapter because both of you were sexually abused as children. I could see someone saying, "Oh, that's why they're queer."
Tito: Why don't you talk about that assumption: that sexual abuse is or is not a factor that "makes" someone gay. You interviewed other people who were not sexually abused, right?
Rob: Only a few students told me they were abused as children. [Four students indicated they had been sexually abused.] But you've heard the theories: that children who were sexually abused or who had distant fathers are more likely to be gay. I even interviewed a couple of students who buy into that.
Tito: Why does it matter? Yes, I was a victim of sexual abuse and yes, I had a distant father. But the fact is I'm a bisexual/queer activist and that's a way for me to be happy. Who cares why? This is what I am.
Rob: But some people do care why.
Tito: The fact is that we have a very Western, twentieth-century conceptualization of what sexuality is--of what gay and lesbian means. I mean, are people really straight or gay? One or the other?
Rob: I don't think so, but the fact is that society defines people that way. I guess my concern is over the way in which people who identify with same-sex attractions get defined and my fear that my study might be used in some way to perpetuate oppressive definitions. You know, like "Tito's queer because he was sexually abused."
Tito: No one is Beaver Cleaver happy. Maybe sexual abuse does contribute in some way to sexual orientation. Maybe it doesn't. But the fact is that straight people also were sexually abused. Straights also had distant fathers.
Rob: Yes. But no one is saying, "Oh, that's why he is straight."
Tito: No. It's only those people who don't fit certain norms whose lives are scrutinized. The so-called "normal" people do not have to explain who they are. Or why they are the way they are. So it wouldn't surprise me at all if more queer people *report* being

sexually abused than straights.

Rob: What do you mean?

Tito: If you're fucked up, as in not normal, then you're more likely to try and figure out why you're fucked up. When someone doesn't fit into society's definitions they are more likely to examine their lives, to think about their childhood in serious terms. They are more likely to turn up sexual abuse. Remember, many people who were sexually abused as children suppress those experiences. What I'm saying is that it may be the case that queers are more likely to uncover their sexual abuse.

Rob: But queers argue that they aren't fucked up. It's society's definitions that are fucked, right?

Tito: Yeah. You're right. That's the difference between someone who is gay or lesbian and trying to fit in, and someone who is queer who is trying to change the system. We're saying that we're not fucked up but that society is. The system is. And we're going to point it out and change the system. We put the illness on a society that does not acknowledge the diversity of sexuality.

Tito's last comment highlights the idea of a cultural worker struggling to claim an identity that differs from and even rejects the norm. In the second half of this chapter I return to Tito and Roger as well as other students who are engaged in the struggle to decenter the norms of sexuality. But first, I delineate more clearly what I mean by the politics of silencing.

The cultural production of the closet is a byproduct of the politics of silencing. In this regard, it seems sensible to situate such a discussion prior to or juxtaposed with a discussion of the closet (chapter 4). Instead, I have chosen to discuss silencing tactics in this chapter to bring such a discussion into closer proximity to student activism.

THE POLITICS OF SILENCING

The normalization of society produces attacks upon the body and soul of individuals who, for whatever reason, reject society's norms (Foucault, 1978, 1979). The attacks come not only from the state, in the form of legal authority; social control is also the result of a system of constraints and punishments evident throughout the entire social structure. From the perspective of Michel Foucault, we have all become "our brother's keeper," watching over one another, making sure that norms are not violated, that dominant beliefs and values are upheld. We develop languages and social practices that exclude, order, disperse, and limit any behaviors or characteristics outside the mainstream. The term "queer," used in its pejorative sense to insult gay people, is an example of how language can be used to exclude a specific individual or group of people who do not fit a certain norm--in this case, heterosexuality. Sometimes people even act as vigilantes, correcting wrongdoers and righting the social balance. The totality of these tactics, many of which are outside our own conscious thought, make up what may be described as the politics of silencing. The tactics are political in that power lies at their center, naming or silencing various individuals, groups, or behaviors.

The preceding paragraph relates some of the theoretical aspects of the politics of silencing. Although it is important to understand the far-reaching nature of such a polity, it is also helpful to verify the existence of oppression through real-life voices. In chapter 4 we heard from students such as Tom, Branden, and Shane, who highlighted the confining and oppressive nature of the closet. Chapter 5 focused on how individuals escape the closet by coming out. We heard from Karsch and Roman and their struggles to claim their gay identities. What I discuss in this chapter pertains not so much to individual acts, although there are some that I note; but the primary focus is on identification and involvement as a member of a community--the gay community--and students' engagement as "cultural workers." In the following pages I highlight some of the experiences of the gay and bisexual men involved in this study. Their narratives are rooted in a society that must conceal and silence that which drifts from the norm. In simplest terms, the politics of silencing refer to social relations that depend upon the use and manipulation of power to oppress an individual or group.

Summer 1992

Ben Curry rolled over to check his alarm clock, half hoping that the loud buzzing sound was all part of a bad dream. Unfortunately, it was no dream. The clock read 8:30 p.m.. Friday night was here and although he was tired from having worked all day at the AIDS Project, he was psyched about a party one of his friends was having. He had to get moving, though, because he was supposed to meet Tito and Roger at 9:00.

Today had been much like other Fridays over the past two months. Unlike previous summers, in which Ben took it easy, maybe took a class, worked a little, partied, this summer had been almost all work and little play. Despite a lack of free time, he enjoyed his internship at the AIDS Project. He was especially excited about the opportunity to plan a sexual awareness program for rural men involved in cruising (picking up other men for casual sexual encounters). The program was all but finished; today he wrapped up most of the final plans. There were just a few details to finalize next week and his internship would be completed. Organization was not Ben's strong point, but he had learned a great deal throughout the summer from his supervisor and from others connected with the Project.

He climbed out of bed and shed his work clothes as he headed for the shower. He hoped that none of his roommates were on the same time schedule as he was and that the bathroom would be free. At 5'11" and 160 pounds, Ben is well proportioned. At age 22, he still has the youthful midsection dreamed about by middle-aged men whose once-slender waistlines have turned to "love handles." Ben enjoyed living in the house he and his friends had rented for the summer; it was cool living with four other queers and one straight woman who was a queer supporter. He was free to have his boyfriend up for weekends; nobody cared, and besides, they all had guests from time to time.

Finished with his shower, Ben got dressed and checked himself in the mirror. His recent haircut left about a quarter of an inch of hair, which took practically no grooming; "bad hair days" were a distant memory for Ben.

He met Tito and Roger on one of the street corners a few blocks from the party, just as they had planned. They were thrilled that Ben was only 15 minutes late. When they arrived at the party, the first thing Ben noticed was that he hardly knew anyone and that none of his other queer friends were there. He was disappointed but not surprised: "I knew that the party was going to be straight and that I would have to act fairly straight. When you're queer you know you have to make an adjustment and be bicultural at times." He went on to add, "I didn't go into the party to hit on anyone or dance with anyone. I went in with a certain degree of closetedness. But if someone asks me, then I'm not going to hide it."

They waded through the crowd of maybe thirty or forty people gathered in a smallish two-room apartment and headed to the kitchen, where the keg was. They each got a beer and returned to the living room, where they hung out for about an hour in one corner of the room. Months later, Roger reflected on the party and countless conversations such as the ones they had that night and at other parties.

Tito: Now there's a cutie.
Roger: I didn't think you went for the muscular type.
Tito: He's not that big. Not as big as that guy over there.
Ben: Yeah. I noticed him when we walked in.
Tito: I knew you'd go for the Neanderthal type. Not me. I'm more into personality.
Ben: Yeah, right. That's why you dated what's-his-name.
Tito: Hey! At least he wasn't a closet case.
Roger: Why can't you find a hot guy who isn't afraid to be honest?

They passed the time commenting on other men and each other's taste in men. Eventually Tito left for another party and Roger and Ben stayed in the corner of the living room. They had a few more beers and visited with a variety of people, including the party's host, who was one of Ben's friends. Ben recalled seeing a guy who he thought was attractive. "Look at that guy." "Which one?" asked Roger. "That one that just came in. He's so hot. That big boy with the shaved head." The woman who hosted the party entered the conversation at this point. "What are you guys talking about?" "Oh nothing. I just thought one of your friends is attractive." "Which one? Show me" she asked. "He's over there, in the kitchen." She walked toward the kitchen pointing at various men: "Is it him? Is it him?" Ben followed her and leaned over her shoulder as she stood at the edge of the kitchen. She eventually pointed at the right guy. "Yeah, that's him." "Oh, that's Jim."

Ben went back and talked with Roger while the hostess stayed in the kitchen and responded to questions about why she was pointing at some of the men. There were seven or eight men seated on the kitchen counters, which formed a U-shape around three of the kitchen walls. She told them that someone had found one of them attractive. "Who is she?" they asked. "It's not a she. It's a guy." "Oh, there are gay guys here?" "Why were they invited?" "Why don't they stay in their closets?"

Ben's friend, the hostess, came back in and told Ben and Roger how disappointed she was in her friends. "It's no big deal," Ben replied, although he now felt a little embarrassed that Jim knew Ben thought he was cute.

Eventually Roger, and then Ben, made their way to the kitchen to refill their cups at the keg. "This guy named Jim started talking to Roger about a cross that Roger wore around his neck." Ben thought things were cool, so he walked over by them to get a beer. A friend of Ben's cut in front of him and started filling his own cup and Ben's, which he had grabbed from Ben's hand. At the same time, several men seated on the counter were pointing at Ben and saying, "That's the guy." "I looked up at Jim and he was staring me down." Ben recalled the brief conversation that took place:

Ben: Don't flatter yourself.
Jim: What the fuck did you say?
Ben: I said, don't flatter yourself.
Jim: Don't come in here. Don't talk to me. And don't even think about looking at me.
Ben: I just came in to get a beer.
Jim: If you say one more word I'll deck you.
Ben: Why?

In an instant Jim jumped off the counter and ran toward Ben. He swung at Ben, but he ducked and Jim's fist barely missed Ben's face. Ben's head went under Jim's left arm and Jim had him in a headlock while he swung at Ben's face with his right hand. In the meantime Ben pounded Jim's back with his right fist, but his blows were weak because he was hunched over so far that he had no leverage. No more than 10 seconds had passed when all of Jim's friends piled on and began punching Ben. Soon the crowd in the living room pushed its way toward the kitchen; some grabbed and pushed Jim's friends aside to break up the melee. As guys were separated from the pile, Jim took one more swing at Ben. His fist struck Ben squarely in the eye. Hunching over to collect himself, Ben placed his hand on his face only to catch a handful of blood that poured from a gash just below his eye. Ben's friends sat him down, helped stop the bleeding, then escorted him back to his house.

According to Ben, after this incident Jim was supposed to be suspended; but by the time his hearing came up he had already graduated. Ben said that the university placed a disciplinary record on Jim's transcript and that Jim also got fined $200 in municipal court.

In August 1992, Ben Curry felt the force of the normalizing society. His expression of same-sex attractions were seen as out of place by several students at a college party. Their attitude was expressed as: "It's a straight party. Why are gays here?" Ben's incident serves as a reminder to queer students at Clement University that being lesbian, gay, or bisexual is tolerable by society only if kept behind closed doors. Bring "it" out in the open and pay the price.

Ben's story also highlights the violence often associated with the politics of silencing. Incidents such as the one that happened to Ben lead other gay students to question the safety of coming out, thereby prolonging their lives in the closet. As Tom, who remains closeted, stated, "I'm scared for my life. There are so many hateful people out there. Who knows what they might do?" Silencing tactics are evident not only in homophobic reactions but also in heterosexist behaviors and attitudes. In what follows, I relate student narratives to these dual forms of oppression.

Homophobia as a Weapon

Homophobia involves prejudicial and discriminatory treatment of lesbian, gay, and bisexual people. The following student voices highlight some of the effects of homophobia and, in particular, the violence that gay students at Clement must be prepared to deal with on a daily basis.

Ron: One time I was physically assaulted at The Odyssey. The guy knew I was gay. I think he was looking for a fight that night because he had bothered some of my friends earlier. I was standing close to a friend of mine talking to her, and he walked by and intentionally bumped into me and made me spill my beer on her. He walked away but I walked after him and asked him to apologize to her. He said something like, "Fuck off, faggot!" We got into kind of a shouting match and then someone finally broke it up. I walked away from him, toward my friend, and he called me a "fuckin' nigger." At the same time he jumped on me and hit me on the side of the head. People broke it up pretty quickly and I didn't have any serious damage.

Jimmy: I was physically assaulted once walking by the frats late at night. There were four guys and at first they verbally assaulted me, then one of them shoved me. They thought I was gay because they kept calling me "fag." This one guy drew back to punch me. I hit him in the nose. It was a knee-jerk reaction. I think I probably broke his nose. I took off and they left me alone.

Patrick: One January I was walking out of this downtown night club and these five drunk guys were arguing about something. All of a sudden as I passed by they opened the door to Friendlies [the only gay bar in Hidden Falls] and yelled in "You fuckin' faggots!" I stopped and said, "Did someone yell faggot?" The guy that yelled and the four others got in my face and pushed me down to the sidewalk. One was getting ready to punch me in the face but another one stopped him and said, "You don't want to get any faggot blood on your hands."

Karsch: I went to the George Bush rally with a bunch of other lesbian and gay people. We held signs protesting Bush's policies. We were chanting slogans against him when these fraternity guys came up to us and called us faggots and dykes and started pushing us out of the way. One person got punched in the face. Another woman got knocked down and we had to form a circle around her to protect her. They were trying to take our signs away. It was really pretty scary.

Rich: I was walking home with this guy I was seeing. We were in front of this pizza place downtown. I started to talk to these three guys, just shooting the breeze. I didn't think that I'd said anything that might offend someone, and I didn't think it was obvious that I was gay, but I might have acted a little flamboyant. As two of the guys turned to leave, the third guy started to follow them but all of a sudden he turned around and hit me with his fist right in the forehead. I was pretty drunk, so everything was pretty much a blur until the guy hit me, and from then on I remember everything. The police and an ambulance came. I had to get eighteen stitches.

The preceding examples of homophobia all involved a high degree of physical violence. However, homophobia includes other forms of harassment or discrimination as well. For example, Roman was walking along the main street in Hidden Falls one day with some of his friends when two women stopped them and asked for change. They were "canning" for charity. Roman gave them whatever pocket money he had and moved along. "These guys behind us knew the girls and stopped after we started to walk away. One of them said something like, 'Dude, you asked a bunch of faggots.'" One of Roman's friends, who always tries to protect him, got upset and was ready to fight. But Roman convinced his friend to "leave it alone." "That's kind of my attitude. I'm more of a passivist than a radical or someone who might fight back. Compared to Martin Luther King and Malcom X, I'm definitely more like King."

Another student had some friends change their minds about sharing an apartment with him soon after he came out to them. He and his friends were hanging out at the downtown diner and one of his friends said that she couldn't live with him because she was applying for a job with the federal government and if they found out that she lived with a homosexual, she might not get the job. "Then my other friend said he didn't want to deal with all the harassment that he felt would come up if he lived with me."

Out lesbian, gay, and bisexual students who live in the residence halls frequently face more blatant forms of silencing tactics. One student woke up one morning to go to the bathroom only to look in the mirror and find the following: "Fag in 408. We don't like cocksuckers on our hall." This student often posted information related to gay issues on his door and every now and then they would get torn down, written on, or spat at. "One time I put my clothes in the dryer and this guy got real upset with me because I guess he was next in line or something and so he left a note on the machine 'Hey fag I was here first.'" Tito and Karsch both worked as Resident Assistants (RAs) and had to deal with derogatory notes on their doors all the time. For them, harassment was a fact of life. Another student recalled how his hall started a petition to get the "fag off the hall." The students were reprimanded by the RA, but in the end they got what they wanted: the "fag" moved off campus.

A student remembered being at The Odyssey on a Thursday night and bumping into a friend whom he had not seen in a long time. This student was wearing his "love knows no gender" T-shirt; when he spotted his friend he walked over to hug him, and they kissed each other on the cheek. "It was really no big deal, but one of the bouncers came over to us and said, 'Save it for Sunday night' [alternative lifestyle night]."

Another student recalled taking a Black Studies class on the life of Martin Luther King, Jr. The professor was pointing out three weaknesses of one of King's key advisors, Bayard Rustin. One was that Rustin was a suspected Communist. When the professor said this no one in the class said anything. The second was that he avoided the draft. Again, no one said anything. The third shortcoming was that he was openly homosexual. Everyone in the class gasped. "That was the one unforgivable thing--that he was gay." The point here is not that Rustin's sexual orientation should be avoided in a class discussion, because in large part his gayness was an issue for many conservative Baptist ministers (although King consistently supported him). Rather, the example demonstrates how the politics of a classroom all too often reinforce norms rather than bringing them into discussion. As I discuss elsewhere in this chapter, the classroom and a multitude of other sites (such as residence halls) offer pedagogic moments for learning and liberation if we use them for interpretation rather than the mere telling of facts.

The stories of homophobia seemed never-ending. On one occasion two gay students walked by a fraternity and someone stuck his head out the window and yelled, "Bend over and let me fuck you up the ass." One of the gay students responded, "I'm too pretty to be your girlfriend and I'm certainly not your roommate." This student has a quick and combative tongue and comes across as physically capable of reacting to violence against him. Some of the other men I interviewed were not as physically self-assured. One student described the feelings of fear he experiences on a daily basis: "I don't feel very safe on campus. I don't really feel comfortable. It's something I put up with, something I tolerate. You just never know when a group of frat boys or jock-types, you know, those who are probably most closeted, are going to beat your face in because you remind them of what they can't admit to."

Other students also live in fear. I asked one student if he wears buttons or T-shirts that might identify him as a gay man: "No, I don't feel comfortable declaring myself to everyone that walks by because of the possibility of being harassed. If you tell the world you're gay, you have a good chance of getting harassed." This student went on to add: "I'm not ready yet to be identified to everyone. That would make me nervous. It's almost as if you're asking for trouble when you're that out." This student also described the first time he made contact with members of the queer community. "At the student activities fair I found the table for LGBSA and got information about when and where meetings took place. I did it looking over my shoulder for fear that someone might see me talking to 'those people.'"

The preceding student's fear of being seen and identified as a gay man parallels some of my own fears about the simplest of activities. On one occasion I volunteered to post fliers in the library to advertise Gay Pride Week. I did not realize when I volunteered at an LGBSA meeting that posting fliers would be so threatening. When I walked through the rotating doors of the library, a subtle change in my demeanor began to take place. My "I don't give a damn attitude" slowly faded and in its place a degree of fear and apprehension surfaced. What if students see me? Will they harass me? Worse yet, will they just give me that condescending look as if I am some kind of second-class citizen? Posting the fliers brought back feelings I had as a child when my mother used food stamps at the grocery store. At the checkout line, my sister Kim and I would slowly drift away from her, disown her, so that we did not have to face "those looks"--wrinkled brows, tightened lips, up-turned noses--"What right do they have to buy pop, or candy, with my tax dollars?" Their looks conveyed an attitude that my mother, that we, were somehow less human than everyone else. Concerns such as these ran through my head as I posted the fliers, making sure that the coast was clear before I pulled any out of my bookbag. This feeling, this hard-to-locate fear, was the same fear I felt the first time I stopped at the student center to get the key for the LGBSA office. Later, I talked to other students about my fears and they told me they experience similar feelings on a regular basis. This was even true of some of the most politically active queer students.

Heterosexism as a Weapon

Heterosexism is the belief that everyone is, or should be, heterosexual. As Karsch maintained, "In a way heterosexism hurts more than homophobia. When someone says something or does something homophobic they at least acknowledge you exist. With heterosexism someone is refusing to acknowledge your existence--you remain invisible."

Nearly every student interviewed reported incidents of heterosexism in Clement University classrooms. One student recalled a class in which the students got to ask each other questions on the first day. Almost all the questions related one way or another to what students might look for in dating the other sex. Another student remembered a similar incident, only this time it was the instructor who asked the students what they look for in the "opposite" sex. When the instructor got to this student he said, "What do you mean? What do I look for in the opposite sex as in dating?" The instructor responded, "Yes." "I don't look for anything in women. I date men. I'm gay." At this time a student nearby applauded and said, "I've been waiting for someone to point out the heterosexism in this class."

Roger recalled a human development course he took in which the professor talked about behavior modification as a means to treat homosexuals. "I raised my hand to point out that there are some serious issues that we should talk about in relation to whether this kind of strategy is acceptable. You know, the idea of 'curing' gays." Andrew has witnessed heterosexism in the classroom so often that he quit keeping track of all the incidents. He often says something and sometimes catches professors off guard, but he does not believe they are sincere about rethinking their attitudes: "A lot of times they are apologetic but it's kind of that superficial level, like 'Oh, yeah, I guess you're right.' I'll just get back to my research lab and do what I'm really interested in."

Time and time again we hear the frustrations that gay and bisexual men feel when their lives are excluded from classroom discussions. Teachers and students frequently, unwittingly in many cases, discuss the experiences of themselves and peers as if everyone adopts the norm of heterosexuality. This fallacious assumption limits our knowledge and awareness of same-sex attraction as a form of expression. To reiterate a point made earlier by Karsch, heterosexism is in many ways more painful than homophobia, for at least when people exhibit homophobia they acknowledge a person's existence.

For many of the gay and bisexual students participating in this study, much of the homophobia and heterosexism exhibited at Clement University and Hidden Falls relates to its rural location. As Shane noted, "I think that coming out would be a lot easier in New York City. We live in the middle of nowhere and it's crazy here." Although the preceding statement reflects Shane's perspective, one has to question his assessment that it would be easier to be out in New York City, given the violence committed there against gay people (Gays under Fire, 1992; Minkowitz, 1990).

Shane is probably accurate in his assessment of Clement and Hidden Falls as conservative (I argue the same point in chapter 1). The conservative quality of the area serves as a source of motivation for Shane: "Clement University was not the ideal choice for me, but I feel challenged to make it the right place. That's one reason I'm involved with LGBSA" [this was later in the fall semester when Shane was more out]. The challenge of being at Clement was also expressed by Andrew: "I think that if I were in a more liberal atmosphere, I'd be bored just because there would be less for me to do."

The preceding pages highlight the many experiences of gay and bisexual students related to heterosexism and homophobia, experiences that lead many to remain silent. Silencing tactics revolve around power--who controls discourse, who defines truth, who determines what knowledge is relevant or irrelevant, who speaks, who listens. Critical postmodernists argue that power is relational; power is not the monopoly of any one person or group. Hence, power can be seized. Opposition can be offered. Shane, Andrew, Tito, Roger, and Ben are examples of student opposition to heterosexism and homophobia. In trying to create a more equitable culture at Clement, queer students have seized power and offered their own form of opposition.

QUEER STUDENTS AS CULTURAL WORKERS

Part of the current student movement draws inspiration from the organization known as Queer Nation and in general follows its slogan: "We're queer. We're here. Get used to it." Anthony D'Augelli (1991b) sheds light on the significance of the queer movement: "The first post-Stonewall generation has redeemed the term 'queer' as a tool for unrepentant empowerment. Intergenerational tension in the lesbian/gay population has emerged, an inevitable consequence of the conflict between accommodative successes and impatient fury" (p. 5). He goes on to point out that today's generation of lesbian, gay, and bisexual college students *expect* a place on campus--"they see no reason for shame" (p. 5).

Clement University offers an example of the power of the queer student movement, and LGBSA forms the heart of this movement. The goal of LGBSA, and of queer students such as Tito and Roger, is to instill in all lesbian, gay, and bisexual people an attitude of pride and openness. Solidarity is a key because there is strength in numbers. Adoption of the term "queer" is in this sense a political act intended to unite lesbian, gay, and bisexual people as well as to highlight the positive aspects of gay identities. Roger is helpful here:

I use the term "queer" to make people aware that I'm not excluding bisexuals and lesbians. It's not even in vogue yet among some queers. It's more of an activist, assertive term. It connotes pride in being a homosexual or a bisexual. "Gay" possibly used to imply the same thing. It's adopting a term that was used in a negative way and conveying a different message, a message of pride, happiness, celebration.

Roger discusses "queer" as a term that signifies pride in one's gay identity. He also uses the term to denote the political aspect of being gay in a culture that is best characterized as heterosexist. Tito, Ben, Jerry, and Andrew use the term similarly. Yet for many, queer is not so much about pride as it is about power and empowerment. When Ben claims to be queer and then describes himself as bicultural, there is a bit of inconsistency. For Ben, bicultural means knowing how to act and survive in a straight world (although his survival skills may not be that great, judging by the gash below his eye). Others within the gay community think of "queer" more in terms of *not* assimilating to heterosexual culture.

Ben is not alone in his expropriation of the term "queer" from other more radical gay activists. At least five of the students in this study who consider themselves to be queer are in secret societies and at least two are in fraternities. This is queer, as in inconsistent or strange, but is it queer? My point here is not to pass judgment on how students identify themselves but to raise questions about our use of language. In *The Culture of Desire*, Frank Browning (1993) discusses the "politics of rage" while describing the organized efforts of Queer Nation (QN) to battle inequality and injustice. He highlights a queer demonstration at a restaurant where two lesbians were mistreated by a waiter, who yelled at them, "We don't serve lesbian bitches here!" Browning elaborates how a group of queer patrons arrived early at the restaurant, around 8 o'clock on a Saturday, requested menus, and ordered water over and over again. Oddly enough, one woman kept finding flies in her soup.

Almost half the tables [were] occupied by Queer Nationals. At 8:45--only 15 minutes off schedule--a crowd of pickets and whistle blowers [could] be seen marching up to the restaurant's floor-to-ceiling plate-glass windows, waving signs and fists and raising enough ruckus to stop street traffic. Simultaneous with the demonstration outside, queer diners [blew] their whistles and then read, in unison, from a leaflet entitled, "THE LAURA ACTION: Lashing-out At Unacceptable Restaurant Aggression." (pp. 42-43)

The diners listed a series of demands: that all queers and queer supporters boycott the restaurant, that the waiter be fired, that the case be tried by the district attorney. The manager appeared on the scene and engaged in an argument with one queer man whom she eventually slapped in the face. The man reached back to return the blow but thought otherwise when a police officer approached. "Faced with arrest the activists filed out, but not before one QN man, who [had] earlier taken an emetic, [began] retching, spewing a thirty-foot trail of vomit across the floor and tables" (p. 43). For some lesbian, gay, and bisexual people, this is queer.

The demonstration described by Browning took place in San Francisco. Can we expect the same type of organized, radical action in Hidden Falls, situated in the middle of a conservative rural area? Does what it mean to be queer vary? Throughout this text I highlight the role that culture plays in shaping identity. The culture of San Francisco is quite dissimilar to that of Clement University and Hidden Falls. Even as we must call upon a range of perspectives to understand the complexity of queer identity, at the same time our understanding of queerness must also be informed by the experiences of lesbian, gay, and bisexual students at Clement as they struggle to shape their own queer identities.

Although queer students at Clement rarely organize "queer visibility expeditions" to the local mall or "zap" local businesses, they nonetheless are actively engaged in a struggle to re-create both the institutional and societal cultures. They use politics, visibility, and education to achieve their goals of equality, liberty, and justice. In this sense, they are very much the cultural workers that Henry Giroux (1992) discusses in his book *Border Crossings*.

> The concept of "cultural worker" has traditionally been understood to refer to artists, writers, and media producers. . . . I extend the range of cultural work to people working in professions such as law, social work, architecture, medicine, theology, education, and literature. In doing so, my intention is to rewrite the concept and practice of cultural work by inserting the primacy of the political and pedagogical. The pedagogical dimension of cultural work refers to the process of creating symbolic representations and the practices within which they are engaged. . . . The political dimensions of cultural work inform this process through a project whose intent is to mobilize knowledge and desires that may lead to minimizing the degree of oppression in people's lives. What is at stake is a political imaginary that extends the possibilities for creating new public spheres in which the principles of equality, liberty, and justice become the primary organizing principles for structuring relationships between the self and others. (p. 5)

Giroux extends the definition of cultural work to include professionals such as those in education, but I go one step further and include individuals such as students and volunteers, people not typically classified as "professionals." My point is that queer students at Clement University are actively engaged in contesting the closet, with the goal of changing the culture of the university and of American society. They have three interrelated strategies: politics, visibility, and education.

Politics

For queer students, coming out is more than an individual process meant to claim a public space; coming out is also a political effort designed to create greater awareness and achieve increased rights and visibility for all queer people. In chapter 5 I discussed coming out mostly in terms of the individual. Here I touch upon the political and group ramifications of publicly identifying as a lesbian, gay, or bisexual person.

One student maintained that simply being out involves a certain degree of politics in that out lesbian, gay, and bisexual people at the very minimum serve as reminders to a straight society that gay people exist. "That's why I wear clothing that might tell people that I'm queer, such as a T-shirt with some type of queer saying on it." Andrew argued that if you wake up in the morning with someone of the same gender, then you're political. "That's the bottom line. Everything we do is political, whether we want it to be or not." Andrew's point is not that merely sleeping with someone of the same gender represents a political act; instead, what he highlights is that in a society that relegates gay people to the closet, a lesbian, gay, or bisexual person is almost automatically thrown into a political mine field, whether he or she wants to be or not.

Another student identified himself as a "gay man/political queer." He elaborated: "Political queer is a more blatant way of defining myself as part of the community. Anyone who questions society's gender roles can be defined as queer. It can include transsexuals. It is the gender fuck kind of thing." Jerry also discussed a group sense of identity: "It's one thing to think about being gay and how that affects me, but I think that I've become much more aware of the impact of anyone being gay in society." Jerry finds "the politics of being gay" fascinating. "It's almost a shame that it is so political and that people just can't be gay as if they were straight. But there are politics behind being gay, and I've become much more aware of it." He went on to point out that he has learned to recognize the connection between other forms of oppression: "I've become a lot more aware of oppression in general. For me, racism, sexism, and homophobia are all part of the big three as far as problems go."

For twenty-seven of the students I interviewed, becoming politically involved was a natural progression after initially coming out. One student received great satisfaction when he gave a speech on the steps of the auditorium building during National Coming Out Day. He also was proud of a protest he organized (a "die-in" on the steps of one of the classroom buildings) after a Clement University student sent a computer message that offered a rationale for killing "homosexuals." Jerry discussed the feeling he had after coming out and how political activism seemed like a natural progression:

There's a lack of challenge once you come out. "What is next?" When I first started to come out I put a lot of energy into it; I expected it all to be so difficult. I felt as if I committed myself to much more of a struggle for personal validation and it seemed as if personally it came too easily. "Ok, I'm out. No big deal." It seemed like I set myself up for this long struggle that didn't happen and my only recourse was to move it from a personal level to a political level. If I could do a greater good by serving the whole community, that would be great. I felt as if I had already done it for myself.

Although several students saw no need to make sexual identity a political issue, almost thirty of the students in this project felt that being lesbian, gay, or bisexual was already political, whether one recognized it or not. For many of these students, forming an alliance with other gay students is essential if they are to achieve equal rights and fair treatment. These students see coming out not only as an individual act but also as an initial step toward forging group solidarity.

Visibility

For queer students, being visible is another step in changing people's understanding of lesbian, gay, and bisexual people and is a means to recognize other members of the gay community. By visibility, most students referred in some way to letting others know that they are gay or bisexual. Visibility was discussed in reference to two different populations: the gay community and the general public.

All forty of the students in this project are out to varying degrees within the gay community. Even the five students who consider themselves closeted are out to some members of the gay community. The remaining thirty-five are out to varying degrees to the larger communities of Hidden Falls and Clement University.

Many queer students explained that it is largely the invisibility of lesbian, gay, and bisexual people within the general population that prevents them from assuming their rightful place within society's power structures. One student commented: "One thing that really bothers me is that as a queer person, I find it very frustrating that so few people are willing to be out and active." For this student, being visible implies *publicly* demonstrating one's sexual identity in some way.

The ways that students choose to demonstrate their gay or bisexual identities are diverse. One student talked about wearing T-shirts with queer phrases on them. He also mentioned certain mannerisms such as "snapping," which involves moving one's hand in a Z-like fashion starting above the head and snapping the fingers at the end of each stroke. Another student described some of the mannerisms he incorporates into his behavior: "Just some of the stereotypical things. Crossing your legs a lot, wearing bright colors, laughing really loud in public, in a higher pitch maybe." This student recognized that these behaviors all relate to different stereotypes, but at the same time he acknowledged, "They come from somewhere. Acting out stereotypes I think is a way to identify to each other." Another student mentioned excessive use of the hands in talking as a clue that one might be gay.

One student has a favorite T-shirt that says "nobody knows I'm gay." This student went on to point out: "When I wear my earring I wear it in my right ear, although that probably doesn't have the same meaning that it once did. But some still think it means you're gay." (Some of us grew up hearing the expression "right is wrong.") This student also talked about gestures like "snapping" and putting his hands on his hips. Mostly these are intentional expressions of queer visibility, flamboyant mannerisms: "Hey we're here. Like it or not." The following students also discussed their visibility:

Roger: I wear T-shirts with queer statements on special days such as National Coming Out Day. That's the only time I really dress to make everyone know that I'm gay. I don't modify my behavior out of fear. If anything I do the opposite. I've become very confrontational, and if I hear people bad-mouthing gays or lesbians I purposely act gay so they might confront me about it. Then I can give them a piece of my mind. It's a mission in my life to be as visible as possible.

Karsch: I wear queer stuff on practically every piece of clothing I have. Mainly I wear stuff to let other gay and straight people know that I am gay. There are so many straights who don't know we exist that you have to advertise. My favorite T-shirt is one that has two men kissing and says: "Read my lips."

Branden: One day during Pride Week I wore my "love knows no gender" T-shirt all around campus. I never had so much bounce in my legs. I felt wonderful and proud to be gay. I was full of positive energy for a change. I was happy and people were looking at me like "What is that?" I didn't even feel nervous--it was unbelievable. I hung my "love knows no gender" T-shirt up in my room when I moved in so my roommate would know right away. He asked me if I was gay and I said yes. He didn't have any major problems with it as long as I didn't bring anyone home. In fact, we made that rule for both of us. Not too long after that I went out and bought a scarf and bought some pink cloth and some black cloth and made a circle and a triangle and sewed it on the scarf. My bookbag has nine buttons on it that are all gay stuff. One says "I like men." Another says "If time and space are curved, then where do straight people come from?" Another has two male symbols together. One has a pink triangle. One says "I'm a fag."

Ben: My favorite T-shirt is my "love knows no gender" one and another that has a drawing of two stick figures holding hands and says "Adam and Steve." As far as behaviors, sometimes I might hold hands when me and my boyfriend walk down the

street, at least until we get close to downtown. It's easy to slip up though, and forget;
like the other day we were at the student center and I yelled at him, "See you later
honey."

T-shirts with queer expressions seem to be the preferred statement of
choice.   One student's favorite says "Too cute to be straight [2QT2B
Straight]." Although wearing T-shirts is seen as an expression of queerness
by many of the most politically active gay students at Clement, others around
the country might argue that T-shirts are a rather conservative or at best
moderate expression of queerness. Wearing T-shirts with queer expressions
is hardly queer in San Francisco. Even though we might challenge students'
definitions of queerness, we must also keep the cultural context of Clement
University and Hidden Falls in mind. Culturally speaking, Hidden Falls is far
removed from New York City or San Francisco.

Not all the gay and bisexual men in this study wore T-shirts with queer
expressions or made other public statements about their sexual identity. Jerry
explained why he does not wear buttons and pins:

> I hate to see bookbags covered with political statements. I don't really want
> people to know. I mean, I want them to know on my terms. I have a variety
> of T-shirts that I wear sometimes. Most of the time I don't. I don't want
> someone to make assumptions about me without first talking to me. So I don't
> want people to see me with a pink triangle and think one thing. I guess it would
> be different if I appeared straight. I think it should be obvious to anyone that
> I'm gay. People should know I'm gay.

Recall from chapter 2 that Jerry is the student who is known for his red high-
top sneakers and matching red hair, often worn in a pony tail. Although Jerry
has some flamboyant mannerisms--he waves his hands a lot when he talks and
his voice is a little high-pitched--the notion that he looks gay may not be as
obvious as he thinks.

Another student talked about why he does not have buttons on his bookbag:
"Originally after coming out I did because I needed to make a point--express
who I finally knew I was. It gave me a purpose in life. But as I became more
comfortable with being gay I began to get away from the overt stuff."

Some students emphasize direct confrontation more than adopting certain
mannerisms. One student makes a point to talk to his professors after class to
let them know he is gay. "I let them know that I am going to be open about
being gay and if they have a problem with that then we are going to have a
problem.   If they don't, then I'll be the perfect student." This student
mentioned other visible behaviors, such as turning his head to look when a guy
walks by him, or not lowering his voice when he talks about gay issues. "I
certainly don't go for the flaming behaviors that some like to display--that's
not part of my personality."

Several queer students I interviewed were critical of other lesbian, gay, and bisexual students, whom they described as "social fags," students who do not make a point of being visible outside the gay community. The following comments capture the sentiment of nearly half the students I interviewed:

> Those people who will come to the parties and go to The Odyssey on Sunday night but who won't do anything political are parasites soaking the rest of the gay community. They either don't realize or they don't care that their actions have ramifications for the entire gay community and that when they choose to remain closeted we all suffer.

However, other students talked about the need to respect an individual's choice in terms of visibility and political involvement. On this issue, my research participants were torn: half felt that students should be pressured to become more visible and more involved, and the other half tended to believe students should be left to decide in their own time what role they will play.

Education

There are several strategies queer students at Clement utilize to bring issues into campus discussion. Although I highlight these tactics under the category of education, they obviously are both political actions as well as acts of visibility. There are two events queer students play a major role in organizing: National Coming Out Day (NCOD) and Pride Week. NCOD corresponds to a nationwide event and is celebrated in October of each year. At Clement University, NCOD revolves around a pride rally at which students speak out about their experiences as lesbian, gay, and bisexual people. This event takes place on the steps of the school auditorium and is highlighted in chapter 1. Pride Week is a week-long series of activities that occur during the spring semester. Prominent speakers, entertainers, and programs are planned and sponsored by LGBSA in conjunction with other organizations such as the Graduate Student Coalition, ALLIES, and the Bisexual Womyn's Group.

As we have seen earlier in this chapter, homophobic acts are often anonymous (like notes on doors or bathroom mirrors). To be sure, one student attacked Ben Curry at a party, but we also have heard comments yelled from fraternity windows or shouted by pedestrians. In the relative anonymity of a large lecture class, students are able to ask questions that they most likely would not ask of an individual face to face. In what follows, I offer one such dialogue that two LGBSA students (Janet and Sean) confronted. The dialogue represents another pedagogical tool used by queer students at Clement to make students more aware of lesbian, gay, and bisexual issues and their difficult struggle in dealing with homophobia and heterosexism. This educational tool is referred to by members of LGBSA as a "straight talk."

Student: When did you choose to be gay?
Janet: Well, it's really not a choice. I am a bisexual woman. This is what I am. The only choice is whether to come out or remain in the closet. I knew in high school but I didn't pursue it until college.
Student: Did you tell the guys you dated?
Janet: Yes, and believe it or not, for some it's a turn-on. But I wouldn't have a relationship with a man and not tell him. What kind of relationship would that be for me to hide a fundamental part of who I am from him?
Student: Are you saying that it's hereditary?
Janet: All I know is that I felt it early on.
Sean: I don't really care whether it is biological or sociological. All I know is this is the way I feel--this is who I am.
Student: How do people react when you tell straight people that you are gay or lesbian?
Janet: Well, when I told my friends I got one of two reactions. Either they cried with me out of the relief and warmth they felt for me, or they distanced themselves from me for a while until they could better deal with it.
Student: I don't think it's an orientation but instead I think it's a choice. I think it's a sin and it's something that you choose to do.
Janet: Do you really think I woke up one day and said, "Hey, I think I'll be a lesbian so that I can be victimized by society, persecuted, and constantly called a sinner"? Does that make sense to you? Who in their right minds would choose to be a lesbian or a gay man? Did you wake up one day when you were a teenager and say, "Hey, I think I'm going to be a heterosexual"? No, of course not. You just are what you are.
Student: Sean, have you ever participated in anal intercourse or given head to another man?
Janet: Why are you asking that? Would we ask you questions about your personal life? About your sex life?
Sean: Wait a minute. I agreed to sit up here and answer questions and I'll answer that one. Yes I have. I have done both.
Student: You've taken it up the butt?
Sean: Do you really think that's the issue? Do you think I would ask you a question like that?
Student: I'd just like to praise you both for all the shit you take.
Student: Why is coming out in public so important?
Janet: To end having to come out. That is the goal. To get people to understand that yes we exist and yes we are different, but we still have hopes, and dreams, and feelings like everyone else. We're people too.
Student: Do you usually get this much harassment and abuse when you do one of these?
Janet: No, this is the worst one I've ever done.

A variety of issues arise with such a discussion. One wonders about the pedagogic encounter in which students are brought into a classroom as experts and then must discuss their lives in such a fashion. In effect, the students are reduced to a single identity in much the same way that African American students or Latino/na students are reduced so that they and they alone speak about "their" condition. By the same token, without such efforts, how many straight students will take the time to educate themselves about sexual orientation and related issues? Straight talks, like other actions by lesbian, gay, and bisexual people that seek to educate heterosexuals about queer lives, run the risk of essentializing identity--reducing the host of complex sources of identity to one, sexual attraction. Yet how else can lesbian, gay, and bisexual people achieve equality, liberty, and justice without organizing around the part of their identity that has resulted in their oppression? This is basically the same question Steven Epstein (1987) poses and one that I discuss in detail in chapter 8.

SUMMARY

The queer student movement at Clement University is an attempt to organize around the social category of "homosexual." Categorized as deviant or abnormal, many lesbian, gay, and bisexual people seek to decenter the norms of society. To achieve their goal, they battle the politics of silencing centered around homophobia and heterosexism. Lesbian, gay, and bisexual people are left with two options: remain closeted and physically safe, or come out and face social scrutiny, rejection, or even violence.

Although being open about one's sexual identity poses certain challenges and dangers, as the narratives of the students in this project reveal, a degree of openness also offers certain rewards. The benefit for many is an improved sense of self and a sense of obligation and identification with other members of the gay community. Students spoke of this commitment in terms of the politics of being gay. At times, the politics of gay identity has been a great burden for many, yet it is a burden none have openly regretted.

In battling the politics of silencing, queer students have stressed politics, visibility, and education. These students seek to create a campus environment that is safe and equitable so that closeted lesbian, gay, and bisexual students will be free to come out. Their efforts require not only educating heterosexuals about heterosexism and homophobia but also confronting the attitudes internalized by other lesbian, gay, and bisexual students.

As we have seen, chapter 4 cites stories of the closet and how students struggled with their self-doubt, self-hatred, and guilt. Chapter 5 highlights the coming-out process as a way to erase the negative feelings associated with the closet. But in coming out, students open themselves up to harassment and discrimination. The emphasis in chapters 4 and 5 is on the individual. In this chapter I focus more on the group and how students have forged a sense of solidarity in battling against the politics of silencing. Taken together, these three chapters serve one of the major goals of this text: to highlight the experiences of gay students as they struggle to develop a sense of identity. But chapter 6 has a dual purpose: it introduces the notion of a group identity and also discusses gay students as a cultural collectivity that provides members a basis for identification. This is touched on in chapter 6 and is central in the next chapter.

A third goal of the book is to elaborate the paradoxical nature of gay identity--the contested terrain of queerness is only one example--and how these issues relate to building communities of difference. In delineating the confusion surrounding gay identity, I call upon the essentialist/constructivist debate. Even though I have alluded to these issues (such as the essentializing tendency of queer students), I save much of the discussion for chapter 8. Finally, in chapter 9 I connect issues related to gay identity to building communities of difference.

7

Culture/Subculture

> Borders are set up to define the places that are safe and unsafe, to distinguish us from them.
>
> --Gloria Anzaldua, *Borderlands*

Lesbian, gay, and bisexual people exist in a borderland defined by their sexuality. Their borders are both unclear and in a continuous state of redefinition. Homosexuals, homophiles, gays, and queers are all labels that have been used at one time or another to name people who identify with same-sex attractions. Additionally, many lesbians, bisexual men, and bisexual women reject gay or queer as a self-identifier. In short, people who identify by their same-sex attractions are often easier to name by what they are not: non-heterosexuals. In this sense, lesbian, gay, and bisexual identities exist in and are largely defined by their opposition to heterosexuality. Randy Shilts (1993) maintains: "In truth, homosexuals in this time and in this culture have very little control over many of the most crucial circumstances of their lives. Control resides with the heterosexual majority, which defines the limits of freedom for the homosexual minority" (pp. 6-7). Diana Fuss (1991) points out that "any identity is founded relationally, constituted in reference to an exterior or outside that defines the subject's own interior boundaries and corporeal surfaces" (p. 2).

George Herbert Mead (1934) argues that identity (the self) is formed out of the interaction between the "I" and the "me," where the "I" is our internalized sense of self and the "me" is our sense of self as we imagine how others might see us. Through social interaction, the self emerges as we move back and forth between the "I" and the "me." Culture frames social interaction and is reshaped by that interaction. Culture establishes the roles that individuals might adopt as they engage in social interaction. In this light, not only is culture the stage upon which the actors weave their narratives, but culture is also the script (Goffman, 1959). As a white male born and raised in a lower-class American family, I have never assumed the role of shaman or tribal initiate. Frequently, though, I have adopted the roles of older brother, teammate, or student. My culture defines these roles for me even though there is a degree of individuality I bring to these roles.

Erik Erikson (1968) discusses identity development as a sense of self that emerges from the interaction between the individual and the social. His view is referred to as a psychosocial view of identity. Erikson recognizes the role that society and culture play in shaping how we think of ourselves, how we define ourselves. Both Erikson and Mead highlight the fundamental role culture and social life play in the process of identity formation. Keeping in mind that lesbian, gay, and bisexual people reside on the borders of sexuality, and as Shilts (1993) and Fuss (1991) maintain, are defined to a large degree by the heterosexual majority, how do we make sense of queer students who have staked their identity claims?

In considering the preceding question, my intent is threefold. First, I offer evidence to suggest that a *contraculture* has formed around and in conjunction with lesbian, gay, and bisexual students at Clement. Second, I highlight the points of contention within this diverse contraculture. Points of contention, or differences, create a dynamic tension within the contraculture. Third, I examine the contraculture in terms of identity issues such as liberal versus radical and gay versus queer notions of identity.

QUEER STUDENTS AS A CONTRACULTURE

In the last chapter I dealt primarily with the political ramifications of a queer identity. To some students, the word "queer" serves as a unifier for lesbian, gay, and bisexual people. One student highlighted this other meaning: "I prefer to say 'the queer community' because it is more inclusive than the term 'gay community.' Queer includes lesbians and bisexuals, whereas gay in its strictest sense only refers to men. So in that way queer has two meanings--the political one and the more inclusive one." Another student noted: "When I hear 'gay' I think about gay men and lesbians. 'Queer' includes lesbians, gays, and bisexuals." Queer used in an inclusive sense underscores the bond that exists among lesbian, gay, and bisexual students at Clement University. This bond forms a social collectivity frequently described by the students as "family."

Queer students as family call attention to the idea that many lesbian, gay, and bisexual students form a unique subculture. A subculture is a group of people engaged in ongoing social interaction who exhibit similar values, beliefs, and attitudes that create a shared sense of meaning. A contraculture is a specific type of subculture, one that exists in opposition to the dominant culture. Because of their oppositional stance to heterosexuality, queer students at Clement are best described as a contraculture.

In the following sections I highlight the shared meanings of the queer student contraculture. The intent here is not to discern what function various practices might serve in contributing to a sense of group identity. Instead, I examine the symbolic or interpretive quality of these social practices. Again, culture frames the narratives people weave and in turn is reconstituted by those narratives. To examine culture, subculture, or contraculture from such a perspective requires coming to terms with the meaning people ascribe or might ascribe to particular practices. Therefore, in examining the queer contraculture I emphasize an interpretive view of culture, framed by three qualities of social interaction: *space*--sites of social interaction; *style*--nature of social interaction; and *substance*--content of social interaction. In other words, where do queer students interact, how do their interactions differ from the heterosexual culture, and what do their interactions concern? In examining the social interactions of queer students, the focus is not on how these interactions differ on the surface; instead, my concern is with the meanings students bring to their actions in light of opposition to heterosexuality.

Space

Observing students "hanging out" in bars, coffee shops, diners, or even street corners is a common sight in any college town in the United States. Like other students at Clement University, lesbian, gay, and bisexual students also congregate in public settings. But although on a superficial level their interaction patterns may be similar, there is an underlying difference in these actions. The significance of being seen in public has little meaning to most heterosexuals, who do not face the possible confines of the closet. But for queer students, hanging out is in part a signification to both a heterosexual and a queer world that lesbian, gay, and bisexual people exist. To the heterosexual world, hanging out might be interpreted as an act of defiance against the social imprisonment of the closet. To a queer world, hanging out might be seen as a way of building community, of letting others with same-sex attractions know that they are not alone.

Downtown Hidden Falls has two coffee shops, which are both popular sites for members of the gay community. One tends to attract more graduate students and professionals, while the other tends to draw an undergraduate clientele. A number of students mentioned these sites as places where lesbian, gay, and bisexual students gather without fear of social retribution. Some discussed the coffee shops as "intellectual retreats" or "safe havens" from public spaces that are almost entirely dominated by heterosexuals and heterosexism. On the several occasions I visited the coffee shops, nearly every time there was at least one student from my study present; frequently, there were several. One student explained the popularity of the coffee shops: "They have kind of a Bohemian atmosphere. Kind of the European idea of the coffee shop as a place for marginalized people--intellectuals, artists, queers."

Another popular social site is the downtown diner, especially late at night. The diner is situated along the main thoroughfare in Hidden Falls, directly across from Clement University. It is open all night long, and serves meals, non-alcoholic drinks, and pastries. For a number of students who go to The Odyssey on Sunday evenings, going to the diner is a pre-Odyssey ritual. Like the coffee shops, the diner has evolved into a safe space for members of the queer contraculture. Not only do queer students frequent the diner for late-night snacks, drinks, or companionship, but many of the staff are queer students as well.

The reason why the diner is queer-friendly is not clear, but apparently a gradual evolution has taken place in which many highly visible queer students have made themselves at home. This has not gone unnoticed by straight students. On one occasion a student passed by, opened the door, and yelled inside, "Fuckin' homos." Such an act is clearly an expression of resentment toward queer students who have staked their claim to a piece of public turf. They have threatened heterosexual hegemony.

Certainly not all the students I interviewed like to hang out at the coffee shops or the diner. I asked one student about hanging out at one of the coffee shops and he told me, "I can't stand all those hair fags! You know, guys that just sit around talking about their hair, or their clothes, or fashions. People who try to toss their gayness around just so everyone will say, 'Hey look, some gay guys!'" Shane offered a different critique: "The coffee shops are too cliquey. I don't want to join a clique and be treated like the new guy on the block. You know, start out at the bottom of the heap."

The Odyssey is another site queer students at Clement have fought to claim as their space. Although the Odyssey is primarily visited on Sunday evenings (on "alternative lifestyle" night), a number of queer students frequent this nightclub on other nights as well, occasionally dancing in all-male groups.[1] In Hidden Falls, gay men dancing at The Odyssey on nights other than Sunday is somewhat akin to the visibility expeditions in which queers in metropolitan areas such as New York or San Francisco often engage.

The Odyssey is contested turf, whereas Friendlies is absolutely queer space. Few heterosexuals go to Friendlies and those that do are often treated poorly by the bartenders. On one occasion I visited Friendlies with two female friends and a male friend who before this evening had never been to Friendlies. I had been there on several occasions with Tito and felt comfortable enough to go there with three straights. I am sure the bartender assumed that we were heterosexual couples (which we were not) as he served everyone else at the bar (about ten other people), and when it came our turn he informed us that the bar was now closed, 2 a.m. had arrived. Because

Friendlies is queer space, hanging out there does not have the same meaning as going to The Odyssey (especially on a "straight" night). As I have noted elsewhere, entering the door to Friendlies requires a degree of visibility; but once inside, the door closes and conceals this world of queer space. A large rubber tree plant in the front window protects patrons from visual penetration by would-be heterosexual intruders. The hidden-away quality of Friendlies is why some closeted gay men frequent it and why many queer students resent the atmosphere there.

The less-than-friendly treatment afforded straights (or people thought to be straight) by some of the bartenders at Friendlies calls attention to the following point: space is moveable, definable, and re-definable. The bartenders at Friendlies seek to retain the queer space their bar signifies to lesbian, gay, and bisexual people. To be overly hospitable to heterosexuals is a possible threat to its queer denotation. Likewise, when queer students seek to claim new turf, such as The Odyssey on Thursdays, they run into heterosexual opposition that seeks to retain the club's heterosexual signification. For example, a queer student was confronted by a bouncer for hugging another gay man: "Save it for Sundays" was the message the bouncer conveyed. Words and meanings are continually defined and re-defined; the same is true of locations. Spaces that are queer-friendly today may be re-defined tomorrow as hostile ground. By the same token, space that is dominated by heterosexuals may be claimed by queer students through extended acts of visibility.

Style

In the preceding section a student expressed resentment toward other gay men who toss their "gayness" around. What this student refers to is an attitude of style that some gay and bisexual men bring to their public lives. Some discuss the behavior as camp, camping, camping it up, or camp culture. Camp essentially reflects an attitude about one's sexual orientation and how that gets enacted in public. More specifically, camp involves acting in a flamboyant and effeminate manner. Jerry discussed how he occasionally acts with a group of his friends: "I don't think of myself as a screaming queen, but I do think of myself as fairly effeminate. Sometimes when I get with a group of friends we get very campy." Jerry described camping as "being a flaming gay person acting out all the stereotypes." He went on to point out that sometimes he and his friends camp it up just to get a reaction from straight people. He gets "pissed" at other gay students who do not like to hang out with Jerry and his friends when they camp it up.

For Branden, camp culture is a source of identity to which straights do not have access. He elaborated on camp culture and on his impressions of straight people:

I have this attitude that gays are more refined, more cultured, more mature, more intelligent than straight people. I know it sounds a little condescending but sometimes I think it's true. I mean, sarcasm and cynicism go right over most straight guys' heads. I had a blast this past year watching the Academy Awards with a bunch of gay men. Talk about camp culture at its best. Camp follows the rule that if we didn't laugh about it or make fun of something we would probably have to cry. It's a form of cynicism that allows us to kind of celebrate that we are different. If you look at these straight people and laugh at them, they can't hurt you. You know, like, "Look at Barbara Striesand's hair. It's awful. Who is her hairdresser? And Whoopie, where did you get that horrendous dress? At the Salvation Army?" It's a way of making fun of straight people for a change. A step up on them for once.

Most of the students in this study who camp it up argue that camp culture offers visible evidence to the straight world that queers exist.

Not all gay students, or queers for that matter, are into camp. One student is completely "turned off" by camp culture. "Feminization" is the word he used in reference to gay and bisexual men who for whatever reason "somehow need to act like women." He elaborated:

Sometimes the "flamers" feminize their behavior and it really bothers me. I mean, I sit around and watch hockey games and drink beer and I don't see anything wrong with that. I think there is a tendency to overcompensate because of the gender fuck. But it comes off as denying one's masculinity, which should have nothing to do with being gay.

Another student explained gender fuck: "It refers to someone who completely defies what it means to be a certain gender." Thus, for some gay and bisexual men, one way to resist mainstream sexual scripts is to adopt what traditionally have been defined as feminine characteristics. This is what some argue camp is all about.

Gender is a social construction linked to sex. Masculinity and femininity are the models typically assigned to males and females through their socialization. Men are supposed to be strong, logical, and in control. Women are often portrayed as weak, emotional, and vulnerable. These are socially assigned traits that are reproduced from generation to generation through social interaction. By accentuating feminine traits, camp is in a sense a rejection of a particular construction of gender and the traditional meanings of masculinity. Brian Pronger (1992) claims that in coming out men are forced in part to fit into the socially constructed category of homosexual or gay man. As a result, gay men go through a process of reinterpreting their social worlds. An important aspect of reinterpretation involves confronting masculine and feminine prescriptions. "Gay men can come to see that the power relations for which the semiotics of masculinity and femininity constitute a strategy have little to do with their lives. The meaning of masculinity, consequently, begins to change" (p. 45). In this light, camp may be seen as a recognition on the part of some gay or queer men that traditional feminine and masculine traits are inappropriately used to coerce male and female behavior. Their rejection of traditional masculine characteristics may be seen as an act of resistance.

Another reading of camp relates to visibility: camping it up is a way of signifying to others one's gay identity. Stereotypes about gay men being more feminine than straight men have been advanced over the years. A belief by many in gender inversion (that gay men are really more like women than they are like men) has reinforced such a view. Consequently, some gay men act out certain stereotypes in order to be visible to other members of the gay community. One student explained: "Anything that deviates from the norm of the heterosexual community can be seen as a sign that someone is gay. For me personally, I act very effeminate."

Camping it up, like any behavior, has multiple interpretations. What camp signifies to one person may be entirely different to another. One interpretation is that camp culture is merely another vehicle for men to reinforce their dominance over women by making femininity the target of ridicule. For example, some queer men use the term "bitch" in a snide manner in reference to male partners or close friends. "Come over here, bitch, and sit on my lap" conveys the usage I highlight here. Use of "bitch" in this manner not only expresses an attitude of superiority toward one's partner or friend, but it also signifies an attitude of domination toward women in general. In this interpretation, queer men who camp it up run the risk of contributing to the continued oppression of women. Their sarcastic treatment of gender may be seen by some as a "putdown" of women.

I offer one more interpretation of camp highlighted by Tito. Notions of masculinity and femininity are posed as dualisms in which men have one trait or another and women typically exhibit the opposite one. But life is not so clear, and many of the traits typically associated with men or with women are often quite apparent in the other sex as well. Tito sees camp not only as resistance to gender prescriptions but also as a way to highlight that which he already feels but has been forced to suppress: sensitivity, caring, compassion. For Tito and other gay and bisexual men, camp is more than resistance to gender codes; it is freedom to experience and share a range of emotions and feelings, especially those socially restricted to women.

How is one to make sense of camp? Alexander Doty (1993) theorizes that interpretations of camp hinge "upon the gender and sexuality agendas of the camp reader, as well as the particular example of camp she/he is faced with" (pp. 83-84). Along this line, one student expressed resentment at how some gay men describe others and themselves as "woman" or "girl." As this student explained, "I'm not anyone's girlfriend. Just because I like men doesn't make me a woman." This student reads camp as offensive, not because it makes fun of women but because camp equates gay men (including himself) with women. Here, the student's reading of camp indicates a degree of sexism in that it is offensive to him to be equated with women. If we accept Doty's explanation, then camp must continually be deconstructed with two concerns in mind: the nature of the act and how various readers might interpret the act.

Camp culture is a significant aspect of the queer contraculture at Clement University. Few students camp it up all the time, and many reject camp entirely. Nevertheless, camp culture depicts behaviors and practices that even those students who resent camp understand and recognize.

Substance

Several of the students I interviewed indicated that they have different types of interactions depending on whether they are with straight friends or queer friends. Jerry commented: "I spend a lot of time in both communities and the subjects of conversation are definitely different. Almost all my conversations with gay friends are about being gay and the politics of it. It's very strange to have a conversation in which gay issues don't come up." Deandre, a gay student with a biting wit (who is a major character in chapter 8) enjoys conversing with straights more so than other gay students: "With my gay friends our conversations are much more commiserating." Another student described conversations with gay friends as "a lot more explicit and sexual. We talk about other interesting things too, like politics, but they are just more open to things that many of my straight friends seem to have a hard time talking about." One student claimed that there is a lack of common ground between gays and straights: "There are topics that just do not come up among straight students." This student, as well as several others, expressed the view that gay and bisexual men are more open when it comes to issues related to sexuality. Another student offered the following perspective:

> I talk about sexual things and experiences with gay friends. With straight friends I try to joke more about women, or who someone is dating. Where if I'm with a gay friend I'll tease him about some guy: "He's checking you out." So I monitor my communications out of respect. That's different than watching what you say when you're closeted. Then it's more out of fear to protect yourself. I like being respectful about sexuality.

In talking about different types of conversations he has with straight versus gay friends, Branden provided additional insight: "I like to talk about the same things in different ways. The subjects will be the same but the discussions are somewhat different." He went on to argue that there are two different worlds: a straight world and a gay world. "Let's say I watch the same film with some straight friends and then the same film with some gay friends. The gay friends are going to pick up on things that will go right over the heads of the straight guys." Branden argued that directors or actors do subtle things that only gays might notice. For example, certain colors for a flag or for some other object might be used, like pink and lavender (colors often used in queer emblems). He offered another example from popular culture: "Look at Madonna's video and song *Vogue*. Do you think the straight world knew or even knows now that that song is about the queer ball scene in New York City? No, of course not." Branden also talked about "all the gossip" that goes on among gay men, an aspect of queer interactions described by many as "dishing."

Another student offered his rationale for having both straight friends and gay friends: "I like to have a healthy mix because it helps me to know what's going on in both worlds and to understand how straights think about gays." Along this line, Ben considers himself bicultural in that he believes he interacts proficiently in both queer and straight settings.

Is sex and sexuality a central concern for members of the queer contraculture, or are queer students simply freer to discuss such issues? As a result of their own marginality, queer people are forced to make sexual orientation a critical aspect of their self-identification. As Erving Goffman points out (1963), this is the nature of social stigma. Thus, when an individual's primary source of identity is rooted in his (I am speaking primarily of gay and bisexual men here) sexual orientation or attraction, it is hardly surprising that sexuality is central to many discussions with others in a similar position. Here it is noteworthy that at least seven of the forty men involved in this study plan careers in human sexuality or a related area. Roger and Ben both want to work as counselors so they can deal with issues related to human sexuality and AIDS prevention. Similarly, Tito and Andrew plan careers in psychology in which they can help other queer people deal with issues of sexual identity and community. For these students, sexuality is not a fixation but an important aspect of making sense of their lives.

What about the question of openness to sexual issues? Again, having continually to confront sexual identity and sexual orientation issues, gay and bisexual men may deal more openly with such topics than do straight men. As Tito noted earlier when he discussed being sexually abused as a child, he is not surprised that more gay and bisexual men uncover sexual abuse, as they are forced (because of their marginality) to explain why they are the way they are. Heterosexuals usually have little explaining to do.

The concepts of space, style, and substance call attention to the fact that queer students at Clement share common understandings that revolve around their opposition to heterosexuality. I have portrayed some general themes and patterns that are evident in the behavior of many students. But not every gay or bisexual man camps it up. In fact, probably only a small percentage are into camp culture: of the forty students in this study, about fifteen to twenty are into camp. Likewise, not every gay or bisexual man hangs out in coffee shops or goes to The Odyssey on Sunday evenings. And certainly, gay and bisexual men who are entirely closeted do not engage in different conversations with their straight friends and their gay friends, because their sexual identity is something they choose to keep hidden from both groups.

The point is not that everyone within a subculture or contraculture must adopt the cultural characteristics that set that social collectivity apart. The question that must be examined is whether gay and bisexual students at Clement University have shared understandings of certain social interactions and whether they consciously choose to participate or not participate for reasons that other members of the contraculture understand. Shane, for instance, does not like to hang out at the coffee shops because he feels they are too cliquey. Certainly, other members of the queer contraculture understand Shane's apprehension, although they might disagree with his assessment. Likewise, another student does not go to one coffee shop because too many "hair fags" hang out there. The chances are good that other members of the queer contraculture understand this student's complaint, although they may disagree with his terminology. And although most students describe different conversations that take place depending on whether one's company is gay or straight, Tito tends to carry on the same conversations regardless of whom he is with, yet he fully understands why so many others modify their behavior.

As well as the shared meanings that I have highlighted in this section, I have alluded to difference and disagreement. Cultural groups are constituted by similarity; they are also marked by difference. Penelope Eckert (1989) makes this point in her discussion of student culture: "A culture marks and elaborates certain internal differences, and it is the recognition and interpretation of these differences that is shared by members of the culture" (p. 21). In the next section I highlight the differences that stretch the fibers of solidarity and challenge the queer contraculture to continually rethink individual and group identities.

SOLIDARITY/DIFFERENCE

From a modernist perspective, communities are bound together by common threads. Traditional research on communities has focused for the most part on identifying these common threads and how such connections function to maintain cohesion. From a critical postmodern perspective, difference and conflict are seen as essential ingredients of communities (Tierney, 1993b). Difference, however, is not seen as something that threatens group cohesion and therefore needs to be eliminated. Instead, difference is seen as an element that brings people into dialogue. Although a critical postmodern perspective emphasizes an examination of difference, this is not to say that common cultural elements do not exist within communities. The point of a critical postmodern perspective is to focus not only on the commonalities of culture but also on those points of divergence, where tension and conflict reside.

The first half of this chapter highlighted some of the common cultural threads that are part of the queer student contraculture at Clement University. Clearly, bonds exist among lesbian, gay, and bisexual students at Clement. Yet disagreement does as well.

Several students shared their views on the lesbian, gay, and bisexual community at Clement University. Their narratives provide clues into the constant struggle between unifying and dividing forces. One student described the gay community as the "visible gay community." He went on to note: "I mean, if you're not out, how can you identify with the rest of the community? I didn't until I came out. I see the community as those who contribute. I think it is those people who participate in some way or who contribute in some way to group life." Another student focused upon the diversity of the lesbian, gay, and bisexual student community at Clement:

> I think there are different levels within the queer community. You have your social fags, people who identify as queer politically, men, women, age differences. I definitely think there's a difference between lesbians and bisexual women, more so than between bisexual men and gay men. Women who define themselves as lesbians are more identified with a women's space, a women's community, than bisexual women. There seems to be more of a division between them than when you compare bisexual men and gay men, where I think the differences get blurred.

Another student echoed this view but added: "Even though we all have separate groups based on gender, race, and orientation, there is a way of coming together." This "way of coming together" was alluded to by other students. "The gay community here is like a secret society. There is this attitude that gays have for each other that if something happens to you I'll protect you no matter what." Branden made a similar point: "You know what makes the gay community? You and me against the whole world. The only way we can keep from being pushed into the corner or back into our closets, our cages, is to unite, to stand together. We have to stand together or be crushed. It's that simple."

For many of the students I interviewed, LGBSA forms the heart of the queer student contraculture at Clement University. In discussing LGBSA, one student noted: "They give me a certain satisfaction that a lot of things continue to happen. They've become a larger and stronger organization--expanding in meeting students' needs. I find that very satisfying. The social network is helpful too. The political network as well. It keeps me connected to others in the queer community." For this student, and for many others, LGBSA is the glue of the queer student community at Clement. Shane described the positive impact of LGBSA in his own life: "The people in LGBSA make me happy. I don't feel like I have to hide. They make me want to be more out almost in a logarithmic way--the more I open up, the more I want to share."

Not everyone agreed about the role of LGBSA. In fact, several students had problems with LGBSA. One student offered his opinion: "I feel that LGBSA is quite closed, almost cliquey. They tell you to come out and everything will be ok and that they will be there for you, and it really isn't like that." This student maintained that many of the political stands of LGBSA are offensive to other lesbian, gay, and bisexual students. "There are officers from LGBSA speaking in the newspaper for the gay community when they really don't represent how everyone feels." This student complained about having to fit a "certain mold" in order to be accepted by LGBSA and in general highlights some of the tension that exists within the queer student community at Clement University. With this in mind I highlight three points of conflict: queer controversies, cultural differences, and bisexuality. Whereas racial differences as a source of conflict relate in part to my research design (something I wanted to learn more about from the beginning), the other two sources of tension emerged from the data and reflect issues brought up by students.

Queer Controversies

In many respects this work is about what it means to be queer in college. The problem is that few can agree on what the term means. Some completely reject "queer" as an identifier. A student explained: "My first reaction to the term 'queer' is negative. I can't really explain why. I generally don't like to hear that term used. It helps to solidify a stereotype that's already in place, the flamboyant, effeminate type, the cross-dresser."

Other students saw the term "queer" as a unifier of lesbian, gay, and bisexual people. Although Andrew believes there are many lesbian, gay, and bisexual communities, he still uses the term "queer community" as a unifier: "I don't like the notion of a single community. I like 'communities' because we have several within what I usually refer to as the 'queer community,' which I see as more inclusive." Andrew went on to add that there are certain contexts in which he would not use the term "queer": for example, if he were meeting with the Board of Trustees over an important issue such as the sexual orientation clause. As Andrew noted, "Most people don't really understand the significance of it." Andrew, in effect, uses the term as an in-group identifier; but many queer people use it outwardly, regardless of their company. Andrew highlights the fact that most of the queer students in this study tend to use queer within certain settings, more or less as an in-group identifier. However, some students, such as Tito, use the term as both an in-group identifier as well as an outward signification regardless of company.

Another student noted that "gay" is frequently used as a "blanket term" to include the many groups that compose this difficult-to-name community. But the student went on to add: "'Gay' could include the bisexual community and the lesbian community but they might be offended by that. They might prefer 'the queer community' as the term that includes us all."

One student focused on the political aspect of the term "queer." He offered a critique of the queer movement and queer politics in general. "It goes back to political affiliation and stereotypes. Whenever you hear of a queer political event it's basically looked at very negatively, because you always think of Queer Nation and ACT-UP and they all have the 'shove it in your face' kind of attitude." This student prefers a slower, more educational approach. "Maybe there have to be two different approaches, but I think queers turn a lot of people off and they make themselves a lot of enemies. I don't think we need any more enemies."

Ben differentiated between the terms "gay" and "queer" based upon the political connotation of "queer". He argued that even straight people can be part of the queer community: allies, radical feminists, and other supporters who are political enough to be involved in gay rights. He also pointed out that not all gays are queer: they have to be political to be queer. For Ben, queer is not so much about sexual orientation as it is about political ideology. For him, gays are more mainstream than queers. "Gays are more or less the group that gets things done through the system. It's like comparing NGLTF [the National Gay and Lesbian Task Force] with Queer Nation." He believes that groups such as Queer Nation and ACT-UP help to legitimize NGLTF. "These groups make politicians want to work with NGLTF. They can get along with the Bill Clintons of the world. Queers are people who aren't afraid to screw with the system."

These two students shed light on the political aspect of being queer, although few students in this study would agree with Ben's assessment that one can be straight and also be queer. In fact, the issue of being straight and being queer was posed to several of the research participants, and their response was unanimous: straights can be queer advocates, allies, or supporters, but they cannot be queer.

The political aspect of the term "queer" extends beyond students' participation in protests, elections, and causes; this aspect of queer relates to the politics of language and discourse. As I have already noted, the adoption of the term "queer" as an identifier is a means to expropriate the discourse of sexual identity. By supplying the term with a positive meaning, lesbian, gay, and bisexual students believe they can ultimately diffuse the negativity associated with previous notions of homosexuals and homosexuality. A student opposed to the use of the term "queer" noted: "I've heard arguments in the community that they are actually taking the word back and empowering themselves. I guess that's great. But I don't particularly want to do that." Another student added: "Maybe I'm a little old-school. Maybe the queer movement is a little ahead of me. Maybe attitudes will change in time, but I don't know. I guess I can see people using 'queer' to depolarize its negative meaning. But that doesn't change the fact that it's a derogatory and negative word." Although this student seems to recognize the politics of language, his last sentence is contradictory. Depolarizing the negative meaning of queer most likely will remove much of its derogatory associations. The simple fact is that the meanings of words are socially constructed and that their derogatory denotations and connotations can be changed.

There is a problem, though, in the efforts of students to "depolarize" the negative meaning associated with the term "queer": students may also "depolarize" its radical connotation. Recall how Ben compared gay and queer to NGLTF and Queer Nation, respectively. He argued that gays are the ones who accomplish things by working with the "system." There is a contradiction here in that students at Clement University who describe themselves as queers for the most part work within the structure of the university. They form coalitions with student government, Black Caucus, and other student groups; and they seek positions on university committees, on which they represent gay concerns. Does this fit within a queer political strategy? Again, my point in this text is not merely to challenge self-definitions offered by the gay and bisexual students, but also to highlight the contested nature of words in particular and language in general. Certainly, the meaning of "queer" is contested both within the queer contraculture at Clement and in relation to other queer groups around the country.

Racial Diversity

People from diverse cultural backgrounds face significant barriers in identifying with the gay community. James Sears (1991) highlights how people of color who are also gay frequently are forced to elevate one source of identity over the other. When a person of color who also is gay identifies with one community, that individual may face a marginalized identity within the other community. Steven Seidman (1993) points out: "Lesbian and gay men of color have contested the notion of a unitary gay subject and the idea that the meaning and experience of being gay are socially uniform" (p. 120). A black student at Clement highlighted the difficult choice that faced him when he came out: "When I came out as a bisexual man I disowned all my black friends with whom I had been politically active. I thought they would reject me when they found out, so I didn't give them the chance. I rejected them first. Most of my friends then became white people in the queer community."

If a queer student of color decides to maintain dual identities, he or she may experience difficulties. Another student offered insight in this regard: "It's kind of like dealing with two forms of oppression. My job is doubly hard. I have to help educate not only the straight community about gay issues but I also have to educate the black community, and that's next to impossible. Homophobia is really strong within the black community."

This student calls attention to a serious problem other black students raised: the pervasiveness of homophobia within the black community. One student elaborated, "Black people in general don't have a history of being very accepting of gays within their community. So that presents a problem, because we face alienation for being black in relation to the whole society and alienation within our own community--the black community--because we are gay." This student went on to offer an explanation for homophobia within the black community:

> I think this relates to the fact that black men have in many ways been stripped of their masculinity by a white-dominated society that tends to demean what they accomplish. Within the black community there is this related attitude that being gay or bisexual is giving in to white society--we are seen as willingly giving up our masculinity. They fail to realize that being gay is not a choice, and, on top of that, it has nothing to do with being masculine or feminine.

A second black student saw the church as the principal source of homophobia. "The black church is the foundation of the black community. On the one hand, the ministers preach all kinds of morality and then they participate in homosexual relationships all the time. It's hypocrisy. There's a lot of saying one thing and doing another." A third offered his explanation: "One issue is that black men frequently have been invisible in the family so when a black man comes out he is seen as contributing in some way to a weakening of the black family." This student also mentioned the church as a source of homophobia.

Homophobia is by no means unique to the black community. Other students from diverse backgrounds face similar fears within their respective communities and families. I asked an Asian American student involved in this study if he was out to his family: "No. They don't know. That's the hardest part. I think for Asian people continuing the family is very important, and for me to come out as gay would seem like a threat to our family."

Tito identifies as a Puerto Rican/Hispanic and commented about his perception of gays in his homeland: "As long as it's kept secret and not discussed in public, then no one seems to care. As long as queers appear 'shamed' and remain hidden, everything is ok. But come out and go public, create noise, and the church and all the conservatives will go to lengths to put 'homosexuals' back in their proper place--the closet." Tito also mentioned the fact that homosexuality is regarded differently in Puerto Rico than in the United States. One example is the notion that men in Puerto Rico who engage in sex with other men do not consider themselves to be gay if they take the role of the aggressor, the role of the penetrator. "There's an attitude that if you're doing something you usually do with women, then you are not gay." Such a perspective exists throughout much of Latin America (Adam, 1993), where *activos* (sexual aggressors in same-sex encounters) are typically not considered to be gay, whereas *pasivos* are seen as subordinate and are considered to be gay.

Queer students from diverse cultural backgrounds not only face possible rejection from their racial communities for being queer, but they also face racism within the gay community. A student commented: "On top of everything there is the issue of racism within the queer community, which tends to be dominated by whites. I feel somewhat comfortable but at times I'm uncomfortable around blacks and gays." Another student offered the following: "Quite honestly, I feel very tokenized. I guess I have allowed myself to be. When LGBSA wants a black, it's me or my roommate." A third student talked about his first encounter with members of LGBSA:

> When I first came here I tried to reach out to LGBSA, and when I went to one of the meetings it took me a half hour just to work up the courage to walk into the room. When I got there I saw that there was nobody else who was black except maybe for one other person. After the meeting not a single person walked up to me and introduced themselves. No one said anything to me. Then this guy on my floor who claimed to be straight was doing a paper for a class on gays and so he went to a LGBSA meeting. He is tall, has good features, and is attractive and white. He went to a meeting and after it was over he said two or three people came up to him and introduced themselves and were very friendly to him. He talked about his paper on our hall one time, and I remember thinking to myself, "this can't be the same meeting I went to." It really woke me up to the white gay community and its racism.

The preceding view was supported by another student who believes students at Clement have negative feelings about people of color. "There are a lot from very rural areas where they have had little to no exposure to diverse peoples." Another student supported this opinion. He claimed that there is a lot of ignorance among gay white men. Gay white men might say that they always wanted to date a black man. When this student hears that kind of talk, he gets suspicious. "Then later they say something else and you realize that they're racists because they have bought in to all these stereotypes about black men and their sexuality. They'll say something like, 'I'm really into black men.'

As if all black men are alike. That tells me something right there."

Two issues are highlighted within this section: racism by gay whites within the gay community, and homophobia within various minority communities. Students who are both gay and members of a minority community not only face dual forms of oppression but also have to come to terms with conflicting sources of self-identification.

Bisexuality

Within the queer community at Clement, like many other communities, hierarchies have evolved. One such hierarchy is the higher status accorded being gay as opposed to being bisexual. In chapter 3 Jerry Sandaval alluded to biphobia when he noted that he identifies as a gay man even though he knows he has some other-sex attractions. "I am making a choice to be gay, which I do mostly for political reasons. I think it makes a stronger statement if I say I'm gay." Another student added: "I think being a bisexual confuses a lot of people because they tend to think you're either gay or straight. Sometimes you get the feeling that people think, 'Oh, thank god he's bisexual; he can still date the same sex.' Others will say, 'I wish he would decide.'"

One student described himself as a closeted bisexual man. This student believes that a lot of bisexuals either stay closeted or are more likely to continue to claim they are straight and brush off feelings for the same sex because of what it means in our culture. "There is no real room in our culture for falling anywhere in the middle. There is a lot of pressure to be one or the other." A second student supported this view: "I think because of the politics of it all it's much more difficult for a man to come out and say he's bisexual. Being a bisexual man is second rate compared to being a gay man. It's like if you're going to do it you might as well go all the way." This student believes there are a lot of men within the gay community who would come out as bisexuals if it were not for the pressure to be gay. "It's a conforming sort of thing." Besides Jerry, another student stated up front that he feels he is a bisexual, but for political reasons he identifies as gay/queer.

Few issues within the queer community highlight the complexities of sexuality more than bisexuality. Some students argued that sexuality is flowing, and that bisexuality is one indication of how people move from straight to gay or vice versa. Others disagree and see bisexuality as one of three fixed sexual orientations, along with homosexuality and heterosexuality. A third stance was offered by four or five students who argued that everyone is bisexual; some of us just lean in one direction or the other.

Dennis Altman (1971) advances the third stance when he discusses the "enormous amount of libidinal energy devoted to repressing our inherent bisexuality" (pp. 72-73). Altman argues: "Men are so concerned to deny any homosexual feelings that they tend to adopt extreme postures of aggression so as to reject feelings of tenderness or love as well as sexual desire for each other" (p. 73). Sex roles and sexuality become blurred, and men, out of fear of their own same-sex attractions, strive toward a hyper-masculine identity. In other words, in order to prove their "maleness"--and most important, their lack of attraction for other men--they adopt machismo behaviors and take on extreme masculine identities (Rhoads, 1991, 1992). The sports arena is the most obvious site of male aggression and machismo identification: as Pronger (1992) points out, it is replete with homoerotic signification.

Altman's argument advances the classic Freudian perspective in which bisexuality is originally present in children and becomes reconfigured through resolution of the Oedipal complex (Freud, 1923/1961). For Freud, heterosexuality is the "positive" resolution: the son identifies as a male with the father, the mother becomes the love object, and later, another woman is substituted for the mother. Homosexual development relates to the "negative" side of the Oedipal complex in which identification with the father is so strong that the father becomes a love object.

But Freud's analysis is constrained by his heterosexual bias in that he positions heterosexual development as "positive" and homosexual development as "negative." Another interpretation of the Oedipal complex sees identification with the father as evidence of early same-sex attraction. As Eric de Kuyper (1993) maintains, "It [identification with the father] is necessarily a love-relation or it would not be possible to have identification at all. Love is, as we know, a specific variety of identification: here it is a relation to the same sex, a homosexual relation" (p. 140). De Kuyper, and Altman as well, build upon Freud by rejecting the idea of homosexual development as "negative" and instead highlight homosexual identification as a "natural" quality of sexual development.

For Altman (1971), and for many of the students involved in this study, the goal is sexual liberation from socially enforced sexual categories: "With liberation, homosexuality and heterosexuality would cease to be viewed as separate conditions, the former being a perversion of the latter, but would be seen rather as components of us all" (p. 89). The irony, of course, is that liberation only seems likely through the emergence of a group consciousness, which is only possible through homosexual identification. I return to this issue in the next chapter.

SUMMARY

Culture shapes identity. Gay and bisexual students at Clement University look to the queer contraculture as a source of identity. As Clifford Geertz (1973) notes, culture is also shaped by people engaged in interaction. Among queer students and the queer contraculture there is an ongoing interactive effect between social interaction and identity. As queer students continually redefine themselves, the queer contraculture is reshaped. As the queer contraculture changes, students' definitions of identity change.

Queer students at Clement stand in opposition to the heterosexist culture that characterizes both the university and Hidden Falls. Their oppositional stance is beyond the scope of student resistance explicated in other research studies of student culture (Holland & Eisenhart, 1990; Weis, 1985). This oppositional quality to their lives has marked effects on how the self gets defined. The meaning that gay and bisexual students bring to the places they claim as their own (space), the way they interact (style), and what they interact about (substance), all affect identity.

Some students "hang out" at the coffee shops and the downtown diner. Visibility is testimony of their existence to other closeted and out lesbian, gay, and bisexual people, as well as to the heterosexual world. Hanging out is in part an act of visibility. Some queer students add a touch of flamboyancy (camping it up) to their public behavior to ensure they are noticed. However, most queer students in this study do not camp it up. Those that do perhaps form their own subculture within a subculture. But even queer students who reject camp recognize some of the complex meanings camp culture raises. Gender fuck comes to mind, as do various criticisms some students offered about the feminization of gay identity.

Interactions within the queer contraculture often focus on issues removed from heterosexual culture. Branden highlighted how he and his gay friends pick up on different cues during movies. Ben described himself as bicultural in that he believes he interacts proficiently in both cultures: straight and queer.

What I have described as the queer contraculture is only a snapshot in time, a portrait of a quickly evolving and constantly changing cultural enclave. Issues of difference are paramount within the queer contraculture. Differences challenge understandings of both culture and identity. This chapter highlights three differences that continually challenge gay students at Clement: queer controversies, racial diversity, and bisexuality. A fourth relates to gender, which I discussed in reference to camp culture.

There is perhaps no better example of the diversity within the queer contraculture than the debate over the meaning of the term "queer" itself. It is a term whose meaning varies and is still in formation. I have noted two meanings: a political and a unifying one. But even in these two senses the meanings converge in that queer as unifier is a political statement. Controversy surrounds what it means to be queer and the whole notion of a social identity based on sexual orientation. For most queers (the political sense), sexual orientation forms a central aspect of their identity. Being queer is essential to how they define themselves. For others, who perhaps might identify as gay or lesbian, the notion of a queer identity may be too restrictive;

there are many other components to their identity. To identify as queer involves, in part, rejecting other sources of self-definition. For women and people of color, being queer may marginalize other notions of the self. In this light, queer is seen as too essentializing. This raises a question about sexual orientation and identity: How should sexual orientation be addressed, as socially constructed or as an essential aspect of identity? Chapter 8 addresses this question.

NOTE

1. Lesbians and bisexual women might also dance together at The Odyssey, but women dancing in groups is more widely accepted and generally speaking does not have the same meaning as men dancing in groups.

IV

REDEFINING CULTURAL BORDERS

> The only way we can keep from being pushed into the corner or back into our closets--our cages--is to unite, to stand together. We have to stand together or be crushed. It's that simple.
>
> --Branden Conners, 21-year-old sophomore

The borders of sexual identity frame the lives of lesbian, gay, and bisexual people. As we shall see in chapter 8, whether or not those borders are rooted in the nature of people or their nurturing is debatable. But regardless of where the ultimate source of sexual identity rests and where sexual borders begin and end, queer people face discrimination and persecution and have few alternatives but to organize around their marginalized status. As Branden Conners points out, lesbian, gay, and bisexual people must either stand together or face the ongoing oppression of the closet. In the concluding two chapters, I focus on how cultural borders might be reconceptualized so that all people, regardless of sexual orientation, have the opportunity to participate in a truly democratic society.

8

Identity and Socialization

> What goes to make up the organized self is the organization of the
> attitudes which are common to the group. A person is a personality
> because he belongs to a community.
>   --George Herbert Mead, *Mind, Self, & Society*

THE CONSTRUCTIVISM/ESSENTIALISM DEBATE

In recent years, researchers have examined sexual orientation as a social
construction (Greenberg, 1988; Halperin, 1990; Kitzinger, 1987). Social
constructivists argue that identity forms out of social processes and interactions
occurring throughout one's lifetime. Social life frames how we see ourselves
and how others think about us. Although the effects of these processes often
extend beyond our conscious awareness, we nonetheless play a significant role
in shaping who we are as a person through the social interactions in which we
engage.

Sexual identity, like other identities, is rooted in the symbolic meaning
people ascribe to various behaviors. These meanings form as a result of the
interaction between culture and sociation. People, then, are not inherently
lesbian, gay, bisexual, or straight; but through socialization they learn to take
on these identities--identities that are themselves the byproducts of history and
culture. Social constructivists *do not* argue that sexual identity is a preference
as opposed to an orientation; they merely situate the basis of sexual identity
in the complexities of culture and social life.

From a constructivist perspective, one can argue that all people are
inherently similar and that only after years of socialization do they become
differentiated. The following student's comment lends support to a
constructivist position: "I got kind of depressed after the euphoria of coming
out ended. It's kind of like I got to make up for nineteen years of defining

myself one way and now I've got to redefine who I am." Another added, "I haven't figured my sexuality out yet. I think it changes. I notice that most of my fantasies for a month will be about men, and then I won't have a fantasy about men for about two or three months." Neither student conveys an image of sexual orientation as a static component of his identity. Instead, their comments allude to the role they play in shaping their own sexual identity: "I've got to redefine who I am" and "I haven't figured my sexuality out yet."

Of the principal characters in this work, the following three tended to fall on the constructivist side of the sexual identity debate:

Jerry: Basically, I think everyone is bisexual. For me, bisexuality is not the point in the middle but is almost all the points in the middle.
Roman: I never really sensed as a kid that anything was different about me.
Tom: I don't see any reason why people have to say they are gay. Just because I'm attracted to men doesn't make me any different from straight people.

The preceding comments support the idea that sexual orientation emerges from social experience. Jerry argues that everyone is bisexual. It follows that observable differences in people must be tied to social experience and/or choices they make in life. In pointing out that gays are no different from straights, Tom supports a position similar to Jerry's. Roman notes that he never felt there was anything different about him as a child. His statement hints at sexual orientation as something that forms later in life.

An opposing view may be termed "essentialist." Essentialism falls closely in line with the nature side of the "nature versus nurture" debate. Social constructivism falls in line with the nurture side of the same debate. Essentialists argue that sexual orientation is biologically rooted (or formed very early in life) and reflects a fundamental difference between heterosexuals and homosexuals (Fuss, 1989; Harry, 1982, 1984). The emphasis on difference is one reason why some gay activists adopt the term "queer," defined as "different from." Queer, for them, underscores the belief that lesbian, gay, and bisexual people are "essentially" different from heterosexuals. Two student voices are helpful here: "I'm probably a five or a six on the Kinsey scale. I've never really been attracted to women or sexually aroused by them." "All my life I remember having same-sex attractions. I remember I would always try to hang out on the corner with this newspaper boy I liked. I was only two or three when I did that." These students convey essentialism's emphasis on difference as well as the idea that such differences form early in life or are already formed when life begins ("all my life" and at "two or three"). Others also expressed essentialist views of sexual identity.

Branden: I've never had any particular desire to have sex with a woman; the idea kind of repulses me; it turns my stomach. I've never actually thought about why. I guess that's just the way I am.

Ben: Since about five I felt attraction for boys, but it probably wasn't until around 11 or 12 that I really knew who I was. I heard "fag" and "homo" and I remember asking my mom what those words meant. I pretty much knew that that was what I was.

Tito: As a child I was known for being unusual, complex. . . . I don't know why I'm queer--I just am. I don't see the need anymore to try to explain it. It's just who I am.

Branden, Ben, and Tito believe they are essentially different from straights. They also support a view that differences are revealed early in life. Their experiences raise questions about the constructivist position, although they by no means refute it entirely, as socialization begins at birth: "from womb to tomb" as John Van Maanen (1983, p. 213) argues. Yet questions are raised about both essentialism and constructivism when some students do not recognize their sexual orientation until they are adolescents and young adults, whereas others recognize this aspect of their identity early in life; and when some students see their sexual orientation as firmly planted, whereas others describe it as changing throughout life.

I argue here that a stark social constructivist and essentialist dichotomy falls short in explaining the complexities of sexual identity. Another way of conceptualizing sexual identity builds upon social constructivism and essentialism but avoids an either/or distinction. Comments from Shane hint at the idea that sexual identity may include inherent and socially derived qualities:

I say I'm bisexual. Others in the gay community would be upset, but that is a social thing. They expect everybody to define themselves as either straight or gay. But things aren't so black and white. I do know that I've always been attracted to males. People aren't so clearly defined. Maybe a long time ago they were, but not anymore.

One of the central aims of critical postmodernism is to construct emancipatory theory. Indeed, a principal goal of this work is to build a view of sexual identity that assists students in organizing diverse academic communities in which lesbian, gay, and bisexual students no longer face discrimination and persecution. Although the queer contraculture at Clement University arguably forms the heart of the gay student community, a vast majority of students do not identify with the queer contraculture. For many students, queer students serve to divide the gay community. Recall that one student felt queers inspire more "enemies" than allies. This student and others such as Tom Beal choose to distance themselves from queer students. With this in mind, the central mission of this chapter is to highlight a view of group identity: one that is inclusive of the diversity of the lesbian, gay, and bisexual community and contributes to group solidarity. I ground the discussion by introducing two more students: Andrew Lempke, who first appears on the steps of the school auditorium in chapter 1, and Deandre Witter, who enters only briefly in chapter 7 in discussing his preference for interacting with straights (because of the "commiserating" nature of conversations he has with gays).

ANDREW LEMPKE

Andrew Lempke is a tall, solidly built senior who enjoys sports, especially shooting "hoops." Looking at Andrew, one wonders if he played football in high school. Andrew, as I note in chapter 1, is one of the leaders of the queer student movement at Clement University. Prior to coming out, he studied mathematics. Later on his interests shifted and his concern for gay issues led him to select psychology as a major. Now Andrew's career goal is to get a Ph.D. in clinical/community psychology through which he hopes to research the struggles faced by lesbian, gay, and bisexual people.

Even though Andrew never self-acknowledged as gay until his first year in college, in high school he felt he was keeping something from his family. "I always felt that I wasn't really being honest with my family. Especially with my father. I mean, I always had a pretty strange relationship with him just because I felt uncomfortable." Andrew will never forget coming out to his parents. He came out to his sister during his first year in college, and she was fairly accepting.

Later that year Andrew's mother questioned his sister during a phone conversation about why he had broken up with his high school girlfriend. Finally, his mom came right out and asked: "Is Andrew gay?" Andrew's sister nearly dropped the phone. After the long silence, she did not need to answer. Andrew's parents jumped in their car and began the three-hour trip to Clement University. In the meantime, Andrew's sister called and warned him that they were on their way.

"It was horrible waiting for them to come up to school because I had no idea what was going to happen. I didn't know whether they were going to take me back home with them and throw me in a hospital." Andrew hoped that the long ride would calm them down. "It was always the biggest fear for me, coming out to my parents." When his parents arrived, Andrew was surprised. They were calm and rational. Their biggest concern was for Andrew's well-being and the fear of his getting AIDS.

Once his parents finally knew, Andrew's life changed dramatically. "I started to get really involved with LGBSA and I started to do a lot of political work. At that time, we were trying to get the sexual orientation clause passed. That was our main project. I really got involved with that." Andrew worked on the sexual orientation project for more than a year and eventually was elected to a leadership position within LGBSA.

For Andrew, everything about being gay is political. Identifying as queer is Andrew's way of stressing the political side of gay identity. He gets frustrated with other lesbian, gay, and bisexual people who are not out or who will not become politically involved. "I don't want to be the embodiment of what it means to be queer, but I also want people to realize that every time they're ashamed of who they are, they send that impression to other people." On some days he gets angry. On others, he sees no point in blaming people within his own community: "I mean, they're victims. It's like blaming the victim. I guess I should really blame the people that are causing us to be closeted and hate ourselves."

Although Andrew identifies as a gay/queer man, he expressed considerable concern over having to define himself based on his sexual orientation: "I describe myself as gay. But, you know, the whole idea of creating categories kind of bothers me." Andrew believes that because of the oppression faced by individuals whom society labels as homosexual, identifying publicly is necessary to battle marginality. Adopting a politically oriented queer identity is one way Andrew believes he can fight gay marginalization.

DEANDRE WITTER

Deandre Witter contrasts the serious political perspective Andrew brings to his sexual identity: Deandre depends upon a biting sense of humor to survive in a heterosexist world. For example, in discussing his career goals, Deandre responded in a cynical and lighthearted tone: "I'm going to be a French teacher and a full-time prostitute." Deandre probably has the personality and good looks to make a lot of money if he chooses the latter profession.

Deandre is about 5'11" and on the thin side. He has straight blonde hair that he parts on the side. His hair is cut short, except in the front, where he has to brush it back to keep it out of his eyes. Deandre has a sparkle in his hazel eyes that makes one wonder if he is keeping a secret, one that he will only share with intimate friends.

Deandre is a senior and about to graduate. He has spent a good portion of his life in a large eastern metropolis. As a result, he has had a great deal of exposure to gay culture and finds little excitement in the gay community at Clement University and Hidden Falls.

He recalls having same-sex attractions early in life. "Even in elementary school I felt weird changing in front of boys. Maybe it didn't become real until around eleventh grade." He also discussed his childhood and his relationship with his family: "I basically was very temperamental. I never got along with my parents. As I look back, I think my sexuality was probably the cause of my poor relations with them. There was always this thing that they didn't know." Deandre is still not out to his parents, although he knows they suspect. One time while staying at home he left his driver's license at a gay bar and someone from the bar called Deandre's house. When his dad found out, he asked Deandre what he was doing at that "faggot" bar.

Deandre does not identify as gay or bisexual: "I don't describe myself. I'm attracted to men and I could be attracted to women." He went on to elaborate:

> I hate words and definitions. You can never stick to them. They are like a New Year's resolution. Once you start to attach labels to something it makes you want to get away from it that much more. I feel that once I accept a label then that's what I have to be. Like if I said I was gay to my parents, then that's what I would always be to them.

Whether Deandre's comments are rationalizations about being closeted to his parents or if he really does experience the confinement of socially derived identities is unclear. What is clear, however, is that Deandre is not out to many people and that he is highly selective about whom he comes out to.

Deandre is only out to people with whom he shares a close bond: "Coming out is not a public thing with me. It's personal." He rejects most notions of what it means to be gay and refuses to wear gay-identifying symbols. Deandre responded to a question about how he would feel walking with someone else who was wearing a pink triangle on his or her clothing: "I'd be embarrassed to be with that person. It represents weakness. That you have to prove to yourself that it's ok to be gay. They're basically trying to convince themselves that it's ok." He does not agree with most of the politics of LGBSA and other queer students: "I think a lot of people get upset and put off by the symbols, the newspaper articles. People are really turned off by this stuff and it ends up doing more harm than good."

For a variety of complex reasons (internalized homophobia might be one) Deandre tries not to define himself by his sexual orientation, yet he faces a bind in that he exists in a society in which social definitions of people are strongly linked to sexuality. His resistance to sexual scripts has only resulted in a different type of marginalized status: in his sexual identity, Deandre is a man without a community. Andrew, on the other hand--although he recognizes (as Deandre has) that identities should be based on a multitude of factors, not merely sexual attraction--has chosen to identify with the gay community.

How might we make sense of Deandre and Andrew vis-a-vis essentialism versus social constructivism? Andrew's statement about being bothered by "the whole idea of categories" reflects an understanding that some aspects of identity are socially derived. Nonetheless, Andrew identifies as both a gay man and a political queer; the latter term is perhaps the most essentializing category of all for people with same-sex attractions, since being queer is about *accentuating* difference based on sexual orientation.

What about Deandre? Oddly enough, Deandre recognized at an early age that there was something about him that was different, which he believes served as a barrier between himself and his family. Yet Deandre does not see his same-sex attractions as the defining point in his identity. For him, identifying as gay is akin to creating a caricature of who he is as a person. Labeling himself as gay is too restrictive, in that he would forever be defined that way by his family and by society. Whereas Deandre's stance may be a rationalization for staying closeted, the point here is not in how we might define Deandre and Andrew, but how they themselves do.

There is an interesting paradox in the stories of these two men. One recognized at an early age that he had same-sex attractions, yet as an adult (Deandre is 22 years old) he defines his same-sex attractions as something that are not an essential aspect of who he is. Andrew, on the other hand, struggled over whether he was gay. He had sex in high school with a male friend, but he also had a girlfriend. Finally, during his first year in college, he came out to himself. For the first time in his life he admitted that he was gay. Yet for Andrew, who has only been out for three years, being gay is the defining point in who he is. The examples of Andrew and Deandre raise questions about whether sexual orientation is ascribed (essentialism) or acquired through life's experiences (constructivism); and whether sexual orientation imposes fundamental differences (essentialism) or people are all similar (constructivism). In the following pages I elaborate on this issue and present an alternative view of gay identity as ethnicity.

SEXUAL ORIENTATION AND ETHNICITY

Steven Epstein (1987) argues that the strict essentialism/constructivism debate is a forced dualism between nature versus nurture and does not reflect the experience of lesbian, gay, and bisexual people. Strict constructivist views of sexuality emphasize that gay people are inherently similar to straight people and that difference reflects varying choices and experiences occurring throughout one's lifetime. From a constructivist perspective individuals play a role in creating who they are, not only in terms of sexuality but also in relation to other identity issues. When Roman determined at the age of 20 that he was gay, he sought information on what such an identity means: "One of the first things I did was go to the library and look up all the books that I could find on gays. I remember going to a bookstore and buying this book called *Being a Homosexual* and how I proudly put it on the counter." Roman's simple act of pride and the research he conducted reflect his role in shaping his sexual identity.

The strict essentialist position is that people are inherently different: lesbian, gay, and bisexual people are different from heterosexuals. Furthermore, people are constrained by the biological forces that shape sexual orientation. We do not shape our own sexual identities. When Roger came out he was able to make sense of his tumultuous life. "Being gay finally was something that I knew for sure. It was certainty. It was a sense of identity." Roger alludes to the idea that his gayness was already present; his sexuality is not something that society has constructed for him: it is part of who he is, part of his essence.

Roman and Roger offer conflicting support for either an essentialist or a constructivist stance. Additionally, each individual offers internal contradictions to either argument: Roman also spoke of the game of "mugger," which he played as a child with a friend in which they would jump on each other and then roll around on a bed together. For Roman, who often reflects on his childhood, the game of mugger was an indication of his predisposition toward same-sex attraction. His experience in this case belies a strict constructivist view. Similarly, although Roger now recognizes various clues that indicated as a child that he might be gay (like hanging around the "cute" guys when he was in school), he nonetheless is actively engaged in shaping his present gay identity: "It's a mission in my life to be as visible as possible." T h e experiences of Roman and Roger as well as Andrew and Deandre highlight the inadequacies of an either/or essentialist/constructivist debate. Two of the most significant works on the history of human sexuality, and in particular homosexuality, add to the confusion. As I noted in chapter 2, in *History of Sexuality* Michel Foucault argues that the notion of a homosexual identity is a fairly recent phenomenon, which emerged during the late 1800s when the medical and psychiatric professions coded human behavior in terms of overarching categories. Homosexual acts, which existed previously as aberrant behaviors (in most cultures), began to be classified as characteristics of a deviant class of people. A homosexual identity was thus constructed. Over time, discourse circumscribed by power relations has continually reshaped our definitions of homosexual identity. The research of Alfred Kinsey (1948, 1953) is one example of a how scientific discourse has helped shape notions of the homosexual. Proclamations by Anita Bryant are another.

Whereas Foucault sees homosexual identity as the byproduct of the emerging social forces of the nineteenth century, John Boswell (1980) offers a view of gay identity dating back to the urbanization of the eleventh century. He argues that evidence, such as gay literature, more than suggests that there was a "substantial gay minority." "Gay people were prominent, influential, and respected at many levels of society in most of Europe, and left a permanent mark on the cultural monuments of the age, both religious and secular" (p. 334). For Boswell, the gay minority of the eleventh century was not a byproduct of society's classificatory schemes, but more or less represented an essentially distinct group of people.

To say that Foucault represents the social constructivist stance and Boswell the essentialist position is to do injustice to their complex analyses. Nonetheless, their works offer an overview of the constructivist/essentialist dualism, a dualism that Boswell succinctly summarizes: "Do categories exist because humans recognize real distinctions in the world around them, or are categories arbitrary conventions, simply names for things which have categorical force because humans agree to use them in certain ways?" (1982/1983, p. 91).

Epstein (1987) considers the constructivism/essentialism dualism as sameness versus difference and choice versus constraint. The strict constructivist position emphasizes sameness and choice: people are basically the same, and any difference reflects choices made (and the subsequent changes) during one's life. The essentialist position is that people are different and have little choice in affecting those differences. When we move away from the dualism of identity as either socially constructed or essential nature and focus on the concepts of sameness/difference and choice/constraint, we see there are four possibilities (see Figure 8.1):

1. sameness/choice (strict constructivism)
2. sameness/constraint (constructivism and essentialism)
3. difference/choice (essentialism and constructivism)
4. difference/constraint (strict essentialism)

Figure 8.1
Epstein's Model of Constructivism/Essentialism Debate

	choice	constraint
sameness	1 strict constructivism *Deandre	2 *Tom
difference	3 *Andrew	4 strict essentialism *Tito

Consequently, when Deandre discusses same-sex attractions as something upon which he chooses not to base identity differences, he is working from the strict constructivist perspective (position 1). When Tom points out that as a child he was attracted to boys, and at the time argues that there are no differences between gays and straights, he is operating from a constructivist/essentialist stance (position 2). When Andrew discusses his distaste for categorizing people, yet chooses to identify as queer, he highlights an essentialist/ constructivist view (position 3). Finally, when Tito goes to elaborate lengths to express what he feels is a fundamental difference between himself and heterosexuals, and yet believes that difference to be beyond his control, he reflects a strict essentialist perspective (position 4).

Certainly, I could borrow other statements from these four students that might reflect different perspectives in Epstein's model. The point is not that people fall forever in specific locations; instead, the point is that multiple interpretations of gay identity exist.

Epstein situates political movements related to gay rights within these four positions. For example, he identifies the "Post-Stonewall gay liberation" movement with strict constructivism (position 1--sameness/choice). He argues that this movement reflects the view that all people are bisexual (essentially the same) and that a degree of choice must be made in identifying as a lesbian or gay person. In position 2, he places the "homophile" movement of the 1950s and 1960s, which emphasized the view that sexual orientation is not a choice and that same-sex attractions do not make one fundamentally different from heterosexuals. Position 3 is occupied by "political lesbians" who reflect the view that sexual identity is a choice (in this case a political statement) and fundamentally different. Position 4, the strict essentialist position, emphasizes the view that sexual orientation is innate and that lesbian, gay, and bisexual people are fundamentally different from heterosexuals. In this quadrant, Epstein includes the "gay civil rights movement."

Once we drop the strict constructivist view that identity is an arbitrary acquisition and the strict essentialist position that identity is fixed forever, another logical possibility emerges: "sexual identities are both inescapable and transformable" (Epstein, 1987, p. 34). Michael Warner (1993) speaks to this very issue: "Identity as lesbian or gay is ambiguously given and chosen, in some ways ascribed and in other ways the product of the performative act of coming out" (p. xxv). Such a perspective describes what we frequently think of as ethnic identities, in which ethnicity represents a form of group identification that one is both born into as well as socialized to adopt. Ethnicity is more than a generational connection passed on through blood; it also encompasses social customs and practices such as language and religion.

An ethnic model of gay identity allows for a great variation in how lesbian, gay, and bisexual people define themselves, while at the same time it provides a common bond. Gay ethnicity allows for the fact that some people recognize same-sex attractions early in life but others do so at a much later stage. Gay ethnicity also allows for the degree of variability by which people identify with their same-sex attraction; just as for ethnic groups, in which one's ethnicity is central for some but not central for others, lesbian, gay, and bisexual people also identify to varying degrees.

When we reject the dualism of constructivism and essentialism, we move toward a view that gay ethnicity reflects both choice and constraint and sameness and difference. In essence, gay ethnicity exists along two axes: a vertical axis ranging from sameness to difference and a horizontal axis ranging from choice to constraint. Figure 8.2 is my modification of Epstein's model (I have moved the choice/constraint axis to the bottom of the schematic). Here, instead of four possibilities, there are an unlimited variety of gay representations.

Figure 8.2
Gay Ethnic Identity

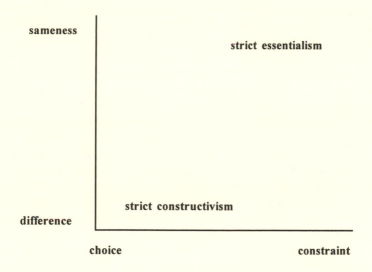

If we take two extreme examples, the utility of a gay ethnic model becomes more apparent. For example, the Post-Stonewall gay liberation movement can be juxtaposed with the current queer movement. Many gay liberationists stressed that all people are basically bisexual and that differences reflect a certain degree of socialization and choice. A strict queer stance is that lesbian, gay, and bisexual people have essential differences that are ascribed. Both of these fundamental beliefs about identity are included in an ethnic model; instead of an either/or idea of identity, we have a range of perspectives that constitute gay ethnicity. This makes sense in that there certainly are queers who believe sexual orientation is acquired through social experience and gays who believe fundamental differences exist.

By creating a model that describes gay identity, one runs the risk of essentializing such identities. The model addresses people who identify as gay and excludes straight people. If straights cannot be situated within the model, then does that mean heterosexuals are essentially different from gays? The solution lies in the notion of group identity. Regardless of one's understanding of individual sexual identity (whether it is essential nature, socially constructed, or a combination of the two), no one can deny that heterosexuals and gays as social categories are defined differently within our society. Although the ultimate source of individual sexual identity is debatable, clearly group identities are socially constructed based on a belief that gays are essentially different from heterosexuals. The category of gay already exists, and people who exhibit same-sex attractions face marginality. Even though people who have same-sex attractions may not be different from people with opposite-sex attractions, our society has already designated gays to be *treated* differently by denying them basic rights and privileges. With regard to a group model of gay identity, a lesbian, gay, bisexual, or queer person has two choices: continue to endure as an individual in a society that oppresses people who exhibit same-sex attractions, or organize around one's marginalized status.

In chapter seven, I discussed the queer contraculture. I highlighted the common threads that connect gay students at Clement as well as differences (queer controversies, racial diversity, and bisexuality) that threaten group solidarity. The concept of ethnicity highlights the unique experience of lesbian, gay, bisexual, and queer people while at the same time forming a common ground for self-organization around a socially imposed categorization.

An ethnic model of gay identity is compatible with a critical postmodern perspective in that critical analyses stress theory building that is empowering. The goal of the researcher/theorist is not merely to describe social phenomena; from a critical postmodern perspective, the theorist is challenged to link theory to praxis in a way that aids in the self-organization of marginalized groups. As Steven Seidman (1993) accurately assesses, "Gay identity politics moves back and forth between a narrow single-interest politic and a view of coalition politics as the sum of separate identity communities, each locked into its own sexual, gender, class, and racial politic" (p. 105). Accordingly, an ethnic model of gay identity encourages the development of a community of difference by including diverse members and at the same time advancing a common sense of identity. Judith Butler (1991) warns of the dangers of identity categories because they often serve as "regulatory regimes," yet she admits to participation in political activities "under the sign of lesbian" (pp.

13-14). She resolves her apparent inconsistency by suggesting identity significations that are permanently unclear. Her suggestion is well taken but we must continually remind ourselves that many in this country who wield significant power have clearly delineated conceptions of heterosexuals and homosexuals and have exhibited little restraint in using that power to oppress queer people. Although the question of who is queer and who is not--and whether the question should even be asked--may be forever debated, there must be some sense of common identity in order to organize large-scale resistance. I maintain here that gay ethnicity, or perhaps queer ethnicity, is one possibility.

In suggesting an ethnic view of gay identity, I drift from poststructural critiques of sexual identity politics, which tend to stress the deconstruction of theoretical categories of sexual identity. From a poststructural perspective, the signification of social identities must be deconstructed continually in order to reveal the deployment of power and, ultimately, social domination. In other words, instead of creating new categories of sexual identity, the solution lies in tearing apart current categories and the basis for their construction in the first place. However, once the basis of oppressive categories and constructions is revealed, the poststructural alternative is unclear. What is clear, however, is that poststructural accounts that avoid identity as a source of difference run the risk of whitewashing difference. Seidman (1993) elaborates on the weakness of a poststructural analysis of sexual identity:

> Refusal to anchor experience in identifications [identity] ends up, ironically, denying differences by either submerging them in an undifferentiated oppositional mass or by blocking the development of individual and social differences through the disciplining compulsory imperative to remain undifferentiated. . . . In other words, it [poststructuralism] fails to theoretically engage the practices of individuals organized around affirmative lesbian and gay identities. (pp. 133-134)

I do not question that poststructural critiques are helpful in understanding the origins and implications of social categories. My concern is that a critical emphasis upon praxis and the ongoing day-to-day struggles of lesbian, gay, and bisexual people may be lost in the deconstruction of sexual identity. The reality is that "whether we like it or not, the crucial if now somewhat contradictory battles for civil rights and for destabilizing the homosexual signification that becomes fuel for medical, social, and 'private' policing still depend on theorized and deployed notions of identity" (Patton, 1993, p. 175).

One remaining concern is that traditional ethnic groups are socialized into an ethnic identity largely through the family. As Brian McNaught (1988) notes, lesbian, gay, and bisexual people are like orphans in comparison to "those communities of people whose oppression is a family affair. We are like strangers who have been dropped on an island together" (p. 82). How then do lesbian, gay, and bisexual people come to adopt an ethnic identity? How are they socialized?

SOCIALIZATION AND IDENTITY

Socialization is *the process of learning the values, beliefs, and attitudes of a group to which one either aspires or is ascribed* (Van Maanen, 1976). Primary socialization relates to those learning experiences that occur during formative years, which take place predominantly in close-knit groups such as the family.   Ethnic identities are largely conferred through primary socialization.   In terms of gay ethnicity, lesbian, gay, and bisexual people typically are not socialized to their sexual identities during their youth through their families. Recall how one student knew at the age of four or five that he had same-sex attractions, but he also knew he should keep those feelings hidden. When he was 12 years old his parents confronted him about being gay, and before he could respond he was told he would be sent away if he was. Such an experience does not socialize a child into gay ethnicity. (If anything, it does the opposite and reinforces the closet.) Likewise, Ben recognized his attractions at an early age (around 11 or 12) but did not come out to his family until he was nearly 20 years old.

Socialization that occurs after much of one's identity has already been formed is described as secondary socialization. Socialization into a gay ethnicity occurs when other fundamental aspects of identity are in place. When Shane came out he was challenged by queer students to assume a greater role in the queer contraculture. They had great expectations of him. Their expectations pushed Shane toward increased openness and activism. The pressures he faced were a source of anxiety and trepidation. Shane had already developed a good idea of who he was as an individual, and now people expected him to be a different person. Shane's example highlights the fact that a sense of identity is largely in place when students come out. Identification with sexual orientation is in many ways a process of reshaping one's sense of identity; as we have witnessed throughout this text, it is a process that involves great personal investment. When one student came out he had to re-define himself after nineteen years of defining himself in one way. Roman and Ben both went in search of information and reading materials about what it meant to be gay. Ben commented: "I didn't know that I didn't have to get my ear pierced or become a drag queen. I had to educate myself."

I have pointed out how queer students at Clement University have played a fundamental role in creating and maintaining a sense of community. Queer students are the primary organizers of rallies, dances, parties, and other social and political events. They are the ones who represent lesbian, gay, and bisexual students in campus and national politics as they seek cultural change.

Because of their preeminent role in the campus life of Clement University, the queer contraculture forms the principal agent of secondary socialization for lesbian, gay, and bisexual students.

Regarding the queer contraculture, a student who comes out at Clement faces three general alternatives:

1. become involved in the queer contraculture and adopt a queer identity
2. become involved in the queer contraculture but resist a queer identity
3. reject the queer contraculture altogether.

The third choice implies the rejection of a queer identity as well, because the contraculture plays such a vital role in defining what it means to be queer at Clement. Andrew falls into category one. He is actively involved in the queer contraculture and describes himself as a gay/queer man. Even though he does not want to be the "embodiment of what it means to be queer," he also wants people to realize that when they are ashamed of their sexual identity, they give that impression to other people and it affects all queer people. Shane initially epitomizes category two and at the end of the year fits more into category one. When we first met Shane, even though he attended LGBSA meetings, went to rallies, and identified with many queer students, he was still uncomfortable about being out: "The people I've told I can count on two hands--no, one hand. . . . I don't advertise that I'm gay. I don't do anything to give people a clue." Category three describes Deandre Witter. "I don't feel I have to fit into any of what the political groups do." Of the students in this study, twenty-seven fall into category 1, ten fall into category 2, and three fall into the third category.

Category 1: Involved in Queer Contraculture/Accept Queer Identity

Because the sample for this study was selected through connections with LGBSA, which is dominated by queer-identified students, quite naturally the majority of students actively participated in the queer contraculture and identified as queer. Students such as Roger, Tito, Jerry, and Andrew highlight the political quality of the socialization offered by the contraculture. Being queer is a way of life for these students. As Roger noted, "In many ways I identify the queer community as my family of choice." Roger hints at the degree to which the queer contraculture shapes his own socialization, nearly approaching the level of the primary socialization offered by his family. For Tito, Jerry, and Andrew, everything about being gay is political. This is why they identify so closely with the queer movement in general and the queer contraculture at Clement in particular. For the students in this category, being queer is an essential aspect of their identity. Although they may not agree on whether their queerness is something that emerged through complex social processes (essentialism/constructivism) or is something they were born into (strict essentialism), being queer makes them essentially different from straights.

Category 2: Involved in Queer Contraculture/Resist Queer Identity

A second option for students who come out is becoming involved in the queer contraculture but resisting self-identification as a queer. One student stated: "I choose to be a very active member of the gay community, although I have a problem with 'queer.' I've heard it used in relation to Queer Nation and I've heard some students here use 'queer.' I have a problem with it. It's a very ugly word. It's hard on my ears." This student went on to equate the use of queer with a name used by gays to insult straights--"breeder." Another student also has difficulty with the word itself: "'Queer' to me means different but in a negative way."

One student who is actively involved in LGBSA and in the politics of sexual identity disagrees with many of the methods adopted by queers in general and queer students at Clement in particular. He feels their methods are alienating; he prefers slower and more educational approaches. This student is turned off by queer students who stress difference over "common ground" and prefers to work within the system and not be labeled as different. He highlights a point of divergence within the gay community that is in part explained by constructivist/ essentialist views of gay identity. Another student sheds light on this distinction:

> To me "queer" has political connotations to it. Queers make a point about being different and being proud of it. Highlighting that we are unique. The gay community more or less wants to fit in. I see myself more in the gay community. Sometimes I feel as though we need a more explicit effort to be vocal, like the queer community.

The four students highlighted in this section reject an essentializing view of gay identity; they see themselves as no different in any significant way from heterosexuals. From their perspective, being gay is not something that should dictate every aspect of one's life or identity. These students participate actively in the queer contraculture but resist the adoption of a queer identity. They tend to prefer a more traditional gay stance regarding politics and social change. For these students, any differences between straights and gays are socially constructed and therefore can be rejected.

Category 3: Reject Queer Contraculture

A third option that students who are out[1] might choose is to reject completely the queer contraculture. Only three of the forty students in this study fall into this category. The queer contraculture has a limited impact upon the secondary socialization of these students. Deandre expressed his rejection of the queer contraculture:

> I've already chosen my friends and therefore I don't have to fit into any of what the political groups do. They are out coalition building, building alliances with Black Caucus, Women's Concerns, etc. . . . Fuck it! If you're going to represent gay then deal with the issues that matter, not the issues related to other groups. Like they've aligned themselves with pro-choice groups. What does that have to do with sexual orientation?

Two other students reject the queer contraculture more for reasons of fear than disagreement over political agendas. Tom explained: "I don't want to be associated with queers at all. I don't want people to know I'm gay." A second stated, "I sort of isolate myself so that other people don't get the wrong idea and figure out that I'm gay."

For the vast majority of students in this study (thirty-seven), the queer contraculture serves as a significant source of secondary socialization into gay ethnicity. The contraculture has become a second family for many. Roger even identifies the contraculture as his family of choice. Even though there is a range of difference in terms of involvement, the queer contraculture impacts students in many ways. Through their own visibility, queer students establish to a large degree the space, style, and substance of social interactions. Although some students choose not to become involved, escaping the reach of the queer contraculture is difficult, because queer students form the center of gay ethnicity at Clement University. Even when students reject the queer contraculture, their identities, in part, become defined by their resistance, just as gay ethnicity is defined by its opposition to heterosexual culture.

SUMMARY

Social constructivism and essentialism as dichotomous theories of sexual identity are conceptually inadequate in explaining the diverse experiences and self-definitions of lesbian, gay, bisexual, and queer people. Whereas social theorists have tended to adopt constructivist perspectives, practitioners of sexual politics (queer activists) have tended to adopt essentialist views. The conceptual lag between the two has prevented a union of theory and practice. A solution exists in the notion of gay ethnicity. A gay ethnic identity moves

away from the either/or dualism of the constructivism/essentialism debate and
provides for variability in how lesbian, gay, and bisexual people make sense
of their lives. Yet at the same time, a common ethnic identity provides for the
unification, the sense of solidarity, necessary to overcome oppression.

Human life is in part a process of sense making. Like gays, straights also
struggle to understand who they are and what life is about. But because
socially imposed categories such as heterosexual and homosexual have
emerged, which privilege some and marginalize others, the challenges of
making sense of one's life are different; although the essential nature of gays
may be the same as straights, the demands of life are clearly dissimilar. As
a result, lesbian, gay, bisexual, and queer people have few options but to
organize around their common marginality.

Unlike other ethnic identities, lesbian, gay, and bisexual people only
experience secondary socialization; a gay ethnic identity typically forms later
in life. One student maintained: "If you decide to establish a positive identity,
then you need to interact with gay-affirming people. You just don't get it on
your own." For gay students at Clement University, the queer contraculture
forms the primary agent of secondary socialization. The majority of lesbian,
gay, and bisexual students at Clement have little direct involvement with the
queer contraculture. But because queer students at Clement are the primary
change agents for lesbian, gay, and bisexual students, all students in one way
or another are shaped by the queer contraculture. For the students in this
study, most (twenty-seven) are actively engaged in the queer contraculture and
identify as queer. Others (ten of the forty) participate in the activities of the
queer contraculture but do not identify as queer. Still other students (three in
this study) reject both the queer contraculture and the notion of a queer
identity.

An underlying theme throughout this chapter and the entire text relates to
issues of difference. The queer contraculture at Clement highlights the
different ways in which lesbian, gay, and bisexual people define themselves.
The conceptualization of a gay ethnicity is largely based upon the need to
organize a diverse group of people whose strongest bond is their opposition to
heterosexuality.

Queer students at Clement are part of the gay ethnic community while at the
same time they seek membership in two other communities, the Clement
University community and the larger community that is American society.
Through their political and cultural work, queer students at Clement seek to
build communities of difference in which their identities are a visible part of
the cultural mosaic. In the concluding chapter of this work, I focus on the
idea of communities of difference and the role queer students play in shaping
such communities.

NOTE

1. In an earlier chapter I pointed out that thirty-five students are mostly out and five are mostly closeted, yet here I am describing all forty as being out. To clarify, I classified five students as closeted, based on their discussion of coming out as something they may do in the future. In other words, they consider themselves still to be closeted. Yet all five of these students are out to some members of the lesbian, gay, and bisexual community and therefore are faced with deciding to what degree, if any, they will participate in the queer contraculture.

9

Toward Communities of Difference

Freedom is never voluntarily given up by the oppressor. It must be
demanded by the oppressed.
      --Martin Luther King, Jr., "Letters from the Birmingham Jail"

Queer students at Clement University have staked a claim to power and have
gained a voice in cultural change. Their goal is to create a diverse academic
community and society in which lesbian, gay, and bisexual people are full
participants in the democratic process. But "conflict is inevitable if the
multiple voices of different groups are to be heard. The lack of conflict either
means that particular groups have been silenced and made invisible or that a
democratic [community] based on the acceptance of difference has not been
reached" (Tierney, 1993b, p. 64).

There has been much conflict at Clement University. Roger stated: "The
administration has been forced to do almost everything that has been positive
for us. They wouldn't see any reason to change anything if we didn't always
kick and scream." In the forceful way queer students have raised issues of
equality, liberty, and justice, they have helped elevate the consciousness of the
campus with regard to gay rights.

In this final chapter, I have four goals. First, I highlight the participation
of queer students in the march on Washington as an example of their
commitment to change the culture of American society. I then summarize
their local efforts to achieve a more diverse academic community. From a
critical postmodern perspective, research is praxis-oriented. Social change
should be the ultimate goal of the researcher/theorist. In this regard, my third
goal is to focus on praxis. To do so, I discuss the problems raised by the
students in this project as well as possible solutions. Finally, I summarize this
work and return to the idea of communities of difference.

SOCIETAL CHANGE

Queer students at Clement University are committed to ending the oppression of lesbian, gay, and bisexual people on a societal level. One student elaborated: "My ultimate goal would be for someone to be walking around and someone else call them a name like 'fag' or 'queer' and have it sound as silly as me calling someone straight." The comments of this student seem to reject an essentialist view of gay identity in that he dreams of a day when the term "queer" would be trivial. Branden offered a different vision: "I would like to see less of a negative attitude toward gay people on this campus and throughout the rest of the world. I'd like for more people to understand what gay is--that it's not something evil, that some of their closest friends are gay." Similarly, Roger dreamed of seeing "less of the idea of tolerance and more of the notion of celebration." The narratives of Branden and Roger reflect an essentialist position: difference is heightened. They may not desire assimilation into mainstream society, but they seek to be respected.

We should not be surprised that different students have different dreams, because, as I emphasized in Parts II and III, identity and socialization are individual and group undertakings. Individuals shape and are shaped by the contraculture I have described here. Yet these dreams get played out in any number of arenas--on the dance floor of The Odyssey, in a "straight talk" with students, or "dishing" with other guys during a late-night visit to the diner. In what follows I turn to a larger event that moves us beyond the parochial borders of Hidden Falls and into the national arena.

The 1993 March on Washington

A group of over 150 students and staff sat on the mall lawn across from the White House awaiting their turn to march. The Clement delegation was one of many from their state among hundreds of other groups. Groups were organized by states, and Clement's was not scheduled to join the march until later in the day. Many of the students who had participated in my research project were there. I visited with them as we waited our turn.

For Roger, the march was a "moment in history" of which he would be a part. Ben offered a similar view, although he worried about the "conservative backlash" he believed the march would generate. The whole event was overwhelming for Branden: "It's almost beyond words. I have never seen this many queer people at one place in all my life. I just don't know what to say. When we came out of the subway it was like every single person was lesbian, gay, or bisexual. People were even cheering."

Roger sat on the grass with his new boyfriend, who sat in front of him. From time to time, his boyfriend leaned back against Roger's chest while

Roger draped his arms around him. Andrew was with his boyfriend, as was Ben. Their smiles seemed incapable of containing their joy. "It's like a fantasy world where you don't have to be concerned about holding hands. It's like what the world should be like," noted Roger. His boyfriend added: "I can be myself for a while. I can be who I am." Another student, who is mostly closeted back at Clement, began to speak, then paused. He looked around him, at the vast crowd, and simply stated: "I feel proud here."

The atmosphere on the lawn across from the White House was a stark contrast to earlier in the day when we had gathered at the student center at Clement University for the trip to D.C. Students were still in a defensive mode and were careful about expressing affection publicly. Once on the bus, however, students began to clasp hands, kiss, embrace one another. There was a sense of relief in their faces, as if they were being catapulted through time to another place in history where same-sex attractions were in the same league with other-sex attractions. In a way they were. But only for a moment.

Nearly ten hours after leaving Clement University, the time had finally arrived for the delegations from Clement's state to join the march. Getting all the groups together was chaotic and many of us got separated. A number of students from Clement had splintered off into smaller groups. None of them seemed to care as long as they were able to join the march, even in groups as small as two or three.

For a while I walked with a friend, a Christian minister from Clement University, and a few other students from Clement. Eventually I separated from them only to join up again later in the day. I dropped out of the march to observe other groups passing. A group from Georgia sang a song: "Hey, hey, ho, ho. Sam Nunn has got to go." Behind them a shirtless, goateed man in tight bluejeans held a sign that portrayed Bill Clinton with a long nose. The sign read: "Played for fools. Time's up. Shut up. Put up." A middle-aged woman followed him and held her sign: "Love makes a family. Nothing else. Nothing less." One woman carried a sign that read: "I Love My Gay Son." She was beckoned and then hugged by another woman standing along the march route. Their cheeks red and their eyes teary, both women gleamed with pride and emotion.

After an hour or so of standing and watching groups pass by, I walked along the sidewalk against the march so that I could observe as many groups as possible. There was a point along the route where the march slowed nearly to a halt. Something was obstructing the march.

"Repent perverts, repent perverts," chanted a group of seven or eight men standing on the sidewalk. Judging by their signs quoting Biblical scripture and the collars that some wore, they were affiliated with various Christian ministries. These men were there to protest the march on Washington for lesbian, gay, and bisexual equal rights and liberation. On this day, April 25, 1993, they were the counterprotesters.

As lesbian, gay, and bisexual people and supporters marched by, they responded to the counterprotesters by chanting, "No more hate! No more hate!"

In turn, the counterprotesters replied, "Back to the Bible! Back to the Bible!"

"No more hate! No more hate!"

"Read the Bible while you're able! Read the Bible while you're able!"

"Jesus loves queers! Jesus loves queers!"

A man wearing a collar pointed at different individuals in the crowd, which had now slowed to a snail's pace. He yelled out at them, "Sinner! Sinner! Sinner!" His favorite targets were the topless women scattered throughout the march. At one time he looked straight at me and shouted, "Sinner!" I momentarily froze as I looked back, but with notebook in hand I continued to write. He stood on the sidewalk behind several police officers who had placed their motorcycles between themselves and the marchers. Beyond the motorcycles was added protection: a yellow dividing strip separated the motorcycles from several parade marshals, who stood in front of the security zone surrounding the counterprotesters. The parade marshals tried to keep the marchers moving. "They want you to stop and yell back. Keep moving. Don't give in to their hatred."

I observed the interactions between the marchers and the counterprotesters for about a half an hour and then once again joined the march. My research as well as this day were coming to a close. Like the students from Clement University, I sensed that a moment in history and this study were about to end. I wondered how we would be remembered. Would the march on Washington be heralded in the same way as the civil rights march led by Martin Luther King, Jr., some thirty years earlier?

I flashed back to what I had observed and learned in nearly two years of research. What stuck in my mind were the students who had helped me with my research. There was Shane, who was mostly closeted when we met and now was a leader in LGBSA. Tito had graduated and taken a job in New York City working with disadvantaged families. Andrew was about to leave for graduate school. Roger was offered a job at Clement working as an AIDS counselor. Tom had disappeared into the darkness of his closet and the hidden recesses of gay life at Clement. What would become of him and all those other young men who still must deal with the power and fear of the closet?

The involvement of students from Clement in the march on Washington symbolizes their commitment to societywide social change. But the march by no means was the only action taken by queer students at Clement. There were letter-writing campaigns to support lifting the ban on gays in the military. Some queer students protested the policies of President Bush toward gays when he spoke on the steps of Old Main at Clement University. Others participated in conferences at other institutions in the region where issues of homophobia and heterosexism were central topics.

LOCAL CHANGE

Although Clement University students exhibit a great deal of concern about societal issues, the local culture of Clement University and Hidden Falls is that which touches them daily. The local culture forms much of the focus of the political efforts of Clement students. Many of the political and educational activities of queer students are discussed in chapter 6; I briefly summarize those activities here. Throughout the academic years 1991-1992 and 1992-1993, queer students at Clement engaged in several significant political activities. They played an integral role in documenting the problems of lesbian, gay, and bisexual students; their finished product was a 400-page report. This report, along with lobbying efforts and committee work conducted by several members of LGBSA, helped lead to the addition of a sexual orientation clause to the university's statement of non-discrimination.

Another political activity was their involvement in promoting a fair housing ordinance in Hidden Falls that included protection based on sexual orientation. After extensive letter writing and participation in town meetings, the amendment was adopted. A number of queer students committed 1992-1993 to protests to force the university to remove the ROTC program from campus. Although this effort has not yet succeeded, many of the students plan to continue their involvement until either they succeed or the military ban is lifted.

Educational efforts have also been central. Organizing National Coming Out Day in the fall and Pride Week in the spring were central projects designed to raise awareness and change attitudes. Additionally, the ongoing straight talks coordinated by LGBSA continued to provide learning opportunities for the Clement University community.

All these efforts highlight a fundamental point: queer students at Clement University have refused to accept the definition of themselves offered by society. They have cast aside the limitations placed upon them by both the institutional and societal culture and have staged opposition through the use of language and by their refusal to remain silent. Queer students have fought the politics of silencing through educational and political efforts aimed at both achieving power for themselves and altering the perception of others.

The adoption of the term "queer" as identifier symbolizes the students' commitment to altering others' perceptions of lesbian, gay, and bisexual people. Their expropriation of queer, however, has not been without its drawbacks. In many ways, students at Clement have dulled the sharp edge of the radical nature that is queer. Around the country, the term "queer" is most often used to accentuate the essential difference between straights and gays, as well as the difference between liberal and radical gays. In this light, queer students at Clement have clouded an already murky distinction between essentialist and constructivist views of gay identity. But the meaning of words and phrases, and of language, is "up for grabs" and queer students at Clement have staked a claim to their own conception of a queer identity.

The notion of gay ethnicity allows for the diversity of lesbian, gay, bisexual, and queer identities to develop some sense of unity, of solidarity. A collective identity is necessary in the struggle for equal rights and social justice. At Clement University queer students are the primary means of socialization into gay ethnicity. They constitute a contraculture in that they are largely defined by their opposition to mainstream cultural norms associated with heterosexuality. Students who identify as lesbian, gay, or bisexual are shaped to a large degree by the queer contraculture even when they reject the contraculture, as Deandre Witter has.

The queer contraculture is the leading student voice at Clement in achieving a community of difference in which all lesbian, gay, and bisexual students are democratic participants. Even though much has been accomplished at Clement University, more work lies ahead. Lesbian, gay, and bisexual students continue to face harassment and discrimination. Their experiences continue to be excluded from much of the academic setting. In what follows I summarize the problems students in this study have revealed. I then discuss solutions, relying both on suggestions from students and on my own observations and understanding. Although these suggestions relate primarily to Clement University, I venture to say that many apply to higher education institutions across the country.

PROBLEMS AND SOLUTIONS

Many of the problems experienced by lesbian, gay, and bisexual students at Clement revolve around different forms of oppression related to heterosexism. Educational institutions play a significant role in the socialization of youth. Clement University socializes students into various fields, careers, the middle class, and so on. But Clement also socializes students into heterosexism: by the way professors speak of "opposite-sex" relationships in classes, by the way the university offers benefits to "opposite-sex" partners, and by the way students and staff are permitted to make disparaging remarks about "those people."

Heterosexism is based on a belief that other-sex relationships are superior to same-sex relationships. Heterosexist ideology is deeply ingrained within the fabric of Clement University. Andrew has witnessed so many heterosexist remarks from his professors that he quit counting. Likewise, Roger has had to question a professor who spoke of counseling techniques to "cure homosexuals." And Karsch had a professor criticize his choice of "coming out" as topic for an in-class speech.

Heterosexism is not only revealed by what gets spoken; it also exists in the unspoken. When a professor makes a history point about an advisor to Martin Luther King, Jr., being gay and the class responds negatively, a pedagogical moment passes that cannot be reclaimed unless students or teachers challenge disparaging reactions. Likewise, when students hold a coming-out rally on the steps of the school auditorium, adjacent to Old Main, and no senior administrators speak or even pass by, the unspoken reveals a great deal.

Homophobia is also a serious problem, one that confronts Clement University students on a daily basis. Caustic remarks, condescending looks, and outright avoidance are some of the less violent forms of homophobia gay students face. Tom remains closeted in part because he cannot deal with all the offensive words his classmates use when they discuss those "rug munchers" or "fudge packers." Tito looks right through people as he leaves Friendlies because he is so tired of "that look they give you." And when Roman came out to his friends, most accepted him with no problems, except for one friend who was so uncomfortable that Roman rarely sees him anymore.

Physical violence is another form of homophobia that confronts gay students at Clement. Ben will never forget the time he got beat up at a friend's party, all because he said some guy was cute. Karsch is still angry that he was assaulted at the President Bush rally when he and other queer students held signs in protest of Bush's policies toward gays. Andrew has come to despise most aspects of fraternity life because of the time several brothers physically assaulted him while other gay brothers stood by and watched.

The problems just described have been either highlighted by students in direct conversation or raised by their experiences at Clement. These problems relate essentially to the complex issues of how knowledge gets defined as truth, or seen in another light, whose social experience gets legitimated and whose gets marginalized. Power lies at the center of this issue. I discuss this question first in a theoretical sense and then relate it to solutions to the problems at Clement University.

The work of Michel Foucault (1980) calls attention to the interconnectedness of knowledge and power. That which gets enacted as truth is tied to power. The same can be said for social experience; those experiences that are seen as legitimate are those associated with sources of power. The dominant culture of U.S. society and Clement University have defined heterosexuality as the norm and homosexuality as deviant. The lives of lesbian, gay, and bisexual people have, in effect, been defined as illegitimate. Power plays a central role in the marginalization of gay people. Seizing power, then, is the most important step in ending heterosexism and homophobia.

The queer contraculture has re-defined gay identities as legitimate expressions among its own members. They stand in direct opposition to the dominant norms of heterosexuality reflected in the cultures of Clement University and American society. The goal of queer students at Clement is not merely to create an island sanctuary in the midst of a sea of hate; queer students also have sought to change the very nature of that body of hate. They have forced their agenda into the discourse of the university. In this way they have seized power for their own cause. Yet oppression still exists and lesbian, gay, and bisexual students still face ongoing harassment and discrimination. Social change does not occur overnight, and queer students at Clement must continue the efforts they have already started.

Based on discussions with the students who participated in this study and my interpretations of the political and cultural dynamics at Clement University, I recommend the following strategies for confronting the cultural structures that continue to promote heterosexism and homophobia. I organize these strategies around three aspects of academic life: curricula, organization, and leadership.

Curricula Solutions

The lives of lesbian, gay, and bisexual people need to become a topic of discovery. Research and teaching are interactive processes: that which gets studied gets taught, and what gets taught gets studied. Not only must faculty be encouraged to investigate gay/queer issues, but also discouragements must be removed. When a researcher who studies gay issues fails to get tenure because the topic is seen as irrelevant, a message has been sent about what knowledge is important and what knowledge is irrelevant. When a student proposes to write a speech on gay rights for a public-speaking class and the professor comments, "Not one of those again," another message has been sent.

"There definitely should be a curriculum change to include gay, lesbian, and bisexual people and their contributions," argued one student. To elevate lesbian, gay, and bisexual lives as a topic of discovery, an academic department should be organized to address such topics. Possibilities include gender studies, gay/queer studies, or a cultural studies department. Karsch noted, "We need to add a gay and lesbian resource center and a department. I had a Women's Studies class and there were ninety women and about ten men in it and they were all gay. There's a real need to have learning experiences related to sexual orientation."

Curricula issues relate not only to what gets taught but also to how we think about teaching. Unfortunately for the students in this study, teaching is often thought of in a negative way. As we have seen, students involved in this project often recalled one or more heterosexist classroom experiences. As a possible solution, Jerry suggested that faculty be better informed about lesbian, gay, and bisexual issues. "A lot has to do with the faculty. I don't want to put all the pressure on the faculty, but students have to feel like they are welcomed." Another questioned what good out-of-class diversity learning might accomplish for students if faculty are not sensitized to the same issues: "I think professors' sensitivity training is another idea. Even if students unlearn things outside of the classroom, such as overcoming homophobia, if they come into the classroom and everything is reinforced, then what good is it?"

Organizational Solutions

Programs and activities that deal with heterosexism and homophobia must be increased. These efforts need to come not only from organizations such as LGBSA, the Graduate Student Coalition, and ALLIES; the administration also ought to play a proactive role in planning and implementing programs. Some students suggested a resource center for lesbian, gay, and bisexual students: "I think I would definitely create a center for lesbian, gay, and bisexual students for campus programming directed at both students and faculty. The center would sponsor awareness weeks and programs, and sensitivity training for faculty. It would do the things that LGBSA does now, programs that should really be done by the administration." Another voiced a similar concern: "I would like to see a cultural center for lesbian, gay, and bisexual students. I'd like to see the university take on the educational aspects of LGBSA, such as expanding counseling services. Right now the university lays the brunt of the educational responsibility on us." Similarly, Ben added: "I'd like to see the burden taken off the students. Last night I had to do a program with the student hearing board." Ben explained that although he did not mind doing the program, it was really something the university should provide, not LGBSA.

Many suggested student life in particular as an area that should be a target of concern. Jerry felt that resident assistants and other student leaders play a major role in shaping students' attitudes and therefore need to be especially aware of gay issues. Roger expressed a concern about the Greek system and reflected the views of several other students: "I'd like to see more work done at the fraternities and sororities. I'd say that a large percentage of the negative experiences at Clement related to homophobia comes from the Greeks. They have such a tremendous influence on the social life of this campus." The following were specifically mentioned as areas in which programs on homophobia could do the most good: the Greek system, athletic teams, and the residence halls. Others suggested that the counseling center should be more proactive in helping closeted gay students deal with issues related to self-esteem and coming out.

Violence and harassment against gay students is a serious problem at

Clement University. If one incident a year occurs in which someone is physically or verbally assaulted, then that is a serious enough problem. But at Clement University, lesbian, gay, and bisexual students face physical or verbal assault on a regular basis. Students need an office or a staff person who coordinates information and training related to homophobia. Andrew expressed such a desire: "We need to have a full-time staff person doing stuff on changing the campus climate." Karsch added: "I think what we need is a Queer Czar--someone on the same level with top administrators. Someone who would coordinate everything and can see where the holes are and can represent us when policy issues come up. Someone who will advocate for queer concerns." As it stands now, students do not know where to turn when incidents of harassment occur. Some go to LGBSA and seek advocacy. A student organization should not be placed in the position of advocate for something so serious; the university ought to provide such a service.

Leadership Solutions

Clement University is in need of students, faculty, and staff who recognize the educative quality of leadership. In building upon the work of Henry Giroux, William Foster (1989) discusses "transformative intellectuals" as leaders "who know how to analyze critically modern forms of discourse which disguise power relationships and who can bring to a specific site the ability to inform and educate" (p. 15). Transformative intellectuals challenge their institutions to think about and confront social injustice and inequality. As William Tierney (1991) notes in discussing a critical postmodern perspective, transformative intellectuals emphasize "moral action that promotes democracy" (p. 164).

One student took issue with the lack of moral stance on the part of the President of Clement University: "One thing I would change is the conservatism. It's bringing this place down. The President not coming out immediately in support of the sexual orientation clause was not right. He should have taken a stance right away." This student likened the President's action to that of some conservative leaders of the 1960s: "They did the same thing in the 1960s with civil rights issues. Instead of doing the right thing right away, they postpone everything and go through a long drawn-out process. We need leaders who will take a stance. The President here is just a figurehead."

The amount of impact a president can have on his or her institution is debatable. On the one hand, some raise serious questions about the ability of college presidents to initiate change (Bensimon, Neumann, & Birnbaum, 1989), and others see the president as the center of academic decision making (Fisher, 1984; Keller, 1983). From a critical postmodern view, leadership does not reside in any specific individual but, instead, hinges upon reciprocal relationships within communities.

Although critical postmodern perspectives stress the role that all organizational members might play as transformational intellectuals, nonetheless a college or university president sits in a unique organizational location with certain advantages for making sense of the academic environment. What I suggest here is that presidents, as well as other administrators, use their vantage point to raise moral and ethical issues. A message is sent when the president of a university fails to speak out against inequality and injustice. The president and administrators at Clement University need to be challenged to take a stance on gay rights. As Roger pointed out earlier, every improvement at Clement has been accomplished by "kicking and screaming." Queer students need to "kick and scream" some more and challenge the administration to come out of their own closets of silence and speak out on gay rights.

Again, leadership is not the sole possession of those in positions of authority. Other faculty and staff need to step up, come out, and take charge of other forms of discourse related to sexual orientation issues. When someone makes a joke about "homosexuals" at the water cooler or in the locker room and no one responds, oppression continues. When someone on a search committee makes a remark about not wanting to hire a gay man or lesbian and no one speaks up, oppression continues. Faculty and staff who strive for justice and equal rights need to take a stance in every setting.

In summarizing this section, I repeat a comment made by one of the students involved in the project: "There should be more diversity classes on 'life' and sexual orientation--not theory, but related to real experiences." In making his point, this student calls our attention to one of the most significant problems researchers and academicians face--connecting research and practice. Throughout the research behind this work, I have tried continually to keep the praxis aspect of this project in mind. Critical postmodernism demands that our efforts be linked to social change and human agency. What can we learn from queer students at Clement University that might contribute to more equitable college and university communities and to a more just society in general?

Lesbian, gay, and bisexual students do not ask for special rights, as some in our academic communities would have us think. To request the enactment of policies or laws that provide basic protection is not to request special treatment. All colleges and universities ought to have protective clauses related to sexual orientation. Second, lesbian, gay, and bisexual students ought to have resources and facilities to which they can turn for assistance in dealing with problems unique to them. Identity issues are not the same for gay and straight students. Nor are identity issues the same for lesbians or gay men or bisexual men or women. Gay students need safe places on our college campuses and trained staff who understand gay issues. Third, research and writing on lesbian, gay, and bisexual people must be moved from the realm of marginality. As was the case with Black Studies and Women's Studies, there may be no other alternative for achieving academic legitimacy than creating a Lesbian, Gay, and Bisexual Studies Program or even a Queer Studies Program. When Ben and his best friend came out together, they sought literature, research, and information but found very little.

CONCLUSION

Queer students strive for the day in which other lesbian, gay, and bisexual people will come out and join their struggle. There can be no gay community without a visible presence. And gay rights will always be in peril without a gay community. The need for visibility highlights the importance of coming out. The more students, faculty, and staff who come out, the greater the strength of the movement toward equality, liberty, and justice. Michelangelo Signorile is helpful: "Remember that all those in the closet, blinded by their own trauma, hurt themselves and all other queers. The invisibility they perpetuate harms us more than any of their good deeds might benefit us" (1993, p. 364). But we should also remember that not all of us have the same degree of support. Some of us have affirming, loving families that accept us regardless of what we might be or become. Others are not so fortunate. Remember the story of one student whose parents asked him at the age of 12 if he was gay, and before he answered, told him they would send him away if he was. To borrow from Signorile again, in coming out people need to make sure that supports are in place and that they "come out wisely."

My goal in this text has been threefold. First, I wanted to shed light on an aspect of student life that has gone largely unresearched: the lives of gay students. In discussing the experiences of the gay and bisexual men involved in this study I have focused on three themes: experiences of the closet, coming out, and political involvement. As chapter 4 shows, the closet is a confining place in which developing self-esteem is difficult. For the students in this study, coming out is a way to begin the process of developing a positive sense of self. As chapter 6 highlights, after coming out, some students become involved in the politics of sexual identity, and work to eliminate heterosexism and homophobia.

A second goal has been to highlight the role that the queer subculture, however problematic, plays in providing students with a sense of support and a basis for identity. As I note in chapter 7, queer students at Clement University do not merely resist the norms of heterosexuality; they stand in opposition to those norms. As an oppositional cultural enclave, queer students are best conceptualized as a contraculture. In effect, the queer contraculture provides the cultural ground upon which gay identities reside.

The third goal has been to examine the broader issues of gay identity and what, if anything, constitutes a common bond. I have delineated the shortcomings of strict essentialist and constructivist views of sexual identity and suggested an alternative conceptualization. In chapter 8 I present a view of gay ethnicity. Such a view allows for the diversity of lesbian, gay, bisexual, and queer identities, yet at the same time encourages the sense of solidarity needed to overcome oppression. At Clement University, the queer contraculture serves as the principal source of socialization into gay ethnicity.

Throughout this text the issues of language and power have been central. This is most apparent in the way some lesbian, gay, and bisexual students at Clement have expropriated the term "queer." They have turned a tool used for their own oppression ("queer" used in a derogatory manner) into a tool for empowerment ("queer" as a term to honor). Their political strategy is aimed at creating a community in which people with diverse sexual orientations play a fundamental role in shaping social life.

In their struggle to create a community of difference, queer students at Clement face the possibility of assimilation into mainstream culture and of losing the essential differences many queer students choose to accentuate. Here the constructivism/essentialism debate resurfaces. Are lesbian, gay, and bisexual people different from heterosexuals, or are they more similar than many straights might care to believe?

Sexuality issues are confusing. I have tried to paint a portrait of a complicated and changing cultural mosaic. The terminology itself can be overwhelming: homophile, homosexual, gay, lesbian, bisexual, queer, straight, heterosexual. Once again, underlying this complex terminology is the essentialist/constructivist dilemma: Are people fundamentally different, or are we all similar? In the movie *The Crying Game*, the lead character (Fergus) falls in love with a woman (Dil) he meets at a nightclub. Although Fergus originally locates Dil to explain the tragic death of her lover and his role in that death, he becomes fascinated with Dil. As they spend more time together, Fergus finds himself falling in love with her. Then comes the climactic surprise that no one who has seen the movie is supposed to reveal. They are about to make love when Fergus finds to his dismay that the woman he has fallen for has male genitalia. Fergus is sent into a chaotic state of interpretation and reinterpretation. As time passes and after the initial shock wears off, it seems as though Fergus still may be in love with Dil. Has Fergus been somehow transformed from straight to gay?

This is one of the central questions raised in the movie, and it relates to a point Tito highlights in chapter 6: Are people really straight or gay? Are we one or the other? Are our sexual identities the same today as they will be tomorrow? Finally, can we overcome our cultural differences (whether socially or biologically derived)? I have no definite answers to the first three questions, but to the last question I offer the following response: to build a just society we have no choice but to cross cultural borders. This work was about crossing one of those borders.

References

Adam, Barry D. (1993). In Nicaragua: Homosexuality without a gay world. *Journal of Homosexuality*, 24(3/4), 171-181.

Agger, Ben. (1991). Critical theory, poststructuralism, postmodernism: Their sociological relevance. *Annual Review of Sociology*, 17, 105-131.

Altman, Dennis. (1971). *Homosexual: Oppression and liberation.* New York: Outerbridge & Dienstfrey.

Anderson, Gary L. (1989). Critical ethnography in education: Origins, current status, and new directions. *Review of Educational Research*, 59(3), 249-270.

Anzaldua, Gloria. (1987). *Borderlands.* San Francisco: Spinsters/Aunt Lute.

Bakhtin, Mikhail M. (1981). *The dialogic imagination: Four essays* (M. Holquist, Ed.) (C. Emerson & M. Holquist, Trans.). Austin, TX: University of Texas.

Banzhaf, Jane. (1990). *Role model choice of gay college students: A study of gay white males attending college during the 1960s, 70s and 80s.* Unpublished dissertation, University of Rochester.

Becker, Howard S. (1963). Student culture. In T. F. Lunsford (Ed.), *The study of campus cultures* (pp. 11-25). Boulder, CO: Western Institute for Higher Education.

Becker, Howard S. (1972). What do they really learn at college? In Kenneth A. Feldman (Ed.), *College and student: Selected readings in the social psychology of higher education* (pp. 103-108). New York: Pergamon.

Becker, Howard S., Geer, Blanche, Hughes, Everett C., & Strauss, Anselm L. (1961). *Boys in white.* New Brunswick, NJ: Transaction Books.

Benhabib, Seyla. (1986). *Critique, norm, and utopia.* New York: Columbia University.

Bensimon, Estela M., Neumann, Anna, & Birnbaum, Robert. (1989). *Making sense of administrative leadership: The "L" word in higher education.* ASHE-ERIC Higher Education Report No. 1. Washington, DC: Association for the Study of Higher Education.

Berlant, Lauren, & Freeman, Elizabeth. (1993). Queer nationality. In M. Warner (Ed.), *Fear of a queer planet: Queer politics and social theory* (pp. 193-229). Minneapolis: University of Minnesota Press.

Bernstein, Richard J. (1976). *The restructuring of social and political theory.* Philadelphia: University of Pennsylvania.

Boswell, John. (1980). *Christianity, social tolerance, and homosexuality.* Chicago: University of Chicago Press.

Boswell, John. (1982/1983). Towards the long view: Revolutions, universals and sexual categories. *Salmagundi,* 58/59, 89-113.

Browning, Frank. (1993). *The culture of desire: Paradox and perversity in gay lives today.* New York: Crown Publishers.

Burbules, Nicholas C. (1986). A theory of power in education. *Educational Theory,* 36(2), 95-114.

Burbules, Nicholas C., & Rice, Suzanne. (1991). Dialogue across differences: Continuing the conversation. Harvard Educational Review, 61(4), 393-416.

Bushnell, John. H. (1962). Student culture at Vassar. In N. Sanford (Ed.), *The American college* (pp. 489-514). New York: John Wiley & Sons.

Butler, Judith. (1991). Imitation and gender insubordination. In D. Fuss (Ed.), *Inside/out: Lesbian theories, gay theories* (pp. 13-31). New York: Routledge.

Cass, Vivienne. C. (1979). Homosexual identity formation: A theoretical model. *Journal of Homosexuality,* 4(3), 219-235.

Cavin, Susan. (1987). *Rutgers sexual orientation survey: A report on the experiences of lesbian, gay, and bisexual members of the Rutgers community.* Unpublished manuscript.

Clark, Burton R. (1970). *The distinctive college: Antioch, Reed, and Swarthmore.* Chicago: Aldine.

Clark, Burton R. (1972). The organizational saga in higher education. *Administrative Science Quarterly,* 17(2), 178-184.

Clark, Burton R., & Trow, Martin. (1966). The organizational context. In T. M. Newcomb & E. K. Wilson (Eds.), *College peer groups* (pp. 17-70). Chicago: Aldine.

Cullinan, Roger G. (1973). A "gay" identity emerges on campus amidst a sea of prejudice. *NASPA Journal,* 10(4), 344-347.

Dale, Wendy, & Soler, Darin. (1993, September 7). Class acts. *The Advocate,* pp. 45-47.

D'Augelli, Anthony R. (1988, March). *Anti-lesbian and anti-gay discrimination and violence on university campuses.* Paper presented at the Northeast Regional Conference on Prejudice and Violence, New York, NY.

D'Augelli, Anthony R. (1989a). Homophobia in a university community: Views of prospective resident assistants. *Journal of College Student Development,* 30, 546-552.

D'Augelli, Anthony R. (1989b). Lesbians and gay men on campus: Visibility, empowerment, and educational leadership. *Peabody Journal of Education,* 66(3), 124-142.

D'Augelli, Anthony R. (1989c). Lesbians' and gay mens' experiences of discrimination and harassment in a university community. *American Journal of Community Psychology*, 17(3), 317-321.

D'Augelli, Anthony R. (1991a). Gay men in college: Identity processes and adaptations. *Journal of College Student Development*, 32, 140-146.

D'Augelli, Anthony R. (1991b, August). *Out on campus: Dilemmas of identity development for lesbian and gay young adults.* Paper presented at the Annual Meeting of the American Psychological Association, San Francisco, CA.

D'Emilio, John. (1990). The campus environment for gay and lesbian life. *Academe*, 76(1), 16-19.

D'Emilio, John. (1992). *Making trouble: Essays on gay history, politics, and the university.* New York: Routledge.

de Kuyper, Eric. (1993). The Freudian construction of sexuality: The gay foundations of heterosexuality and straight homophobia. *Journal of Homosexuality*, 24(3/4), 137-144.

Denzin, Norman. (1989). *The research act* (3rd ed.). New York: Prentice-Hall.

Doty, Alexander. (1993). *Making things perfectly queer.* Minneapolis: University of Minnesota Press.

Eckert, Penelope. (1989). *Jocks & burnouts: Social categories and identity in the high school.* New York: Teachers College.

Epstein, Steven. (1987). Gay politics, ethnic identity: The limits of social constructivism. *Socialist Review*, 17(3/4), 9-54.

Erikson, Erik H. (1968). *Identity: Youth and crisis.* New York: W. W. Norton.

Etringer, Bruce D., Hillerbrand, E., & Hetherington, C. (1990). The influence of sexual orientation on career decision-making: A research note. *Journal of Homosexuality*, 19(4), 103-111.

Fay, Brian. (1987). *Critical social science.* Ithaca: Cornell University.

Fetterman, David. (1989). *Ethnography step by step.* Newbury Park, CA: Sage.

Fine, Michelle. (1986). Why urban adolescents drop into and out of public high school. *Teachers College Record*, 87(3), 393-409.

Finnegan, Dana, & McNally, Emily. (1987). *Dual identities: Counseling chemically dependent gay men and lesbians.* Center City, MN: Hazelden Foundation.

Fisher, James L. (1984). *The power of the presidency.* New York: Macmillan.

Foster, William. (1989) [1991]. The administrator as a transformative intellectual. *Peabody Journal of Education*, 66(3), 5-18.

Foucault, Michel. (1970). *The order of things.* New York: Vintage Books.

Foucault, Michel. (1978). *The history of sexuality, Volume I: An introduction* (R. Hurley, Trans.). New York: Vintage Books.

Foucault, Michel. (1979). *Discipline & punish* (A. Sheridan, Trans.). New York: Vintage Books.

Foucault, Michel. (1980). *Power/knowledge* (C. Gordan et al., Trans.). New York: Pantheon Books.

Freire, Paulo. (1970). *Pedagogy of the oppressed* (M. B. Ramos, Trans.). New York: Continuum.

Freud, Sigmund. (1923/1961). The ego and the id. In J. Strachey (Ed., Trans.), *The standard edition of the complete psychological works of Sigmund Freud* (Vol. 19) (pp. 3-66). London: Hogarth Press.

Friend, Richard A. (1993). Choices, not closets: Heterosexism and homophobia in schools. In Lois Weis & Michelle Fine (Eds.), *Beyond silenced voices: Class, race, and gender in United States schools* (pp. 209-235). Albany: State University of New York.

Fuss, Diana. (1989). *Essentially speaking*. New York: Routledge.

Fuss, Diana. (1991). *Inside/out: Lesbian theories, gay theories*. New York: Routledge.

Gays under fire. (1992, September 14). *Newsweek*, pp. 35-40.

Geertz, Clifford. (1973). *The interpretation of cultures*. New York: Basic Books.

Gergen, Kenneth. J. (1991). *The saturated self: Dilemmas of identity in contemporary life*. New York: Basic Books.

Geuss, Raymond. (1981). *The idea of a critical theory*. Cambridge: Cambridge University.

Gibson, Paul. (1989). Gay male and lesbian youth suicide. In M. R. Feinleib (Ed.), *Report of the Secretary's Task Force on Youth Suicide* (pp. 110-142). Washington, DC: U.S. Department of Health & Human Services.

Giroux, Henry A. (1981). *Ideology and culture & the process of schooling*. Philadelphia: Temple University.

Giroux, Henry A. (1983a). Theories of reproduction and resistance in the new sociology of education: A critical analysis. *Harvard Educational Review*, 53(3), 257-293.

Giroux, Henry A. (1983b). *Theory & resistance in education*. South Hadley, MA: Bergin & Garvey.

Giroux, Henry A. (1986). Authority, intellectuals, and the politics of practical learning. *Teachers College Record*, 88(1), 22-40.

Giroux, Henry A. (1992). *Border crossings: Cultural workers and the politics of education*. New York: Routledge.

Gitlin, Andrew. (1990). Educative research, voice, and school change. *Harvard Educational Review*, 60(4), 443-466.

Goffman, Erving. (1959). *The presentation of self in everyday life*. Garden City, NY: Doubleday.

Goffman, Erving. (1963). *Stigma: Notes on the management of spoiled identity*. Englewood Cliffs, NJ: Prentice-Hall.

Goldberg, Jonathan. (1993). Sodomy in the new world: Anthropologies old and new. In M. Warner (Ed.), *Fear of a queer planet: Queer politics and social theory* (pp. 3-18). Minneapolis, MN: University of Minnesota Press.

Grayson, Dolores A. (1987). Emerging equity issues related to homosexuality in education. *Peabody Journal of Education*, 64(4), 132-145.

Greenberg, David. (1988). *The construction of homosexuality*. Chicago: University of Chicago Press.

Habermas, Jurgen. (1973). *Theory and practice* (J. Vietel, Trans.). Boston: Beacon Press.

Hall, Stuart. (1990). Cultural identity and diaspora. In J. Rutherford (Ed.), *Identity: Community, culture, difference*. London: Lawrence & Wishart.

Halperin, David. (1990). *One hundred years of homosexuality.* New York: Routledge.

Harry, Joseph. (1982). *Gay children grow up: Gender culture and gender deviance.* New York: Praeger.

Harry, Joseph. (1984). Sexual orientation as destiny. *Journal of Homosexuality,* 10(3/4), 111-124.

Harry, Joseph. (1986). Sampling gay men. *Journal of Sex Research,* 22(1), 21-34.

Hellwege, Dennis R., Perry, Katye, & Dobson, Judith. (1988). Perceptual differences in gender ideals among heterosexual and homosexual males and females. *Sex Roles,* 19(11-12), 735-746.

Henderson, Ann Fleck. (1984). Homosexuality in the college years: Developmental differences between men and women. *Journal of American College Health,* 32(5), 216-219.

Herdt, Gilbert. (1992). *Gay culture in America: Essays from the field.* Boston: Beacon.

Herek, Gregory M. (1986). *Sexual orientation and prejudice at Yale: A report on the experiences of lesbian, gay, and bisexual members of the Yale community.* Unpublished manuscript.

Herek, Gregory M. (1989). Hate crimes against lesbians and gay men. *American Psychologist,* 44(6), 948-955.

Herek, Gregory M. (1993). Documenting prejudice against lesbians, and gay men on campus: The Yale Sexual Orientation Survey. *Journal of Homosexuality,* 25(4), 15-30.

Higginbotham, Evelyn Brooks. (1992). African-American women's history and the metalanguage of race. *Signs: Journal of Women in Culture and Society,* 17(2), 251-274.

Holland, Dorothy C., & Eisenhart, Margaret A. (1990). *Educated in romance: Women, achievement, and college.* Chicago: University of Chicago.

hooks, bell. (1984). *Feminist theory: From margin to center.* Boston: South End.

Horkheimer, Max. (1972). *Critical theory* (M. J. O'Connell, Trans.). New York: Herder and Herder.

Horowitz, Helen L. (1987). *Campus life: Undergraduate cultures from the end of the eighteenth century to the present.* New York: Alfred A. Knopf.

Horstman, William R. (1975). MMPI responses of homosexual and heterosexual male college students. *Homosexual Counseling Journal,* 2(2), 68-76.

Jay, Martin. (1973). *The dialectical imagination.* Boston: Little, Brown and Company.

Keller, George. (1983). *Academic strategy.* Baltimore: The Johns Hopkins University Press.

Kellner, Douglas. (1988). Postmodernism as social theory: Some challenges and problems. *Theory, Culture & Society,* 5, 239-269.

Kellner, Douglas. (1989). *Critical theory, Marxism, and modernity.* Baltimore: Johns Hopkins University.

Kellner, Douglas. (1990). The postmodern turn: Positions, problems, and prospects. In G. Ritzer (Ed.), *Frontiers of social theory: The new synthesis* (pp. 255-286). New York: Columbia University.

Kinsey, Alfred C., Pomeroy, Wardell B., & Martin, Clyde E. (1948). *Sexual behavior in the human male.* Philadelphia: Saunders.

Kinsey, Alfred C., Pomeroy, Wardell B., Martin, Clyde E., & Gebhard, Paul H. (1953). *Sexual behavior in the human female.* Philadelphia: Saunders.

Kitzinger, Celia. (1987). *The social construction of lesbianism.* Newbury Park, CA: Sage.

Kuh, George D. (1990). Assessing student culture. In William G. Tierney (Ed.), *Assessing academic climates and cultures* (pp. 47-60). New Directions for Institutional Research, no. 68. San Francisco: Jossey-Bass.

Labaton, Stephen. (1993, July 25). Challenge to military's gay policy faces obstacles. *New York Times* (*National*), p. 22.

Lamont, Michele, & Wuthnow, Robert. (1990). Betwixt and between: Recent cultural sociology in Europe and the United States. In G. Ritzer (Ed.), *Frontiers of social theory: The new synthesis* (pp. 287-315). New York: Columbia University.

La Salle, Linda A., & Rhoads, Robert A. (1992, April). *Exploring campus intolerance: A textual analysis of comments concerning lesbian, gay, and bisexual people.* Paper presented at the Annual Meeting of the American Educational Research Association, San Francisco, CA.

Lather, Patti. (1986a). Issues of validity in openly ideological research: Between a rock and a soft place. *Interchange, 17*(4), 63-84.

Lather, Patti. (1986b). Research as praxis. *Harvard Educational Review, 56*(3), 257-277.

Leemon, Thomas A. (1972). *The rites of passage in a student culture.* New York: Teachers College.

Lincoln, Yvonna S., & Guba, Egon G. (1986). But is it rigorous? Trustworthiness and authenticity in naturalistic evaluation. In D. D. Williams (Ed.), *Naturalistic evaluation* (pp. 73-84). New Directions for Program Evaluation, no. 30. San Francisco: Jossey-Bass.

Lorde, Audre. (1984). *Sister outsider.* Freedom, CA: The Crossing Press.

Lorde, Audre. (1985). *I am your sister: Black women organizing across sexualities.* Latham, NY: Kitchen Table Press: Women of Color Press.

Low, Jane M. (1988). *The Davis social environment: A report of student opinions.* Davis: Student Affairs Research and Information, University of California at Davis.

Lyotard, Jean-Francois. (1984). *The postmodern condition.* Minneapolis: University of Minnesota.

Macionis, John. (1992). *Society: The basics.* Englewood Cliffs, NJ: Prentice-Hall.

MacLeod, Jay. (1987). *Ain't no makin' it.* Boulder, CO: Westview.

Marcuse, Herbert. (1972). *Studies in critical philosophy* (J. De Bres, Trans.). Boston: Beacon.

Marso, Joan L. (1991). *Addressing the developmental issues of lesbian and gay college students.* (ERIC Document Reproduction Service No. ED328861)

McLaren, Peter. (1986). *Schooling as a ritual performance.* London: Routledge & Kegan Paul.

McLaren, Peter. (1989). *Life in schools.* New York: Longman.

McLaren, Peter. (1991). Decentering culture: Postmodernism, resistance, and critical pedagogy. In Nancy B. Wyner (Ed.), *Current perspectives on the culture of schools* (pp. 231-257). Boston: Brookline Books.

McNaught, Brian. (1988). *On being gay.* New York: St. Martin's.

McRobbie, Angela. (1978). Working class girls and the culture of femininity. In Centre for Contemporary Cultural Studies (Eds.), *Women take issue* (pp. 96-108). London: Routledge & Kegan Paul.

Mead, George Herbert. (1934). *Mind, self, & society*. Chicago: University of Chicago.

Minkowitz, Donna. (1990, November 6). Gays and lesbians bash Dinkins. *Village Voice*, 35(45), p. 12.

Miranda, Jeanne, & Storms, Michael. (1989). Psychological adjustment of lesbians and gay men. *Journal of Counseling & Development*, 68, 41-45.

Moffatt, Michael. (1989). *Coming of age in New Jersey*. New Brunswick, NJ: Rutgers University.

Mohr, Richard D. (1992). *Gay ideas: Outing and other controversies*. Boston: Beacon.

National Gay & Lesbian Task Force. (1992). *Partial list of colleges and universities with non-discrimination policies which include sexual orientation*. Washington, DC: NGLTF Policy Institute.

Nelson, Randy, & Baker, Harley. (1990). *The educational climate for gay, lesbian, and bisexual students*. Santa Cruz: Student Services, University of California at Santa Cruz.

Nelson-Jones, Richard, & Strong, S. R. (1976). Rules, risk and self-disclosure. *British Journal of Guidance and Counselling*, 4(2), 202-211.

Nieberding, Ronald A. (1989). *In every classroom: The report of the President's Select Committee for Lesbian and Gay Concerns*. New Brunswick, NJ: Office of Student Life Policy and Services, Rutgers University.

Nuehring, Elane M., Fein, Sara B., & Tyler, Mary. (1989). The gay college student: Perspectives for mental health professionals. *Counseling Psychologist*, 4(4), 64-72.

Ogbu, John U. (1988). Class stratification, racial stratification, and schooling. In Lois Weis (Ed.), *Class, race, and gender in American education*. Albany: State University of New York.

Patton, Cindy. (1993). Tremble, hetero swine! In M. Warner (Ed.), *Fear of a queer planet: Queer politics and social theory* (pp. 143-177). Minneapolis: University of Minnesota Press.

Patton, Michael Q. (1980). *Qualitative evaluation methods*. Beverly Hills, CA: Sage.

Pronger, Brian. (1992). Gay jocks: A phenomenology of gay men in athletics. In L. May & R. A. Strikwerda (Eds.), *Rethinking masculinity: Philosophical explorations in light of feminism* (pp. 41-55). Lanham, MD: Littlefield Adams.

Reynolds, Arthur J. (1989). Social environmental conceptions of male homosexual behavior: A university climate analysis. *Journal of College Student Development*, 30, 62-69.

Rhoads, Robert A. (1991, February). *A cultural portrait of fraternity life*. Paper presented at the Twelfth Annual Ethnography in Education Forum, University of Pennsylvania, Philadelphia, PA.

Rhoads, Robert A. (1992, November). *The brothers of Alpha Beta: An ethnographic study of fraternity oppression of women*. Paper presented at the Annual Meeting of the Association for the Study of Higher Education, Minneapolis, MN.

Richardson, Laurel. (1990). Narrative and sociology. *Journal of Contemporary Ethnography*, 19(1), 116-135.

Rosaldo, Renato. (1989). *Culture & truth: The remaking of social analysis*. Boston: Beacon.

Sanday, Peggy R. (1990). *Fraternity gang rape: Sex, brotherhood, and privilege on campus*. New York: New York University.

Schwabish, Rick M. (1990). *Power and intimacy motives of males in same-sex and opposite-sex dating couples*. Unpublished doctoral dissertation, Hofstra University.

Sears, James T. (1991). *Growing up gay in the South: Race, gender, and journeys of the spirit*. New York: Harrington Park.

Sedgwick, Eve Kosofsky. (1990). *Epistemology of the closet*. Berkeley: University of California.

Seidman, Steven. (1993). Identity and politics in a "postmodern" gay culture: Some historical and conceptual notes. In M. Warner (Ed.), *Fear of a queer planet: Queer politics and social theory* (pp. 105-142). Minneapolis: University of Minnesota Press.

Shepard, C. F. (1990). *Report on the quality of campus life for lesbian, gay, and bisexual students*. Los Angeles: Student Affairs Information and Research Office; University of California at Los Angeles.

Shilts, Randy. (1993). *Conduct unbecoming: Gays & lesbians in the U.S. military*. New York: St. Martin's Press.

Signorile, Michelangelo. (1993). *Queer in America: Sex, the media, and the closets of power*. New York: Random House.

Smircich, Linda. (1983). Concepts of culture and organizational analysis. *Administrative Science Quarterly*, 28, 339-358.

Smith, Ruth Bayard. (1993). The rise of the conservative student press. *Change*, 25(1), 25-29.

Spradley, James. (1979). *The ethnographic interview*. New York: Holt, Rinehart and Winston.

Tierney, William G. (1988). Organizational culture in higher education. *Journal of Higher Education*, 59(1), 2-21.

Tierney, William G. (1991) [1989]. Advancing democracy: A critical interpretation of leadership. *Peabody Journal of Education*, 66(3), 157-175.

Tierney, William G. (1992). *Official encouragement, institutional discouragement: Minorities in academe--the Native American experience*. Norwood, NJ: Ablex.

Tierney, William G. (1993a). Academic freedom and the parameters of knowledge. *Harvard Educational Review*, 63(2), 143-160.

Tierney, William G. (1993b). *Building communities of difference: Higher education in the 21st Century*. Westport, CT: Bergin & Garvey.

Tierney, William G.,et al. (1992). *Enhancing diversity: Toward a better campus climate*. A report of the Committee on Lesbian and Gay Concerns, Pennsylvania State University.

Tierney, William G., & Rhoads, Robert A. (1993). Postmodernism and critical theory in higher education: Implications for research and practice. In J. C. Smart (Ed.), *Higher Education: Handbook of theory and research* (pp 308-343). New York: Agathon.

Van Maanen, John. (1976). Breaking in: Socialization to work. In R. Dubin (Ed.), *Handbook of work, organization, and society* (pp. 67-130). Chicago: Rand McNally College Publishing.

Van Maanen, John. (1983). Doing things in old ways: The chains of socialization. In J. L. Bess (Ed.), *College and university organization: Insights from the behavioral sciences* (pp. 211-247). New York: New York University Press.

Wallace, Walter L. (1966). *Student culture: Social structure and continuity in a liberal arts college*. Chicago: Aldine.

Warner, Michael. (1993). *Fear of a queer planet: Queer politics and social theory*. Minneapolis: University of Minnesota Press.

Weeks, Jeffrey. (1988). Against nature. In A. van Kooten Niekerk & T. van der Meer (Eds.), *Homosexuality, which homosexuality?* (pp. 199-214). Amsterdam: Jhr. Mr. J. A. Schorerstichting.

Weis, Lois. (1985). *Between two worlds*. Boston: Routledge & Kegan Paul.

Whyte, William Foote. (1943). *Street corner society*. Chicago: University of Chicago.

Willis, Paul E. (1977). *Learning to labor*. Aldershot: Gower.

Woestendiek, John. (1992, October 27). Oregon's Measure 9 brings the gay lifestyle to a vote. *Philadelphia Inquirer*, pp. A1, A6.

Wright, Loyd, & Fling, Sheila. (1983, April). *Perceptions of self and parents among college students of different sexual orientations*. Paper presented at the Annual Convention of the Southwestern Psychological Association, San Antonio, TX.

Yager, Joel, Kurtzman, Felice, Landsverk, John, & Weismeier, Edward. (1988). Behaviors and attitudes related to eating disorders in homosexual male college students. *American Journal of Psychiatry*, 145(4), 495-497.

Yinger, J. Milton. (1960). Contraculture and subculture. *American Sociological Review*, 25(5), 625-635.

Index

Rhoads, Robert A., 7, 25, 34, 40-43,
    50, 138
Rice, Suzanne, 43
Richardson, Laurel, 55
Rosaldo, Renato, 54
Rustin, Bayard, 107

Sanday, Peggy R., 34
Schwabish, Rick, 37
Seidman, Steven, 134, 154-155
Sears, James, 134
Sedgwick, Eve Kosofsky, 59
Self-acknowledgement, 67-69
Self-disclosure, 67-69
Shepard, C. F., 7
Shilts, Randy, 14, 121-122
Signorile, Michelangelo, 8, 60, 72, 174
Smircich, Linda, 12, 35
Social reproduction, 10, 33
Socialization, 12, 21, 143-161
Soler, Darin, 7
Space, 123-125
Spradley, James, 44, 48-49
Stonewall, 110
Storms, Michael, 37
Straight talk, 118
Street Corner Society, 42
Student culture, 130; defined, 33

Subculture, 11, 20, 21, 26, 33-36
Substance, 128-130
Supreme Court, 13
Style, 125-128

Tierney, William G., 7, 12, 25, 34, 36,
    38, 40-43, 50, 56, 130, 163, 172
Trow, Martin, 33
Tyler, Mary, 35

Validity, 49-51
Van Maanen, John, 145, 156
Visibility, 114-117

Wallace, Walter L., 33
Warner, Michael, 152
Weeks, Jeffrey, 30
Weis, Lois, 34, 139
Whyte, William Foote, 42
Wiesmeier, Edward, 37
Willis, Paul E., 34
Woestendiek, John, 13
Wright, Loyd, 37
Wuthnow, Robert, 27

Yager, Joel, 37
Yinger, J. Milton, 34-35